International Investment Arbitration

Lessons from Developments in the MENA Region

AF754896

JUDGE DR MOHAMED A.M. ISMAIL
LLB, LLM, PhD, FCI Arb
Vice-President of the Egyptian Conseil d'Etat

With a Foreword by Professor Martin Hunter

Routledge
Taylor & Francis Group
LONDON AND NEW YORK

Mohamed Ismail provides an insightful guide for readers providing a better understanding of risks, protections and opportunities available to foreign investors dealing in the MENA region. The book, part historical analysis, part critical review, and part focused on future opportunities, is a must read for anyone practicing or interested in the International Investment Arbitration Sphere.

Doug Jones, AO, Australia and UK

To My Mother's Soul

First published 2013 by Ashgate Publishing

2 Park Square, Milton Park, Abingdon, Oxfordshire OX14 4RN
52 Vanderbilt Avenue, New York, NY 10017

Routledge is an imprint of the Taylor & Francis Group, an informa business

First issued in paperback 2020

British Library Cataloguing in Publication Data
Ismail, Mohamed A.M.
International investment arbitration : lessons from developments in the MENA Region.
1. International commercial arbitration – Middle East.
2. International commercial arbitration – Africa, North.
I. Title
341.5'22'0956–dc23

The Library of Congress has cataloged the printed edition as follows:
Ismail, Mohamed A.M.
International investment arbitration : lessons from developments in the MENA region / by Dr Mohamed A.M. Ismail.
pages cm.
ISBN 978-1-4094-6363-4 (hardback)—ISBN 978-1-4094-6364-1 (ebook)—ISBN 978-1-4094-6365-8 (epub) 1. Investments, Foreign—Law and legislation—Middle East. 2. International commercial arbitration—Middle East. I. Title.

KMC747.I83 2013
346.56'092—dc23

2012043602

ISBN 13: 978-1-4094-6363-4 (hbk)
ISBN 13: 978-0-367-60151-5 (pbk)

Contents

List of Figures

About the Author

Dr Mohamed A.M. Ismail is Vice President of the Egyptian State Council (Conseil d'Etat), Judge at the Court of Appeal (contracts circuit), Fellow of the Chartered Institute of Arbitrators (UK), Visiting Professor and PhD examiner at the Egyptian Universities in International State Contracts and Arbitration, particularly on infrastructure projects, lecturer at the Cairo Regional Centre for International Commercial Arbitration (CRCICA) and arbitrator in international construction contract disputes, particularly those concerning international public works agreements. Dr Ismail is a lecturer at the Bahrain Chamber for Dispute Resolution in cooperation with the American Arbitration Association (BCDR-AAA) and lecturer in the Arab League on Arab countries in International Arbitration. Dr Ismail was formerly a senior legal adviser to His Excellency the Egyptian Minister of Petroleum and represented the Egyptian government in state international business transactions in the oil and gas industry, especially in the UK, with law firms such as Shearman Sterling, the international counsel to the Egyptian government. He was formerly a senior legal adviser to His Excellency the Egyptian Minister of Trade and Industry and, before that, a senior legal adviser in the Egyptian investment sector, representing the Egyptian government at the United Nations Conference on Trade and Development (UNCTAD), Geneva, for the bilateral investment treaties (BITs) negotiations in which developing states were involved. In 2011/2012 Dr Ismail was the recipient of the State Prize Laureate in Legal Research. This prize, the highest award in the MENA region, was granted to him by the Arab Republic of Egypt. Dr Ismail has published widely in the UK, Germany, and in the MENA region, for both academics and practitioners.

Foreword

Martin Hunter

It gives me great pleasure to write a foreword to this latest work from the distinguished and prolific author Dr Mohammed A.M. Ismail. Dr Ismail injects into the book his wide experience and his personal knowledge of the region, and of the law and practice of arbitration in the Arab Middle East. Readers will also find his text both well researched and conveniently presented.

The term *arbitration* is used, at least by English-speaking lawyers, to mean a private dispute resolution process, outside the state-sponsored court system, that leads to a *binding* and *enforceable* 'award'. This distinguishes *arbitration* from the classic alternative dispute resolution processes, such as negotiation and third-party-assisted negotiation (mediation, conciliation, etc), which are designed to lead to a signed settlement agreement between the disputing parties. Such ADR outcomes are of course enforceable under the *law of contract*, like any other contractual obligation. However, if the parties do not sign up to an agreed settlement at the end of the process, then the effort, expense and delay involved will have been worthless.

Dr Ismail starts by examining the unique characteristics of the legal systems of the Arab Middle East, including the influence of the French Napoleonic Code on the civil laws of almost all the countries in the MENA region. Like most of Dr Ismail's work, the opening chapter is not limited solely to the legal perspective; he explores the social, economic, cultural and political elements that exist within the region. He then turns to evaluate the manner in which the region has reacted to the 'forces of globalization'. Towards the end of the chapter, he charts the emerging trends of various methods of alternative dispute resolution in the area. Interestingly, Dr Ismail describes the shortfalls of 'western techniques' for dispute resolution, which he considers to be over-reliant on 'foreign' traditions and an institutional and pedantic approach to contract interpretation.

Dr Ismail deals separately (and rightly so) with International Commercial Arbitration and Investment Treaty Arbitration, in Chapters 3 and 4 respectively. He explains, accurately, that arbitration is a novel idea in the region, having gained attention only in the last few decades. The change has been triggered as a result of the growing appreciation of the advantages of referring high-value disputes to arbitration as opposed to determination by the civil courts of the states from which either disputing party originates, or has a close connection to. Where huge sums of money are involved (which is often the case in infrastructure projects), investors tend to have little confidence in the impartiality of the host state's courts, and the host state will have little confidence in the impartiality of the courts of the investor's country of origin.

Chapters 5 and 6 explore ICSID and bilateral investment treaty arbitrations. Chapter 5 commences with a brief history of the emergence of BITs. Dr Ismail confirms that, as in other parts of the developing world, the rise in popularity of BITs heralded a new era for large-scale private investment in countries within the MENA region, as state-to-state investment declined. He comments:

> The emergence of newly independent Arab developing countries, from the early 1950s onwards, brought about economies for which existing treaty arrangements were unsuited … the development

> process, in Arab countries, has increased in the early 1960s and consequently, private foreign investment has thus increasingly come to play an integral role in the development process.

In Chapter 6, Dr Ismail provides a helpful introduction to ICSID arbitration. He goes on to consider the interaction between the Washington Convention and the legal systems of the MENA region, highlighting the obstacles posed in the path of initiating ICSID arbitration.

The work finishes with a series of conclusions which pull together the strands that run through the work. This chapter is of great assistance as it sets out the author's propositions in a succinct manner.

The book covers a wide range of material on the subject. Dr Ismail has provided a well-thought-out work and a wealth of information which will help to promote knowledge and skills in international arbitration in the MENA region. I am happy to be able to recommend it most warmly.

London
December 2012

Preface

Today, international investment arbitration, running parallel with international commercial arbitration, plays a significant role in the legal and economic life of the Middle Eastern and North African (MENA) countries. Economic growth in the MENA region has been considerable in recent decades, presenting a number of challenges to foreign investors, who are normally from developed nations. In the last two decades, some Arab countries have moved away from the socialist ideology and market-led economy and have adopted, instead, the free-market economy. The Arab Spring revolutions, which originated in Tunisia and Egypt, are now spreading into many Arab countries which are drafting new constitutions in order to start a new era of a clean political climate which offers a threshold of protection for foreign investors. The real protection for investors will now be offered through constitutions, and the host state will be responsible for promulgating legislations and adopting fair polices through a regulatory framework. Democracy, constitutional developments and fighting corruption are some of the fundamental tools for increasing inward foreign direct investments (IFDI) in the MENA region. Further, Arab states will be obliged to respect their international commitments through ratifying international treaties and to respect those treaties as valid legislations after ratification. International investment law theory and practice has made significant progress in recent decades not only in the MENA region, but also in the international sphere, as it is the main concern of academics and practitioners in the field as well as private foreign entities(investors) from developed nations.

Cultural globalization nowadays plays a significant role in the flow of Anglo-American legal culture to Arab Middle Eastern civil law jurisdictions. In light of the economic developments in the Arab Middle East, arbitration – whether international commercial arbitration or international investment arbitration – is now playing an increasingly fundamental role in the various economic sectors in the region.

The modernization, liberalization and internationalization of arbitration legislations were fundamental tools in achieving a suitable threshold of protection for foreign investors. These modifications in all Arab civil law legal systems were adopted in accordance with international instruments such as the United Nations Commission on International Trade Law (UNCITRAL) Model Law on International Commercial Arbitration, which influenced all Arab legislation, and the International Centre for the Settlement of Investment Disputes (ICSID) Convention of 1965 (Washington), as well as the 1958 New York Convention. The latter convention is the fundamental pillar, worldwide, for the recognition and enforcement of arbitral awards.

This book focuses on international commercial arbitration as well as international investment arbitration and the nature and extent of protection offered to foreign investors in the MENA countries. It scrutinizes the substantive protection provided to foreign investors through customary international law, BITs and the Washington Convention through the analysis of investment treaty provisions. Nationality, protected investments, expropriation, fair and equitable treatment (FET), most favoured nation(MFN) treatment and other substantive issues are the main concern of the study as these provisions constitute the BITs' common substantive protection. ICSID case law involving MENA countries is also scrutinized in order to learn lessons from developments in international investment law in the MENA region. It is of great importance to draw upon lessons from the ICSID case law in the current leading cases between Arab countries and foreign investors from developed states. The book also analyses the ICSID as a leading institution which plays a fundamental role in investment arbitration both in the MENA region and worldwide.

Although law serves and reflects society, this book is not confined to legal influences but, rather, draws on a wide range of cultural and economic factors in order to discuss the direction in which the law may be heading.

A fundamental question arises relating to whether the arbitrability in *Le Contrat Administratif* in Arab civil law legal systems is still relevant, particularly when the host state signs and ratifies the Washington Convention or a bilateral investment treaty (BIT) which enables the foreign investor direct recourse to international investment arbitration without the Arab host state's consent to start arbitral proceedings.

New means of dispute settlement in *Le Contrat Administratif* in civil law jurisdiction in the last two decades, particularly arbitration, are the direct result of cultural and legal globalization. This book focuses on investment arbitration in detail with special reference to Arab arbitration legislation which has been directly influenced by the UNCITRAL Model Law and the Arab Arbitration Acts, as well as Arab constitutions, Arab civil codes and state procurement laws. Most of these constitutional and legislative instruments have been introduced in recent decades.

As HH Humphrey Lloyd QC pointed out in his foreword to my recent book[1]

> Some Western techniques for dispute resolution are overly formalistic or institutional in nature and ill suited for countries, especially the Middle East where tradition and culture calls for every avenue of discussion, negotiation and assistance from outsiders to be fully exhausted, before embarking upon formal proceedings, including arbitration.

The present book also deals with the time bar in standard forms of contracts before starting arbitration and highlights some issues relating to mediation in the MENA region. It further explores investment arbitration in the MENA region and policies adopted towards foreign investors in Arab countries before the Arab revolutions through scrutinizing ICSID case law. This is the first book in English to deal with such a critical issue.

The Appendices show the most recent trends worldwide and the most recent regional and international instruments in the arbitration world in both theory and practice. They also include some of the Arab world's famous BITs with the USA, UK and China.

Finally, international instruments, practices and national laws of developed and developing countries are assessed, providing conclusions and recommendations for the future.

---

1 Mohamed A.M. Ismail, *Globalization and the New International Public Works Agreement in Developing Countries* (Farnham: Ashgate Publishing 2011) xiv, foreword by HH Humphrey Lloyd, QC.

Acknowledgements

This book started as views and thoughts from lectures given at the Cairo Regional Centre for International Commercial Arbitration (CRCICA). Those views have since been developed in books and articles written in the UK, Germany and the Arab world regarding international infrastructure agreements and international commercial arbitration in state contracts (*Le Contrat Administratif*), but not investment arbitration, that is, until now. I am most fortunate in having the eminent Professor Martin Hunter write the foreword to this book; his excellent advice was of tremendous value when I started the book in 2011. In addition, I would like to express my gratitude to Professors Alan Redfern, Martin Hunter, Nigel Blackaby and Constantine Partasides; their book *Redfern and Hunter on International Commercial Arbitration* (Oxford University Press, 2009) is the leading authority in arbitration law and practice worldwide, and as such was the main source of inspiration during the writing of this book. I also acknowledge the influential book *Law and Practice of International Commercial Arbitration* by Professors Alan Redfern and Martin Hunter. The 1991 second edition played a fundamental role in my career; this was the principal source to which I turned for enrichment of my thoughts and knowledge in the art and science of international arbitration over the decades.

Special thanks and sincere gratitude go to Alison Kirk and Sarah Horsley of Ashgate Law and Legal Studies, to whom I express my deep appreciation for their continual support, help and constructive cooperation. I strongly believe that without their assistance this book would not have appeared. I wish to express my appreciation to Sarah Charters and all Ashgate staff. I recall clearly that it was constructive cooperation which was key to the success of my book *Globalization and the New International Public Works Agreements: An Analytical Perspective* (Ashgate Publishing, 2011), in which I dedicate my views to academics and practitioners around the globe.

My gratitude goes to the World Bank and ICSID staff for their cooperation and support.

Last, but most important, my deep emotions go to my wife, Rania Adel Koura, LLM, USA, to whom I owe so much for her warm and endless support; to her I give my everlasting gratitude.

List of Abbreviations and Terms

AAA	American Arbitration Association
AALCO	Asian-African Legal Consultative Organization
AC	Law Reports, House of Lords (Appeal Cases)
ADR	alternative dispute resolution
All ER	All England Law Reports
Arbitration	Journal of the Chartered Institute of Arbitrators
BCDR-AAA	Bahrain Chamber for Dispute Resolution in cooperation with the American Arbitration Association
BITs	bilateral investment treaty
BOO	build, own, operate
BOOT	build, own, operate, transfer
BOT	build, own, transfer
CA	Court of Appeal of England and Wales
Conseil d'Etat	State Council (Egypt)
CRCICA	Cairo Regional Centre for International Commercial Arbitration
CIA	Chartered Institute of Arbitrators
CIF	cost, insurance and freight
Con LR	Construction Law Reports
DIAC	Dubai Arbitration Centre
DIFC	Dubai International Financial Centre
EC	European Community
ECT	Energy Charter Treaty
EPC	engineering, procurement, construction
EPPPL	*European Public Private Partnership Law Review*
EU	European Union
FAA	United States Federal Arbitration Act
FDI	foreign direct investment
FET	fair and equitable treatment
FIDIC	*Fédération International des Ingénieurs Conseils*
FOB	free on board
FY	financial year
HL	House of Lords
IBA	Rules IBA Rules on the Taking of Evidence as amended in 2010
ICC	International Chamber of Commerce
ICDR	International Centre for Dispute Resolution
ICLR	*International Construction Law Review*
ICSID	International Centre for the Settlement of Investment Disputes
IFDI	inward foreign direct investment
IIA	international investment agreement
LCIA	London Court of International Commercial Arbitration

MENA	Middle East and North Africa
MFN	most favoured nation
MIT	multilateral investment treaty
Model Law	UNCITRAL Model Law on International Commercial Arbitration adopted in June 1985 and amended in 2006.
New York Convention	The 1958 New York Convention on the Recognition and Enforcement of Foreign Arbitral Awards
OECD	Organization for Economic Cooperation and Development.
PC	Privy Council
PCA	Permanent Court of Arbitration (The Hague)
PIL	Private International Law (Switzerland)
PPP	public–private partnership
RCADI	*Recueil des Cours de l'Academie de Droit International de la Haye*
Rev Arb	*Revue de l'arbitrage*
SCC	Stockholm Chamber of Commerce Arbitration Institute
SIAC	Singapore International Arbitration Center
UAE	United Arab Emirates
UNCITRAL	United Nations Commission on International Trade Law
UNCITRAL Rules	UNCITRAL Arbitration Rules as Amended 2010
UNCTAD	United Nations Conference on Trade and Development.
UNIDEROIT	International Institute for the Unification of Private Law.
Washington Convention	Washington Convention on the Settlement of the Investment Disputes between States and Nationals of Other States, 1965
WIPO	World Intellectual Property Organization

Chapter 1
Middle Eastern Legal Systems: An Overview

Introduction

After the First World War and the signing of the Sykes-Picot agreement in 1916 between the United Kingdom and France, the Arab Middle Eastern and North African (MENA) countries were divided into British and French Colonies. This led to the flow of English and French legal culture into the region although Egypt, which had been a British colony since 1882, continued to be influenced by English culture in general. There was minor diversity between other Arab countries, too: for example, the Maghreb countries (Tunisia, Algeria and Morocco) in North Africa were directly influenced by French culture and language whereas the Gulf States completely escaped French influence as they were British colonies. The French influence on the Arab civil codes began to become apparent in the late 1940s and early 1950s. Egypt codified its civil code in 1948 and, later, its code of civil and commercial procedures. Both codes were based on the French Napoleonic Code for, although Egypt was a British colony until 1952, it was greatly influenced by French legal culture. The influence of the French Napoleonic Code then spread from Egypt to all Arab countries which, in turn, codified their civil codes in accordance with the Egyptian experience. Libya, Syria, Lebanon, Sudan, Kuwait, Bahrain, Morocco, Algeria, Tunisia, Iraq, Yemen and other Arab legal systems were directly influenced by the codification, doctrine and practice of the Egyptian Civil Code. At that time, Arab countries did not recognize any other method of dispute settlement except litigation and national courts. Arbitration as a dispute settlement mechanism in international business transactions was neither codified nor recognized in Arab legislations, and the same applied to alternative dispute resolution (ADR) mechanisms. International disputes or investor–state disputes had to be scrutinized by the national courts.

The scope of research in this book covers those Arab Middle Eastern states that currently recognize ADR, commercial arbitration and investment arbitration. Both the international commercial arbitration process and foreign investors are facing various challenges in the Middle East despite the forces of globalization from Anglo-American jurisdictions to the Middle Eastern civil law legal culture.

The rise of arbitration, whether domestic or international, began in the light of the codes of civil and commercial procedures in the Arab region. In Egypt, Syria, Lebanon, Iraq, Libya, Tunisia, Algeria, Morocco, Kuwait, Oman, UAE, Bahrain, Qatar and other Arab countries, codes of civil and commercial procedures played a significant role before these countries codified arbitration acts. Saudi Arabia codified its arbitration act in the early 1980s on the basis of Sharia'a law, and a new Saudi arbitration act was promulgated in 2012. Egypt was the first country to be greatly influenced by the UNCITRAL Model Law of 1985, its arbitration act being promulgated in 1994, before the UNCITRAL Model Law amendments of 2006. Oman promulgated its arbitration act in 1997 and was greatly influenced by the UNCITRAL Model Law and the Egyptian arbitration act of 1994. Jordan promulgated a modernized and liberalized arbitration act in 2001 and, later, Bahrain, Morocco, Libya, Algeria and Sudan followed suit. Some of them were influenced by the UNCITRAL Model Law, and a few countries were influenced by the French arbitration act. Other Arab countries, such as Kuwait and the UAE, incorporated the arbitration legal regime, whether domestic or international, in codes of civil and commercial procedures. A liberal and modern draft of arbitration law has been prepared in the UAE and is on its way to being promulgated.

The institutionalization of the arbitral process in the MENA states began when the Cairo Regional Centre for International Commercial Arbitration (CRCICA) was established in 1979 under the auspices of the Asian-African Legal Consultative Organization (AALCO) and became the leading arbitral institution in the MENA region. Following the CRCICA, many other regional centres were founded in the area, such as the Dubai International Arbitration Centre (DIAC) and the Bahrain Chamber for Dispute Resolution in co-operation with the American Arbitration Association (BCDR-AAA).

It is worth mentioning that, for decades, the CRCICA has played a significant role in codifying the Egyptian arbitration act of 1994, which was followed by other arbitration acts in the MENA region. Before the codification of arbitration legislations in the region, it also played a unique role in the institutionalization of the arbitration process, whether domestic or international. Today, the CRCICA has a reputation in the international arbitration community as an impartial and independent arbitral institution, which is not subject to the influence of any Arab state government. Further, the organization has institutionalized other alternative dispute resolution mechanisms in its rules, which are well recognized in Arab arbitration practice. It also hosts practice and educational branches of international institutions such as the UK Chartered Institute of Arbitrators. Nowadays, DIAC is making a significant contribution to the institutionalization, modernization and liberalization of arbitration in the region, and the BCDR-AAA is playing an increasing part in the ADR and arbitration process. Both institutions are playing a pivotal role as arbitral institutions in the MENA region, particularly in the Gulf States.

In past centuries Arab legislation was based on Sharia'a law or *Fiqh*. Sharia'a law included a legal and religious framework relating to arbitration, particularly in family law and practice. Historically, the law in most Arab countries has been a combination of Sharia'a law and European laws. The legal and judicial system, particularly in Egypt, was influenced by the combination of Sharia'a law and European laws.[1]

The legal framework of the arbitration system in Egypt used to be a combination of Sharia'a law and French laws. Later, during Egypt's First Republic after July 1952, it was influenced by the socialist arbitration system. In the last decade of the twentieth century, particularly after 1994, arbitration law and practice in Egypt were influenced, to a great extent, by the United Nations Commission on International Trade Law (UNCITRAL) Model Law.[2]

The Middle East: A Special Case in the International Legal Order

It is appropriate at this stage to refer to the leading role of the Ottoman Empire in the MENA region centuries ago, which persisted until the region came under the control of British and French imperialism. The Ottoman Empire ruled the Arab countries through Islamic Sharia'a law, and the legal and judicial systems in those countries applied this law. The main sources of Sharia'a law are the Qur'an and the Sunnah.

1 For Egypt, see 'Arbitration in Egypt' in Abdul Hamid El Ahdab and Jalal El Ahdab, *Arbitration with the Arab Countries* (Kluwer Law International 2011) 155–223.

2 For the Egyptian legal system, see ibid.; Fathy Waly, *Arbitration Law in Theory and Practice*, 1st edn (Monsha'at El Maareef 2007) (in Arabic).

The Arab world was divided into British and French colonies during the late nineteenth and early twentieth centuries, as the Ottoman Empire began to decline. This division of the MENA region has diversified its character in many respects. Certainly, the region still retains its Eastern conservative character with regard to family laws, despite the forces of cultural and legal globalization which are reshaping new patterns of dispute resolution that were not previously recognized in the MENA region.[3] The Arab judiciary has a unique history, and it used to reject any form of parallel dispute resolution, particularly when states were involved in disputes. New forms of dispute resolution appeared in the second half of the twentieth century as a result of influence by social trends, particularly arbitration in state contracts. Whereas the division of the Middle East into French and British colonies had a minor influence on legal cultures in various Arab countries, France had a considerable influence on the language and some social and cultural habits in the Maghreb countries (Tunisia, Algeria and Morocco). This French cultural influence is not apparent in Egypt and the Gulf States. Nevertheless, the public law systems in all Arab countries, including Egypt, Morocco, Algeria, Libya, Kuwait, Oman and other Arab states are influenced by the French legal system. These countries have written constitutions and were greatly influenced by the French system, not only in terms of civil codes, but also in constitutional law and administrative law. Some countries, such as Egypt and Morocco, have *dual* judicial systems like the French system – that is, they have ordinary civil, commercial and criminal courts and an independent Conseil d'Etat (State Council) for administrative disputes. Among these administrative disputes are investor–state disputes according to the *Contrat Administratif* theory and practice.[4] Pursuant to the Egyptian constitution the Conseil d'Etat is an independent judicial authority and an essential part of the judicial authority in Egypt. It is widely respected in the regional Arab legal and judicial community as it is one of the guarantors of democracy in Egypt, protecting human rights, liberties and domestic and foreign investments through the state contracts courts circuit. The Administrative Courts in Morocco also play a pivotal role in judicial life as it has been maintaining liberties for decades. Both the Egyptian and Moroccan Administrative Courts were greatly influenced by the French Conseil d'Etat and both play a parallel role in supporting arbitral processes involving states in the MENA region, particularly investor–state arbitration. Despite their differences in terms of cultural influence – the British on Egypt, the French on the three Maghreb countries and, to a lesser extent, the British on the Gulf States – all Arab countries adopted Napoleonic civil codes. Investor–state arbitration is utilized to deal with disputes that have a connection with public and private international law, whether bilateral investment treaties (BITs) or proceedings which come before arbitration or national courts. International arbitration is a method of dispute resolution that involves a complex interconnection of private and public international law.[5] It combines both the elements of traditional litigation customarily attributed to *Contrat Administratif* and private commercial dispute resolution with an international dimension of both private and public

3 Mohamed A.M. Ismail, *Globalization and New International Public Works Agreements in Developing Countries* (Ashgate Publishing 2011); and by the same author, *Public Economic Law and the New International Administrative Contract* (El Halabi Publishing 2010, in Arabic) 49. The latter book was awarded the State Prize in Academic Research by the Arab Republic of Egypt, 2011/2012.

4 *Le Contrat Administratif* is a contract similar to civil and commercial transactions but different in three respects: (1) The state must be party to the agreement (or any of the state's public juristic entities); (2) The substance of the agreement must concern public utilities (its organization and management); and (3) The agreement must contain excessive clauses ('*Les clauses exorbitantes*') in favour of the state, or forfeiture of the letter of guarantee's performance bond.

5 Christian Leathley, *International Dispute Resolution in Latin America* (Kluwer Law International 2007) xv.

international law. Much of this book will focus on processes and systems that are fairly familiar to dispute resolution academics and practitioners.

The MENA region has now begun to recognize international arbitration and other international ADR processes. Initially, this was through the codes of civil and commercial procedures, but in the last two decades, some Arab states have promulgated arbitration acts, although they have not codified ADR mechanisms. ADR mechanisms are currently institutionalized through the regional arbitral institutions which codified ADR techniques through CRCICA and BCDR-AAA rules.

Civil Law Codification and the Influence of the French Civil Napoleonic Codes

Arab civil codes are based on Napoleonic codes. This is related to the historical circumstances that characterized the region's legal order. After the Arab revolutions in the 1950s and 1960s, a new era of political, constitutional and legal order began. Legal experts from Egypt started to codify civil codes for Arab countries based on the Egyptian legislature and on the French Napoleonic Code. The same applied to the Arab codes of civil and commercial procedures, which spread from the Egyptian legislation to the MENA countries.

Cultural, Economic, Social and Geographical Diversity in the MENA Countries

Egypt's cultural influence on the Middle East began around 7,000 years ago when Egypt rose to be the leading civilization in the Middle East and the world. In the twentieth century cultural, moral and legal concepts again began to flow from Egypt to the Arab region in a similar fashion to the spread of modern globalization. Lebanon, Syria and the Maghreb countries played a significant part in this process. Experts from Egypt, such as Dr El Sanhory,[6] played a leading role in codifying most of the Arab civil codes. In the early 1950s this flow from Egyptian legal culture to the region played a fundamental role in reshaping the region's legal order after centuries of applying Sharia'a law as the main source of legislation and litigation. After the codification of Arab civil codes, new patterns of international commercial transactions were created in the region. Until the mid-twentieth century, the MENA region did not recognize ADR or arbitration as dispute settlement mechanisms.

Meanwhile, the economic factor favoured the oil- and gas-rich Gulf States. The infrastructure revolution started early in the Gulf countries, during the second half of the twentieth century, after the discovery of huge oil and gas reservoirs in the Gulf. In parallel to the huge infrastructure projects and developments in the Gulf, there was a considerable revolution in all economic sectors, particularly during the last 50 years. Telecommunication, health, education, civil aviation, ports, energy, construction and other sectors made vital progress through very sophisticated agreements with multinational companies employed as contractors and through the adoption of very advanced technology. Arbitration resulting from disputes in these agreements, throughout the decades, is estimated at tens of trillions of US dollars. Before the establishment of regional arbitral institutions, such as the CRCICA and the DIAC, arbitral disputes were held before the international arbitral institutions such as the International Chamber of Commerce (ICC), the International Centre for

6 Dr Abdelrazak El Sanhory is the founder of the Egyptian and Arab civil codes, which are based on the French Napoleonic Code. He was President of the Egyptian Conseil d'Etat in the early 1950s and the most eminent Professor of Civil Law in Cairo University and Arab countries in the 1940s and early 1950s.

the Settlement of Investment Disputes (ICSID) and the London Court of International Arbitration (LCIA). This includes disputes between private domestic or multinational entities, which are purely commercial disputes, and other state-contract disputes between investors and any of the Arab hosting states through investor–state arbitration.

The social dimension is almost the same in all Arab countries. The entire Arab region, whether Coptic or Muslim, has the same social and cultural traditions as it comprises mainly Eastern conservative countries.[7] Cultural and legal globalization have a considerable effect on international business transactions and dispute settlement mechanisms in the MENA region but do not influence the Eastern social traditions that directly relate to culture.

The geographical factor in North African countries has played an important role in the development of huge tourism projects and their related infrastructure. Egypt (which has the additional advantage of its ancient history), the UAE, Tunisia, Morocco, Jordan and Algeria are the most touristic countries in the region. Lebanon was a leading tourist destination from the 1950s and has become so again over the last 30 years, since the end of the civil war. For many decades, geographical factors, including the Pharaonic history of Egypt, were fundamental in attracting foreign direct investment (FDI) into the region's tourism sector. Over the years huge arbitration cases have resulted from these transactions, whether state contracts, such as in the *Pyramids* case, which started as an ICC arbitration and ended as an ICSID arbitration,[8] and the Siag arbitration in the ICSID,[9] or other commercial transactions. Both the leading cases are investor–state arbitrations.[10]

Dubai in the UAE is a pivotal centre in the MENA region. It is one of the leading centres for inward foreign direct investment (IFDI) in all economic sectors. Most of the international financial institutions, multinational companies in various economic sectors and private foreign investment entities have a presence in Dubai. Indeed, these features are the main factor behind the existence and success of the DIAC as many arbitral disputes originate from huge international business transactions in the Gulf States.

Similarities Characterizing the Entire Region's Political and Legal Order

There are various similarities in the MENA region such as the Arab language, Islamic and Coptic religions, and Eastern conservative culture in some legislations, particularly in family law, regardless of minor religious controversy, as both Copts and Muslims share the same social habits. In brief, all Arab countries share the same culture with some minor liberal exceptions, such countries being Egypt, Lebanon, Tunisia and Morocco. This liberal trend is reflected in

7 Ismail, *Globalization and New International Public Works Agreements*; Ismail, *Public Economic Law*.

8 *SPP v. Egypt*, ICC Case No. 3493, session 16/2/1983, For details on the *Pyramids* case, see Sigvard Jarvin, Yves Derains and J.J. Arnaldez, *Collection of ICC Arbitral Awards, 1974–1985* (ICC Publishing 1990) 124–38. See also Mohamed A.M. Ismail, *International Construction Contracts Arbitration* (Beirut: El Halabi Publishing 2003), 107–8; *SPP v. Egypt*, ICSID Case No. ARB/84/3, https://icsid.worldbank.org (the award was issued on 20 May 1992); Philippe Leboulanger, *Les contrats entre états et entreprises étrangères* (Economica 1985) 94.

9 *Waguih Elie George Siag and Clorinda Vecchi v Egypt*, ICSID Case No. ARB/05/15, 1 June 2009, http://www.kluwerarbitration.org and https://icsid.worldbank.org.

10 For the *Pyramids* case, see Alan Redfern and Martin Hunter, *Law and Practice of International Commercial Arbitration* (2nd edn, 1991); Julian Lew, Loukas Mistelis and Stefan Kröll, *Comparative International Commercial Arbitration* (Kluwer Law International 2003); Ismail, *Globalization and New International Public Works Agreements*; Ismail, *International Construction Contracts Arbitration*.

international business transactions and arbitration. Some critical issues, such as interest rates in monetary arbitral awards, do not face any unpredictability in most Arab countries (i.e. the part of the award including the interest rate is unenforceable). The liberal Arab countries were the first to adopt legislative arbitration tools in accordance with the UNCITRAL Model Law.

The Ottoman Empire reflected the Islamic caliphate which had existed in the Arab world for centuries. The Empire declined after the First World War and the Arab world was divided into British and French colonies. Liberation revolutions started in Egypt in 1952 when the First Republic was set up, followed by another revolution in January 2011, which led to the beginning of the Second Republic. Syria, Libya, Algeria, Iraq, Yemen and Tunisia achieved independence in 1963, 1971, 1954, 1958, 1962 and 1957 respectively, and all Arab countries were against the UK, France and Italy. The Arab League was formed in 1945 as a unified regional organization representing the Arab nations.

There was consistency and harmony in the political, constitutional and legal order in the region after the mid-twentieth-century revolutions, because Egypt, under President Nasser, was leading the political forces in the Arab world. Furthermore, Egyptian legal experts were drafting Arab constitutions in all the MENA countries following their revolutions against British and French colonialism. The leading ideology in Egypt, Syria, Libya and most other Arab countries in the late 1950s and early 1960s, and for the following two decades, was socialism. This led to the nationalization of private-sector assets, unpredictability and difficulties in various economic activities in the Arab world. The Gulf region, however, was far removed from socialist ideology and its possible dramatic effect on the economies of some Arab countries, such as Egypt, Libya and Syria.

Some Arab countries, such as Egypt, Syria, Libya, Tunisia, Algeria, Iraq and Yemen, became republics after their revolutions; meanwhile, the wealthy Gulf States adopted the monarchy system in light of the social historical background of their governing families.

Harmony in political, constitutional and legal patterns led to the emergence of arbitration in regional practice in the MENA countries, administered by the CRCICA and, later, also by the DIAC. This was facilitated by a consistency in the region's constitutional and legal order, particularly with regard to Arab civil codes and codes of civil and commercial procedures. The Gulf Cooperation Council Arbitration Centre and the Bahrain Arbitration Chamber are now playing pivotal roles in the Gulf region in assisting the arbitration process.

Once again, the region is experiencing revolution – this time against dictatorship and government corruption; in 2010 in Tunisia, in January 2011 in Egypt, Libya and Yemen and, currently, in Syria and other Arab countries. Certainly, the newly elected Arab governments will not adopt socialist ideology as was the case in the 1960s. Today, following the collapse of the Soviet Union and the consequent rejection of communism throughout Eastern Europe, all Arab countries will adopt different economic ideologies, which will have a positive effect on arbitration in the MENA region.

The Region's Response to the Forces of Cultural Globalization[11]

Cultural globalization is a cultural socio-economic phenomenon.[12] The first element to be influenced by globalization was culture. Cultural interaction is the main outcome of the flow of ideas and values into Arab countries. Culture represents a set of practices, values, beliefs and

11 Ismail, *Globalization and New International Public Works Agreements*, 1–2.

12 Ibid., 1; Ismail, *Public Economic Law*.

customs acquired by individuals as members of a distinctive society and resulting from interaction amongst people.[13]

Culture has reacted to globalization in two contrasting ways:

1. acceptance of a new global culture; and
2. rejection of a total loss of cultural identity as each distinctive group of people strengthens localization.[14]

In fact, globalization, according to many authors, has two faces. With respect to the economic dimension of globalization, Stiglitz describes the effects of globalization in some parts of the world as follows:

> The current process of globalization is generating unbalanced outcomes, both between and within countries. Wealth is being created, but too many countries and people are not sharing its benefits. They also have little or no voice in shaping the process. Seen through the eyes of the vast majority of women and men, globalization has not met their simple and legitimate aspiration for decent jobs and a better future for their children … Even in the economically successful countries, some workers and communities have been adversely affected by globalization. Meanwhile, the revolution in global communications heightens awareness of these disparities.[15]

These global imbalances are morally unacceptable and politically unsustainable. However, it is also true that:

> Those who are discontented with economic globalization generally do not object to the greater access to global markets or to the spread of global knowledge, which allows the developing world to take advantage of the discoveries and innovations made in developed countries.[16]

It is argued that globalization is a debate with two different views: universalism versus territorialism or globalization versus globaphobia. However, economists used to refer to 'international economic integration' when discussing the growth of overseas transactions whereas today they refer to 'globalization', which has become the popular term. For example, in his 1983 article 'The Globalization of Markets', published in the *Harvard Business Review*, Levitt stated that a powerful force drives the world towards a converging commonality; that force is technology, and the direct outcome emanating from that is a new commercial reality.[17]

Culture is a very complex entity which, in the age of globalization, is seen to be torn between two powerful forces: 'a centrifugal force' and 'a centripetal force'. The latter force works to facilitate cultural homogenization and the formation of a true global society that has dissolved all differences, while the 'centrifugal force', under the influence of national movements and the

13 Joseph E. Stiglitz, *Globalization and its Discontents* (W.W. Norton & Company Inc. 2004). See also Stiglitz, *Making Globalization Work* (W.W. Norton & Company 2007); Brian Snowdon, *Globalization, Development and Transition* (Edward Elgar 2007); Mohamed S. Wahab, *Cultural Globalization and Public Policy: Exclusion of Foreign Law in the Global Village* (Oxford University Press 2005) Vol. 8, 306.

14 Ibid., 364.

15 Stiglitz, *Making Globalization Work*. See: *Globalization and New International Public Works Agreements*, 1.

16 Ibid. See: *Globalization and New International Public Works Agreements*, 1.

17 Levitt quoted in Snowdon.

fear of loss of identity, mitigates the impact of globalization by preserving local identities.[18] The newly advanced telecommunication technology has facilitated, to a great extent, the cultural and globalization phenomena.[19]

In modern Arab civilized systems it is common to find high degrees of differentiation. Differentiation is accepted in the cultural and legal context. When scrutinizing arbitration in state contracts, the *Le Contrat Administratif* theory was a controversial and much-debated issue in some Arab countries, such as Egypt. The Egyptian Conseil d'Etat courts (the supreme administrative courts) and the General Assembly for Legal Opinion and Legislation of the Egyptian Conseil d'Etat had different views on the same issues. The practice of arbitration faced several difficulties regarding permission to start arbitration, whether domestic or international, in state contracts. This critical issue was finally settled by Law No. 9 of 1997 amending the Egyptian Arbitration Act No. 27 of 1994, which permitted arbitration in *Le Contrat Administratif*. This legislative amendment has had a real influence on the Egyptian legislature through its effect on cultural and legal globalization. The Omani, Jordanian, UAE, Kuwaiti and Lebanese legislative powers have been constantly influenced by the effects of cultural and legal globalization through the development and codification of legislative instruments for arbitration. Further, the regional arbitral institutions began to adopt mediation and conciliation as new ADR mechanisms which were not previously recognized in the region. The CRCICA and the DIAC play a leading role in this area. The BCDR-AAA is also growing fast.

Inward of Foreign Direct Investment (IFDI) in the MENA Region in Recent Decades

Within the pattern of regional integration, Arab countries have adopted the UNCITRAL Model Law when codifying arbitration legislations in the MENA region. The UNCITRAL Model Law, which greatly influenced the legislative process for arbitration in the region, created harmonization and integration among Arab legislations. Further, its codification in the MENA region modernizes, liberalizes and internationalizes arbitration legislation and, consequently, arbitral proceedings. The latter processes increase the region's credibility in the eyes of the outside world.

Harmonization and integration in the region appeared as a result of the leading role played by the Egyptian legislature after the promulgation of the Egyptian Arbitration Act in 1994. Following in the steps of the Egyptian parliament, the Omani legislature promulgated its arbitration act in 1997. The Jordanian arbitration act appeared in 2001. Most of the Arab countries – namely, Lebanon, Kuwait and the UAE – have legislative rules on arbitration in their codes of civil and commercial procedures. All Arab countries, whether they have separate arbitration acts or still keep their arbitration regulations in their codes of civil and commercial procedures, are adopting the UNCITRAL Model Law. As arbitration is a transnational, socio-economic and legal phenomenon, the influence of the UNCITRAL Model Law on Arab legislature has unique results in practice. The flow of the Anglo-American legal practice in international arbitration is clearly apparent in Arab arbitration legislation and in the institutionalization of the arbitration process in regional arbitral institutions, particularly through the CRCICA and the DIAC which are adopting the same source in their efforts to unify arbitration practice in the region. The same applies to ADR techniques, which are as yet recognized in the region only at the institutional level. Arab legislature has not codified mediation, conciliation and other ADR mechanisms. For instance, unlike arbitration and litigation,

18 See Wahab, 364.

19 Ismail, *Globalization and New International Public Works Agreements*, 1–2.

ADR mechanisms have no legal effect in terms of interrupting the course of prescription in Arab civil codes.[20]

This integration, harmonization, liberalization and internationalization of arbitral legislative and institutional instruments is the main factor behind the internationalization of the arbitration process in the region. This internationalization is, in turn, the main incentive behind the flow of IFDI into the region in various economic sectors. Among these sectors are the infrastructure sectors which play a significant role in the arbitration process in the MENA region. It is appropriate to refer to one of the statistics which shows that the total value of projects in the MENA region is about USD 2.3 trillion. The statistics show that some other projects might be undisclosed.[21]

Latest statistics show that the total value of construction projects in the MENA region is USD 775.5 billion.[22] Disputes resulting from these projects, as well as other economic sectors, are huge; thus arbitration plays a significant role in the region as a unique mechanism encouraging IFDI in various economic sectors. International financial institutions consider effective arbitration mechanisms including, among others, the enforcing of arbitral awards in MENA countries, pursuant to Arab legal systems, a fundamental pillar of IFDI for the region. Enforceability of arbitral awards, by Arab states' courts against private domestic entities and Arab states' public juristic entities, in favour of the private foreign entities (foreign investors), is the main concern of both international financial institutions, such as the World Bank, and foreign investors. The 1958 Convention on the Recognition and Enforcement of Foreign Arbitral Awards (the New York Convention) is a recognized mechanism and has been a fundamental pillar in Arab countries for decades. The recognition that arbitral awards are final, binding and enforceable is the fundamental factor in the increase of IFDI. Further, the MENA countries' respect for their international commitments, demonstrated by their signing and ratification of international arbitration treaties, increases the region's credibility to the outside world. This respect is playing a pivotal role in increasing IFDI.

In the third quarter of FY 2008/2009 the Egyptian Ministry of Investment announced that the economic growth rate had decreased to 4.1 per cent in the second quarter of the same year compared to 7.7 per cent recorded during the same period of the previous fiscal year (2007/2008). The state budget deficit had decreased from approximately EGP45 billion (9.5 per cent) from February to July of the FY 2007/2008 to EGP38.4 billion (6.9 per cent) for the whole of the FY 2007/2008. The aim of the Egyptian government was to reduce the deficit to 3 per cent by 2011.[23] Unfortunately, unpredictable circumstances prevailed during the last 18 months and after the Egyptian Revolution of January 2011, although the situation is now beginning to improve. The Egyptian government is seeking to set a national policy to generate funds and increase existing private-sector participation in infrastructure projects and other sectors in Egypt.

If one looks at the Latin American experience for comparison, the situation in Brazil is unprecedented. Brazil became the leading Latin American recipient of foreign direct investment in 2007, followed by Mexico and Chile. Although global foreign investment flows declined in 2008 and 2009, developing countries are less likely to be affected by the current financial crises. During the 1990s Brazil did not have the ability to invest due to a lack of government funds. Instead, it

20 For prescription, see Article 374 of the Egyptian Civil Code and Article 375 of the Syrian Civil Code. All Arab civil codes have similar provisions. The concept of prescription stipulates that after a certain period of time, the claimant cannot claim his substantive rights. As a general rule, this period is 15 years in Arab civil codes.

21 http://www.zawya.com, accessed 1 December 2011.

22 http://www.zawya.com, accessed 1 December 2011.

23 Ministry of Investment, *Report on the Ministry of Investment Performance in the Fiscal Year 2007/2008*, 12.

followed an ideological agenda, chiefly targeting efficiency and innovation. Currently, however, Brazil promulgates legislations and public procurement laws governing public-private partnerships (PPPs) as, nowadays, it is facing the challenge of attracting private investment in infrastructure. This is essential to maintaining and proceeding with its development, both in profitable infrastructure facilities such as electricity and transport (roads, airports, underground railways and seaports) and in areas which require government expenditure to repay the sponsors, such as roads and those projects which do not generate enough demand such as hospitals, irrigation, schools and prisons.[24]

The globalization wave of business activities that characterized the 1980s occurred mostly within the industrialized countries. One indicator is the share of developing countries in overall FDI, which is an important indicator of globalization.[25]

FDI Incentives in Arab Arbitration Acts

As previously stated, harmonization, internationalization and integration among Arab legislations were achieved through adopting and codifying UNCITRAL Model Law principles. The Arab legislature is adopting and superseding the party autonomy principle. This trend is clear in many aspects, for instance, the consent of the parties to the dispute to start arbitration in commercial arbitration disputes. Further, proceedings in the arbitration process are very advanced, such as the constitution of the arbitral tribunal, whether in simple or complex multi-party arbitrations, and adopting the principle of *compétence à compétence* in most Arab legislations.[26] The latter principle is exercised by the tribunal; the tribunal is selected by the disputing parties. The judiciary's role in assisting the arbitral tribunal has been maintained in many cases, such as when challenging an arbitrator for lack of independence or impartiality. Further, the concept of interim measures and interlocutory awards is clear evidence that the Arab legislature is aware of how to assist the arbitral tribunal and disputing parties through prompt mechanisms when needed. The ratification of the 1958 New York Convention, so that it became an integral part of the Arab legislations, was a considerable step towards maintaining the arbitration process and enforceability of the arbitral award. This increases the region's credibility in terms of protecting FDI and maintaining a fair and constant mechanism for dispute settlement. Consequently, the IFDI to the MENA region has significantly increased in recent decades.

---

24 Cecilia Vidigal Monteiro de Barros, 'PPPs in Brazil' (2009) 26 *International Construction Law Review*, Part II, 180–81. For a comparative perspective between private education and public policy in Latin America, see Leonardo Villa and Jesús Duarte, 'Concessionary Public Schools in BOGOTÁ: An Innovation in School Management in Colombia' in Laurence Wolff, Juan Carlos Navarro and Pablo Gonzalez (eds), *Private Education and Public Policy in Latin America* (PREAL 2005) 95–130; for the situation in Argentina, see Alejandro Morduchowicz, *Private Education: Funding and (De)regulation in Argentina*, Occasional Paper No. 36 (Columbia University National Center for the Study of Privatization in Education 2001) 39–65; for Chile, see Claudia Peirano and Jaime Vargas, 'Private Schools with Public Financing in Chile' in Wolff, Navarro and Gonzalez, 67–91, and Laurence Wolff, 'Public Policy and Private Education: Where to Now?' in ibid., 247.

25 Jörg Meyer-Stamer, *Technology, Competitiveness and Radical Policy Change: The Case of Brazil* (Frank Cass 1997) 66–7.

26 This principle exists in Arab countries' arbitration legislations and in the English Arbitration Act 1996. It means that the arbitral tribunal is the authority which can issue decisions related to its jurisdiction before starting the substantive issues of the dispute.

BOT, BOOT and States' Procurement Legislations

Arbitration plays a significant role in infrastructure projects in the MENA region. The existing legal framework concerning the granting of concession agreements was promulgated by the Egyptian legislature more than five decades ago. Disputes relating to infrastructure projects are well known in investor–state arbitration.

Legislation has significantly developed with regard to granting concessions to infrastructure projects and public utilities. Laws No. 100 of 1996, No. 229 of 1996, No. 3 of 1997 and No. 22 of 1998 amended long-standing legislations (such as Law No. 129 of 1947) in regard to granting BOOT concessions for the electricity, public roads and highways, airports and civil aviation and specialized ports sectors, respectively. These four new laws mark a new advanced trend in terms of administrative contracts and state international administrative transactions.

At this stage, it is appropriate to refer briefly to the Egyptian legal regime governing BOOT (build, own, operate, transfer) transactions in view of its critical importance in understanding the current situation of PPPs and the proposed modifications and enhancements to related legal regimes. As pointed out previously, the legal regime controlling the concession-granting process for public utilities used to be governed by Law Nos 129 of 1947 and 61 of 1958. The latter was concerned with granting concessions in the area of exploiting and exploring oil, gas and natural resources pursuant to Article 123 of the 1971 Egyptian Constitution. Both laws were promulgated more than half a century ago. However, the Egyptian legislature realized that such outdated laws were not suitable for regulating BOOT transactions because of their more dynamic nature and need for rapid changes and modifications. Therefore, in the late 1990s the Egyptian parliament promulgated the above-mentioned four new laws for granting public utility concessions by virtue of BOOT agreements. The new legislation includes various modifications and enhancements to the previous legal regime governing the granting of concessions in the field of public utilities. The concession-granting period has been extended from 30 years under the previous two laws to 99 years (as a cap) under the four new laws. In addition, the state now plays a limited role in the contractual process; it is merely the technical and financial supervisor of the entire process. It cannot unilaterally amend service prices offered by the concessionaire as was the case in the traditional concession legislation. Service pricing for end-users is subject to contractual clauses as well as to the consent of the foreign contractor rather than to a regulatory clause that could be amended unilaterally by the state.[27] State intervention in the contractual process in terms of BOOT agreements is very limited compared to the old regime in the traditional concession agreements concluded by and between the state and domestic contractors. The aim of the current legislation is to meet the economic expectations of foreign contractors both at the time of tendering and in the course of preparing technical and financial feasibility studies, especially given the fact that this is a long-term agreement which, from the contractor's perspective, requires that a financial equilibrium be maintained during the span of the contract, which may last for decades.[28] Some of the fundamental legislative policies behind the promulgation of the current four laws aim to encourage private foreign entities to tender for international infrastructure projects announced by the Egyptian government. Another aim is to encourage major foreign entities in the sector to generate more FDI, in order to sustain the intensive development of infrastructure that Egypt embarked on a few decades ago. New legislation is urgently required to facilitate good transactions

27 For the regulatory clauses that can unilaterally be amended by the state in Arab doctrine, see Soad El Sharkawy, *Administrative Contracts* (Dar El Nahda El Arabia 2003) 65.

28 Ismail, *Public Economic Law*, 62.

in all sectors, as well as detailed executive regulations that are compatible with each sector's needs.[29]

It is recommended that arbitration should have special legislative provisions in the new Arab legislations to provide a threshold of protection to foreign investors.

Arbitration and Standard Forms of Contracts for Infrastructure Agreements (FIDIC Forms of Contracts)

Various forms of construction contracts can be used in state infrastructure projects in developing Arab Middle Eastern countries. The most common in use in international public works agreements and large infrastructure projects are the FIDIC (*Fédération International des Ingénieurs Conseils*) forms of contracts which include special clauses relating to arbitration.

The *FIDIC Conditions of Contract for Works of Civil Engineering: 4th Edition* (1987) includes arbitration as a dispute settlement mechanism in clause 67.3. The 1999 Red Book, Yellow Book and Silver Book are the main instruments in the field, both in terms of practice and academic research.[30] The 1999 Red Book includes in sub-clause 20.6 arbitration as a dispute settlement mechanism in case of failure to reach an amicable settlement by the parties; the 1999 Yellow Book includes in sub-clause 20.2 details of disputes and arbitration; and the 1999 Silver Book includes in sub-clause 25.2.9 stipulations related to disputes and arbitration.[31]

The adoption of FIDIC forms of contracts, particularly ADR and arbitration mechanisms, highlights the internationalization and harmonization of Arab legal systems, as well as the flow of Anglo-American legal practice into Middle Eastern civil law legal systems.

Mediation and Conciliation: Emerging ADR Mechanisms

Cultural Globalization

The forces of cultural and legal globalization were the reasons for the flow of ADR mechanisms to the MENA region in recent decades. ADR has not been codified but it has been institutionalized through CRCICA and DIAC institutional rules. Dispute resolution is an adversarial process in that parties use pieces of evidence or arguments against each other to prove their case before a judge who imposes a decision which usually leads to a win–lose situation. However, ADR theory and practice, particularly in negotiation and mediation processes, try to achieve a win–win situation that will not violate any of the disputing parties' expectations to any great extent. Despite the fact that negotiations and mediation have restricted applications in Middle Eastern Arab countries, the concept is significant.[32]

Economic Growth

A factor in the economic growth of the MENA region is the use of conciliation and mediation to maintain a fast and effective dispute resolution mechanism which respects party autonomy.

29 Ibid., 64.

30 See generally Nael G. Bunni, *The FIDIC Forms of Contracts*, 3rd edn (Blackwell 2005).

31 Ismail, *Globalization and New International Public Works Agreements*.

32 Ibid.

The terms 'mediation' and 'conciliation' are used interchangeably in the MENA region. Unlike arbitration, mediation does not violate any of the disputing parties' expectations in terms of the arbitral award. Instead, it leads to an agreement between the parties and is subject to their consent. Thus, the codification of mediation in the institutional rules of bodies such as the CRCICA and the BCDR-AAA is of great significance to economic growth as mediation may constitute an easy method of dispute settlement. Mediation may also avoid arbitration, which is often a costly and lengthy process.

Reduced Workload for the Judiciary

The ADR legislative and regulatory framework in the Egyptian Conseil d'Etat and Arab jurisdictions has played a considerable role in reducing workload for the judiciary.

Article 28 of the Egyptian Conseil d'Etat Law No. 47 of 1972 stipulates that the Commissaire d'Etat shall find a mechanism for amicable settlement for disputes between parties. Despite the fact that this article was promulgated in 1972, few applications have been issued to date. Furthermore, the president of the Egyptian Conseil d'Etat has issued an administrative decree to regulate procedures relating to the implementation of Article 28. Decision No. 35 of 2003, dated 1 February 2003, set out in detail procedures for amicable settlements in light of the Egyptian Supreme Administrative Court principles, as this court is highest in the Egyptian judicial hierarchy. The decree stipulates that, if the Commissaire d'Etat suggests an approach for an amicable settlement and either party, whether the state or the private entity, rejects the settlement without justifiable reason, then the rejecting party may pay a fine pursuant to the Commissaire d'Etat decision. To date, the Egyptian Conseil d'Etat has not exercised amicable settlement on a wide scale.[33]

In another attempt to achieve ADR and to reduce the workload for the judiciary, the Egyptian legislature promulgated Law No. 7 of 2000 on conciliation between individuals and the state in disputes between both parties. The law stipulates that any party who wishes to start a dispute against the state must begin conciliation through retired judges who are appointed as conciliators by the Minister of Justice. In case of failure of conciliation, the conciliation committee has to issue a legal opinion (a recommendation) that a party can start litigation if the outcome of conciliation is not satisfactory to him and it violated his expectations.

However, the outcome of conciliation is always unsatisfactory for one of the parties as it is an imposed decision rather than an agreement between the disputing parties. The aim of this legislation, as stated above, is to reduce workload for the judiciary. In practice, the public juristic entity does not follow the decision of the conciliation committee; thus the foreign private entity has to start arbitration proceedings. This procedural step is not required before starting arbitration. However, the new parliament of the Egyptian Second Republic, which was elected in January 2012, annulled Law No. 7 of 2000 as it has not proved to be successful in practice; it merely caused delays to the litigation process. It is obligatory to go to the conciliation committee before starting litigation, but it is not obligatory to follow the recommendations of the committee; thus, the public juristic entity and private persons are not obliged to follow the committee's recommendation. Because the committee's recommendation is not enforceable, the law failed to achieve its aim of achieving an amicable settlement and avoiding a long litigation process.

---

33 Mohamed Badran, 'ADR for Administrative Dispute in Egyptian Administrative Law' (undated unpublished paper); Announcement by the President of the Conseil d'Etat, *El Ahram* (Cairo, 21 February 2003) 13; for further suggestions see: Mohamed A.M. Ismail, 'The Suggested Role of the Egyptian State Council', *El Ahram* (Cairo, 31 July 2001) 32; and Ismail, *Globalization and New International Public Works Agreements*.

The Distinction between Mediation and Conciliation in the Middle Eastern Countries

In most developed legal systems, negotiation and mediation play a significant role in attempting to avoid arbitration which is costly, particularly with the growth in cross-border transactions where the potential for dispute is high.[34]

Because the international infrastructure agreements differ from domestic public works agreements, developing states have tended to create new mechanisms over the last decade. The new trend was imposed by modifications and developments to the public economic law and state procurement law in civil law jurisdictions in Arab Middle Eastern states. Privatization of public-sector utilities, developments in the infrastructure sector and the promulgation of investment legislation in recent decades have considerably influenced the legal culture in developing countries. The growth of inward foreign direct investment (IFDI) requires new dispute settlement mechanisms beyond ordinary litigation.

Centuries ago, before litigation became the means of dispute settlement,[35] disputes were generally settled by village priests and family friends. During the past 30 years, the increase in negotiation and mediation and related processes in developed states was often referred to as the alternative dispute resolution (ADR) movement. Arbitration has been used in most American jurisdictions for more than 75 years and its use was favoured by law.[36]

Negotiation was one of the most important tools for dispute settlement in the pre-contractual steps before the dispute reached the national courts. Pre-trial adjudication, rather than the national courts, played a significant role in dispute settlements, especially in the United States. Mediation started in the United States with a very limited scope compared to arbitration which was, until then, the main mechanism for dispute resolution. In the mid-twentieth century, the courts began to encourage the mediation process; the term used was 'conciliation', particularly in family law disputes. The use of ADR mechanisms grew significantly in the 1970s, especially when judges and lawyers took into account the delays and increased costs involved in the litigation process.[37] ADR began to look like an effective alternative to normal litigation.

The main advantages of ADR mechanisms[38] are that they are low-cost, fast and maintain confidentiality for huge multinational companies; in addition, disputing parties can choose a specialized negotiator or mediator. They are used not only as a means for reaching an amicable settlement, but also for preventing further disputes in the future.[39]

Mediation[40]

Mediation is the central, most frequently adopted ADR technique worldwide.[41] It is 'the use of a third party to help those in conflicts to do things and breach agreements which, unaided, they may never be able to do or may do so much later in the conflict when each side will have suffered further

34 Karl Mackie and David Miles, *Commercial Dispute Resolution: An ADR Practice Guide* (Butterworths 1995).

35 Ibid., 3, 6.

36 Ibid., 6.

37 Ibid., 7.

38 For the advantages of ADR, see ibid.

39 Hani Salah Sarie-Eldin, *Consortia Agreements in the International Construction Industry* (Kluwer Law International 1996) 202.

40 Ismail, *Globalization and New International Public Works Agreements*, 138–40.

41 Mackie and Miles, 41.

harm'.[42] Its aim is to open doors to help disputing parties achieve a rational and problem-solving approach, to clarify issues and to help negotiations by bringing objectivity to a dispute. Generally, mediation aims to put back responsibility for the outcome into the hands of the parties. There are no unpredictable outcomes as may happen with arbitration or litigation. In a dispute, each party wishes to achieve a 'win' situation for himself or herself and a 'lose' situation for his or her opponent. However, if a mediation agreement is achievable, it is by the consent of both parties who are each trying to reach a 'win–win' situation. Conversely, if either party fails to achieve a 'win–win' situation and agrees to any other scenario, this implies that he or she accepts this approach to the unpredictability of a binding, final and enforceable arbitral award. Legal interpretation differs from other sciences, such as engineering. A single issue is controversial in terms of legal interpretation due to the controversy amongst various jurisdictions and legal cultures; thus, a single issue for consideration and determination may be subject to different interpretations in civil law jurisdictions from those of common law jurisdictions. By contrast, the dimensions of a dam, a bridge or a building are the same, even if measured by different consultancy engineering firms from different countries.

Some scholars use the terms 'mediation' and 'conciliation' interchangeably. Others use the term 'conciliation' to denote less formal procedures than 'mediation'; moreover, they argue that a conciliator is less active than a mediator. However, in the MENA countries, the terms 'conciliation' and 'mediation', which are not accurately defined, are generally used interchangeably.[43]

The process works as follows. All parties to a dispute agree to mediate, then a location and time are arranged, and a mediator is selected. The mediation begins with a joint session which everyone attends. The mediator makes an opening statement explaining the process and his role as a mediator and asks each side in turn to make a presentation of its case and its position. Opening statements, which may be in writing, should last no more than 10 to 15 minutes, after which there is an opportunity to ask questions, both of the mediator and the other side. A mediator will have the opportunity to see each side in a private session.[44]

Mediators' strategies vary widely. Some mediators focus negotiations on satisfying the vital interests of each party whereas others focus on legal rights. The process that experienced mediators use is simple, even in complex disputes. Mediators traditionally enter disputes with little authority; their ability to help bring about settlements depends partly on the willingness of the parties to accept the mediator. When trust has been established, parties can be expected to cooperate with the mediator, disclose their real interest and value the mediator's reaction.[45]

The mediator summarizes the areas of agreement to motivate the parties towards a final settlement. If the parties move to mutual consent and a common position on disputed issues, the mediator begins to draft the agreement. The mediation agreement should preferably be in writing, and may include an enforcement clause which provides for monitoring by the mediator or another party and specifies what the parties will do if they believe the agreement has been violated.[46]

---

42 Bevan, 18.

43 For the purpose of this study, both terms will be treated as synonymous. For the same approach see Sarie-Eldin, 205; and for Arab doctrine see Ismail, *Globalization and New International Public Works Agreements*, 321–4.

44 Bevan; Bunni, 425; Philippe Fouchard, Emmanuel Gaillard and Berthold Goldman, *Traité de l'arbitrage commercial international* (Litec 1996), 16ff; Mackie and Miles, 76–9.

45 Stephen Goldberg, Frank Sander and Nancy Rogers, *Dispute Resolution: Negotiation, Mediation and Other Processes*, 2nd edn, Law School Case Book Series (Little, Brown and Company 1992) 105–6.

46 For a mediation agreement, see, for example, Mackie and Miles, 201; for more elaboration and explanation of the process, see Goldberg, Sander and Rogers, 110. For Arab doctrine, see Ismail, *Globalization*

Mediation is a voluntary process, which means that you can leave when you wish. It is a non-binding process by which a mediator cannot impose a decision.[47] Moreover, it is a confidential process. A mediator may attempt to encourage exchange of information, provide new information, help the parties understand each other's views, promote a productive level of emotional expression, encourage flexibility, let the parties know that their concerns are understood, and stimulate the parties to suggest a creative settlement and invent solutions that meet the fundamental interests of all parties.[48]

Unlike in arbitration, a conciliation or mediation clause is simply a declaration of intent which does not oblige the parties to refer a dispute to a mediator. Mediation is an informal process which may or may not result in an agreement between the parties on the disputed matters. Proposals made by the mediator are not final or binding upon the parties, who are free to accept or reject the expert's recommendations. As the mediator's recommendations and suggestions are not an arbitral award, they are not covered by the 1958 New York Convention on the Recognition and Enforcement of Foreign Arbitral Awards.[49]

A mediator should be a neutral and experienced adviser. Procedures should maintain simplicity, minimum delay, confidentiality and a short period for the conduct of mediation itself. International arbitral institutions such as the International Chamber of Commerce (ICC) and the American Arbitration Association (AAA) provide mediation rules. Regional institutions such as the CRCICA and BCDR-AAA also provide advanced mediation rules. The fundamental principles of ADR (that is, its non-binding nature, flexibility, party autonomy and volition, and confidentiality) are the foundations of the mediation and conciliation rules adopted by the above-mentioned organizations.[50]

If parties fail to achieve a mutually agreed resolution through mediation and if there is an arbitration clause in the international agreement, either party can initiate arbitral proceedings. A crucial question arises when the agreement stipulates that amicable settlement through mediation is a preliminary step before starting arbitral proceedings. If a party fails to start mediation and moves directly to arbitral proceedings, can the other party allege that mediation is a condition precedent to the start of arbitral proceedings?

If either party fails to try mediation in an attempt to achieve an amicable settlement before starting arbitration, it will not deprive that individual of his or her substantive right to start arbitral proceedings pursuant to procedural rules and to claim his or her substantive rights. The same legislative stipulation exists in all Arab civil codes.

Does ADR Affect Prescription and Substantive Rights in Civil Law Legal Systems?[51]

In civil law legal systems, prescription is a fundamental concept by which a claimant cannot claim substantive rights after a certain period of time.[52] Prescription is codified in all Arab codes following the Egyptian Civil Code. This period is 15 years in Egypt (Article 374 of the Civil Code) and most Arab jurisdictions (Article 372 of the Syrian Civil Code).[53] Article 383 of the Egyptian

---

and New International Public Works Agreements, 322–4.

47 Bevan, 18–19.

48 Goldberg, Sander and Rogers, 103.

49 Sarie-Eldin, 205.

50 Ibid., 205–6.

51 Ibid.

52 For Arab civil law doctrine, see Abdel Razek El Sanhoury, *The General Theory of Obligations. Part 3: Expiry of Obligations* (1984) 1162; Abdel Wadoud Yehia, *Obligations' Stipulations* (Cairo, 1987) 370.

53 Ismail, *Globalization and New International Public Works Agreements*, 138–40.

Civil Code stipulates that prescription can be terminated by recourse to litigation or by starting any kind of litigation process before the courts. The claimant retains substantive rights and continues litigation proceedings.

In Middle Eastern civil law jurisdictions, the ADR mechanism does not terminate prescription unless arbitration or litigation proceedings have begun. In other words, unlike arbitration, negotiations and mediation do not terminate prescription and start a new prescription period. If either party claims substantive rights through mediation and the prescription duration has started, such party has to claim substantive rights through arbitration or litigation. The reason is that legislation in civil law jurisdictions, such as the Egyptian Arbitration Act and the Kuwaiti Civil and Commercial Procedural Law, states that arbitration, as well as court procedures, is a means of claiming substantive rights.

Despite the fact that other ADR mechanisms are institutionalized in the rules of arbitral institutions, such as the CRCICA, national legislation has not yet codified them. Commentators differ as to whether or not prescription can be terminated by the agreement of the parties. Some suggest that it is possible as the prescription duration is not a matter of public policy;[54] others believe it is not possible.[55]

Prescription can only be terminated by legislation as this supersedes agreements made by the contracting parties.

It is strongly recommended that Middle Eastern jurisdictions codify negotiation and mediation as effective means of dispute settlements and that they be an integral part of the judicial process as well as arbitration. Furthermore, civil law legal systems in the above-mentioned countries should recognize the legal effect regarding prescription and all other concepts relating to civil law legal culture principles. Until legislation in Arab developing states recognizes ADR mechanisms, courts must consider the legal effect of these mechanisms and apply the party autonomy principle stipulated by the contracting parties.[56]

Arbitration as a New Mechanism for Dispute Settlement in the MENA Region in Recent Decades

Various civil law jurisdictions, particularly in Arab Middle Eastern countries, recognize arbitration as a fast and effective mechanism for dispute resolution as it leads to a final, binding and enforceable award. Arbitration is deemed the alternative means for the settlement of administrative and commercial contract disputes. It plays a vital role in the resolution of disputes. Despite the availability of various other alternatives, arbitration receives significant preference from local and international dispute arenas alike. Thus, parties to a dispute are provided with a judicial mechanism which they may voluntarily resort to for the settlement[57] of any existing or potential conflict that may arise between them. Arbitration in developing countries is surrounded by special circumstances. As a means of resolving disputes, it is distinguished from other means of dispute resolution by pertinent characteristics that have attracted the support of some and the opposition of others.[58]

54 Mohamed Abdel Latif, *Prescription*, 2nd edn (1996) 149.

55 Fathi Waly, *El Wassit in Civil Law Procedures* (Dar El Nahda El Arabia 1986) 40; Abdel Monem El Sharkawy, *Civil and Commercial Procedures* (n.p. 1950), paras 464, 633.

56 Ismail, *Globalization and New International Public Works Agreements*, 138.

57 Lew, Mistelis and Kröll, 1.

58 Ismail, *Globalization and New International Public Works Agreements*; Ismail, *International Construction Contracts Arbitration*.

Arbitration may be classified into domestic arbitration and international arbitration, and each may be further sub-classified into institutional or *ad hoc*.

First, a clear definition must be given to the term 'arbitration' in the MENA countries. Its characteristics, merits and demerits also need to be reflected upon. The next chapters of this book will provide an in-depth analysis on the procedural and substantive issues of international commercial arbitration and investment arbitration processes in the MENA countries.

Chapter 2
International Commercial Arbitration in the MENA Region

Historical Background

Arab legal systems have recognized arbitration only recently.[1] Previously, Arab state constitutions allocated the dispute settlement process to the courts. Recent developments in Arab constitutional and legislative systems and in Arab countries are the main reason for adopting arbitration as a means of settling disputes. Many Middle Eastern and North African (MENA) countries began to accept arbitration as a dispute settlement mechanism, particularly over the last 20 years, in light of their existing constitutions. For example, in Egypt, arbitration used to be conducted pursuant to the Code of Civil and Commercial Procedures, but after the promulgation of the new Egyptian Arbitration Act in 1994, the Egyptian legal system accepted the concept of a parallel mechanism for dispute settlement within the same constitution, leading the disputing parties to a final, binding and enforceable award. A considerable debate arose in the Egyptian judiciary and in the Arab doctrine which rejected arbitration during the 1980s and early 1990s. Concerns were raised regarding arbitration as a dispute settlement mechanism in Egypt in light of the 1971 constitution. When the Egyptian legislature promulgated the Arbitration Act No. 27 of 1994, there was a new interpretation of the current legislative progress in light of the 1971 constitution. However, it is not the constitution which draws up the legal framework for arbitration in the Middle East region but the interpretation of the legislation. In Egypt, the leading legal system in the MENA region, several interpretations were given by the General Assembly for Legal Opinion and Legislation

---

1 For Arab doctrine, see: Fathy Waly, *Arbitration Law in Theory and Practice*; Samia Rashed, *Arbitration in Private International Relations* (Dar El Nahda El Arabia 1984); Samir El Sharkawy, *International Commercial Arbitration, a Comparative Study* (Cairo: Dar El Nahda El Arabia 2011); Abdel Hamid El Ahdab, *Encyclopaedia of Arbitration* (in Arabic) (Beirut: El Halabi Publishing Co. 2009); Ahmed El Sawy, *The Concise in Arbitration* (3rd edn, Dar El Nahda El Arabia 2010); Azmy Abdelfatah Attya, *Kuwaiti Law of Civil Procedures, a Comparative Study with the New French Code, Arbitration Act, Gulf council countries and other Arab countries* (2nd edn, Kuwait: Dar El Kootob 2012); Mohamed A.M. Ismail, *International Construction Contracts Arbitration*; Mokhtar Beriry, *International Commercial Arbitration* (Dar El Nahda El Arabia, 1995).

For international doctrine generally see: Julian Lew, Loukas Mistelis and Stefan Kröll, *Comparative International Commercial Arbitration*; Alan Redfern and Martin Hunter, *Law and Practice of International Commercial Arbitration* (London, Sweet and Maxwell, 2nd edn, 1991 and 3rd edn, 1999); Nigel Blackaby and Constantine Partasides with Redfern and Hunter, *Redfern and Hunter on International Commercial Arbitration* (Oxford University Press 2009); Phillipe Fouchard, Emmanuel Gaillard and Berthold Goldman, *Traitė de barbitrage commercial international* (also in English); Julian Lew, *Applicable Law in International Commercial Arbitration* (New York: Oceana 1978); Mohamed A.M. Ismail, *Globalization and New International Public Works Agreements*; Laurence Craig, William Park and Jan Paulsson, *International Chamber of Commerce Arbitration* (ICC Publishing 1985); The Egyptian Conseil d'Etat, file 54/1/265, session 17/5/1989 and same decision by the Appeal Administrative Court; see also Case No. 486 of Judicial Year (38). These Judgements by the Supreme Administrative court, session 20/2/1990 case (3049) of (32).

of the Egyptian Conseil d'Etat which referred to Article 10 of the Conseil d'Etat. Legislation No. 27 of the Egyptian constitution stipulates that the Egyptian Conseil d'Etat is the only authority in the Egyptian judiciary which has the jurisdiction to make settlements in administrative disputes. Among these administrative disputes are the administrative contracts disputes. Several interpretations of the constitutional ban stipulated by Article 172 became an important issue in the Arab legal community. The importance of this issue justifies the exclusive jurisdiction of the Egyptian judiciary regarding dispute settlements of administrative contracts, prohibiting any dispute mechanism from exercising its power to issue final, binding and enforceable awards. This interpretation prevailed for many years in the Egyptian and other legal systems in the region. However, judicial opinions in 1989 and in 1993 pointed to the fact that Article 10 of the Egyptian State Council Law No. 47 of 1972 had to be interpreted in the light of Article 172 of the Egyptian constitution of 1971. This interpretation emphasizes the importance of the concept of exclusive jurisdiction of the State Council to exercise judicial review upon administrative contracts. This exclusive jurisdiction was exercised pursuant to Article 10 which was promulgated by the Egyptian Parliament in 1972 and in the light of the 1971 constitution.[2] The purpose of this article is to draw the line between the Egyptian State Council courts' jurisdiction on one hand; and the civil and commercial courts' jurisdiction on the other. Article 10 was promulgated to create a distinction between the administrative courts' jurisdictions and civil and commercial disputes, which can be referred to ordinary courts.[3]

To conclude, it was up to the Egyptian Supreme Administrative Court and the General Assembly for Legal Opinion and Legislation in the Egyptian State council to decide on and to create a detailed interpretation in light of the 1971 constitution and the socialist ideology which was adopted upon the promulgation of the 1971 constitution. Arbitration was a controversial process and it was not determined whether to accept arbitration in light of the 1971 constitution or not. The Code of Civil and Commercial Procedures in Egypt and in all Arab countries included some provisions for dispute settlement through arbitration. This particular problem was the reason for considerable debate amongst judiciary in the MENA region, particularly in Egypt. The debate was not completely settled after the promulgation of the Egyptian Arbitration Act in 1994; it was not until 18 December 1996 that the Egyptian State Council issued a leading decision by which arbitration was prohibited in administrative contracts, despite the existence of Article 1 of the Egyptian Arbitration Act No. 27 of 1994. The Egyptian General Assembly for Legal Opinion and Legislation, which is the highest legal opinion authority in the Arab judiciary, stated its famous decision[4] which pointed out that in the light of Article 1 of the Egyptian Arbitration Act of 1994, it is not clear whether the Egyptian legislature's intention is to accept arbitration in administrative contracts or not, as Article 1 of the Egyptian Arbitration Act includes general clauses. The general legislative provisions, in light of the General Assembly's interpretation, make it unclear in the Arbitration Act of 1994 as to whether or not arbitration can be accepted in administrative contracts. Further, the General Assembly pointed to one of the fundamental principles in administrative contracts in Arab jurisdictions. This fundamental principle is that a public juristic entity cannot

2 Article 48 of the Constitutional Declaration, March 2011, after the second Egyptian Revolution.

3 The General Assembly for Legal Opinion and Legislation, the Egyptian Conseil d'Etat, file No. 54/1/265, session 17/5/1989 and the same decision by the Appeal Administrative Court, case No. 486 of the judicial year (38). This case was rejected by the supreme Administrative Court, session 20/2/1990, case (3049) of the judicial year (32). See also: The Appeal Administrative Court, Case No. 5837, of the Judicial year (44), session 9/12/1990.

4 The General Assembly for legal opinion and legislation, session 22/2/1997, file 54/1/339, opinion No. (160).

grant competence to arbitrators as the public juristic entity had delegated its power from the nation pursuant to Arab constitution. Pursuant to administrative law principles, if a public juristic entity has had power delegated to it, it cannot delegate this power to any other entity.[5]

Finally, despite the fact that the Egyptian, Syrian, Libyan, Iraqi, Algerian and some other constitutions[6] adopted the socialist ideology, which rejects arbitration from the Socialist political parties' points of view, there were some interpretations which accepted arbitration in other countries.[7]Meanwhile, decisions of Arab courts rejected arbitration until the promulgation of Arab arbitration acts or until the modernization of the civil and commercial procedures laws took place.

Legislations were promulgated in the light of the existing situation in order to provide a safe environment for investment in Arab countries by adopting arbitration as a dispute settlement mechanism. UNCITRAL Model Law played a significant role in codifying Arab arbitration acts such as in Egypt in 1994, Oman in 1997, Jordan in 2001 and Bahrain in 1994. Other legal systems which have arbitration legislative rules incorporated in their codes of civil and commercial procedural laws such as those of Kuwait and UAE have been influenced to a great extent by the UNCITRAL Model Law. This is a sign of the liberalization of arbitration acts in the Middle East region. Despite previous arbitration practices and in light of the experiences of Arab constitutions, most of the promulgated arbitration acts adopted UNCITRAL Model Law principles towards the internationalization of arbitration in the region. Most of the Arab countries adopted the UNCITRAL Model Law: Egypt in 1994, Oman in 1997, Jordan in 2001 and Bahrain in 1994. Arab arbitration acts are, to a great extent, a liberal and modern step towards increasing Foreign Direct Investment (FDI) in the region. It is worth mentioning that some Arab arbitration acts followed the French arbitration law, such as the act of Algeria in 2008.[8]

International Commercial Arbitration in the Middle East before Arbitration Acts

International Commercial Arbitration had started in the Middle East before the codification of arbitration acts in the region. It is appropriate to refer to the fact that private foreign entities and public juristic entities in the Middle East were party to arbitration disputes before the International Chamber of Commerce (ICC) in Paris, the International Centre of Settlement of Investment Disputes (ICSID) and regional centres such as the Cairo Regional Centre for International Commercial Arbitration (CRCICA), the Dubai International Arbitration Centre (DIAC) and the Bahrain Chamber for Dispute Resolution (BCDR-AAA). The legal framework in international commercial arbitration was governed by the Arab Codes of Civil and Commercial Procedures before codifying arbitration acts in Arab countries.[9] International investment arbitration was subject to the Washington Convention and to BITs as these are valid legislations in Arab countries after ratification, pursuant to Arab constitutions.[10]

5 Ibid., the same legal opinion; Appeal Administrative Court, case 496/ of the Judicial year (5), Session 1/2/1954; Hamdy Yassin, *The Administrative Acts* (Alexandria: Monsha'at El Maaref, 1987).

6 See Egyptian, Lebanese, Syrian, Iraqi and Algerian constitutions.

7 Egyptian Supreme Administrative Court, 3049, of Judicial Year (32), Session 20/2/1990 and Egyptian Appeal Administrative Court at the Egyptian Conseil d'Etat, Case No. (5837) of the Judicial year (44).

8 El Ahdab, 8 (in Arabic).

9 See, for instance, Egyptian Code of Civil and Commercial Procedures No. 13 of 1968.

10 Arab Constitutions, for instance, see Egyptian Constitution, Article 151; Omani Constitution, Article 76 ; Kuwaiti Constitution, Article 177; Lebanese Constitution, Article 52.

Sharia'a Law in Arab countries recognizes arbitration as a dispute settlement mechanism in family law.[11] Arbitration was recognized about 14 centuries ago in Islamic Law as a dispute settlement mechanism and this has continued over the following centuries; the Qur'an, the Muslims' holy book, recognizes arbitration as a dispute settlement mechanism in family law. Since then, arbitration has been recognized in international business transactions, civil, commercial and administrative contracts.

International Dispute Resolution in the MENA Region

In recent decades, arbitration has been the most significant alternative method in dispute settlement in Arab Middle Eastern countries as it plays a significant role in dispute resolution. Arbitration is given significant preference in local as well as international dispute arenas. Given the fact that the disputing parties at the arbitral dispute are the reason for the establishment of an arbitration tribunal, the Arab arbitration acts supersede the party autonomy principle in all newly promulgated arbitration acts in the Middle East region. It is strongly recommended that arbitration is used by jurisdictions to strengthen the scope of application of an enforceable award which might violate a disputing party's expectations; meanwhile mediation, for instance, is a feasible technique that meets disputing parties' expectations. Further, mediation avoids parties' fees, expenses and the time spent in arbitration. It is a feasible technique which meets the disputing parties' expectations through the mediator's agreement.

International dispute resolutions which are currently recognized in Arab countries are mediation and arbitration. It is clear that in the Arab world, the terms 'mediation' and 'conciliation' are used interchangeably. The fact is that arbitration which leads to a final, binding and enforceable award is nowadays very well known in the region. Arbitration has different characteristics to other alternative dispute resolutions worldwide, particularly mediation. The definition of arbitration in the Arab legal system reflects its unique characteristics, which are different from those of any other mechanism. Scholarly opinion, in Arab doctrine, considers arbitration to be an agreement between parties contractual or otherwise, restricting the settlement of a dispute to individuals selected as arbitrators. The parties to a dispute choose the arbitrators; parties may also choose a permanent arbitration centre to manage the arbitration process in accordance with the centre's bylaws and regulations.[12]

International Commercial Arbitration and International Investment Arbitration (Investor–State Arbitration)

International commercial arbitration is based on an arbitration clause/agreement. In Arab arbitration acts, there is a clear reference to the arbitration agreement which is significant in starting the arbitration process.[13] In Arab countries, disputing parties cannot start arbitration in international commercial arbitration without an arbitration clause/agreement. The situation is different in international investment arbitration, where a foreign investor can rely on an arbitration provision in

11 The Muslim holy book, the Qur'an.

12 Beriry, 5.

13 Egyptian Arbitration Act, Article 10; Omani Arbitration Act, Articles 10–12; Kuwaiti Code of Civil Procedures 173; Bahrain Arbitration Act No. 9 of 1994, Articles 7–9, and Bahrain legislation No. 30 of 2009, section 2; Jordanian Arbitration Act, Articles 9–11; UAE Code of Civil and Commercial Procedures, Article 203.

any Bilateral Investment Treaty (BIT) or a Multilateral Investment Treaty. The hosting state, when signing and ratifying a BIT, considers the treaty to be valid legislation in Arab legal systems. Arab constitutions stipulate that an international treaty, whether bilateral or multilateral, upon ratification by parliaments in Arab countries, is valid legislation in these countries.[14] Thus, a foreign investor can rely upon arbitration provision in an international treaty to offer him safe recourse to arbitration as long as the treaty is ratified by the other state parliament without an arbitration clause/agreement. The latter situation provides protection for investors who are not concerned with domestic national investments. It is worth mentioning there may be situations where some procedural steps have to be taken by investors to start arbitration; for instance, the Egyptian Arbitration Act 1994 stipulates that in administrative contracts, an investor, whether domestic or foreign, cannot start arbitration proceedings without the concerned minister's consent. In addition, the domestic investor is not protected by an international treaty offering him safe recourse to arbitration without procedural steps, and the concerned minister's consent is mandatory for domestic investors as well as foreign investors. In other words, the domestic investor cannot start arbitration without the concerned minister's consent as stipulated in the Egyptian Arbitration Act, 1994.

However, the foreign investor can start arbitration by an easier process relying on the international treaty which offers him a threshold of protection and a dispute settlement mechanism through arbitration without recourse to the national courts pursuant to national Codes of Civil Procedures. Arab constitutions stipulate that the international treaty is an integral part of Arab legislation if it has been ratified by Arab parliaments.[15] The hosting states cannot stipulate that the foreign investor must be granted the concerned minister's consent, as long as the foreign investor is protected by an international treaty. Although it is clear that the international instruments provide a threshold of protection to private foreign investments (investors) in Arab jurisdictions, this protection and the possibility of starting arbitration is not applicable to domestic investors, who are subject to procedural stipulations by Arab arbitration acts, such as the concerned minister's consent to start arbitration. The fact is that the threshold of protection granted to foreign investors is greater than the protection provided to domestic investors. Thus, it is strongly recommended that the legislative stipulation should apply to international commercial arbitration and not to international investment arbitration, as there is legislative consent from the state after ratifying a BIT to enable the foreign investor to start investor–state arbitration.

The Art and Science of International Commercial Arbitration in the MENA Region

The art and science of international commercial arbitration lie in the fact that the process is based on party autonomy. Disputes between parties are the reason behind the existence of the arbitral tribunal, its competence, jurisdiction and the powers vested in the tribunal until a final award is reached. This is the main feature of arbitration in Arab countries. However, there are some other scholarly opinions which highlight the judicial theory and the nature of arbitration as it leads to

14 For examples in Arab constitutions see: Egyptian Constitution, Article 151; Kuwaiti constitution 177. It is worth mentioning that the French constitution of 4/10/1958, Article 55, stipulates that an international treaty supersedes national legislation, after ratification. This is on the condition that the other party must apply the same treaty.

15 See the following Arab constitutions: Egyptian Constitution, Article 151; Omani Constitution, Article 76; Kuwaiti constitution 177. It is worth mentioning that the French constitution of 4/10/1958, Article 55 stipulates that an international treaty supersedes national legislation, after ratification. This is conditioned that the other party must apply the same treaty.

a final, binding and enforceable award.[16] It has been suggested that both the contractual nature, which is based on party autonomy, and the judicial nature, which leads to a binding, final and enforceable award, reflect party autonomy in the existence of the arbitral tribunal based on parties' choice.[17] The arbitral award wouldn't exist without the parties' consent to start arbitration.

Definition of International Commercial Arbitration in the Arab Middle Eastern Doctrine

The use of the term 'commercial' usually refers to a subject matter of a commercial nature. In Arab Middle Eastern jurisdictions, trade legislations and commercial transactions having such a commercial nature are seen as being distinct from civil transactions. The significance of the distinction is that commercial transactions are subject to simple evidence rules and a short prescription, a well-known concept relating to the expiry of substantive rights after a certain period of time.[18] The Modern Law stipulates that the term commercial be given a wide interpretation to cover matters arising from commercial relationships. Relationships of a commercial nature include but are not limited to the following transactions: any trade transaction for the supply or exchange of goods or services; distribution agreements; commercial representation factoring; construction of works; consulting, engineering, licensing, investment, agency, financing, banking, concession, joint-venture and other forms of industrial or business cooperation; carriage of goods or passengers by air.

The legislative policy behind this is to maintain a better atmosphere for arbitration. After the prominent promulgation of the Egyptian Arbitration Act in 1994, the Omani Arbitration Act in 1997, the Bahrain Arbitration Act, the Libyan Conciliation and Arbitration Act in 2010, the Jordanian Arbitration Act in 2001, the Sudanese Arbitration Act in 2005 and other Arab legislations, Egypt, Dubai and Bahrain became the centre for international commercial arbitration under the auspices of the Cairo Regional Centre of International Commercial Arbitration, the Dubai International Arbitration Centre and the Bahrain Chamber for Dispute Resolution.[19]

Arbitration Theory in Middle Eastern Legal Systems

Middle Eastern Civil Law Countries and the Acceptance of Arbitration 'Constitutional and Legislative Principles'

International business transactions between states and private foreign entities are the direct result of economic growth within developing countries. Economic growth projects are not only

16 Ahmed Abou El Wafa, *Contractual and Obligatory Arbitration* (Alexandria: Monsha'at El Maaref, 3rd edn, 1978), 18; and in very old eminent Arab doctrine, see Abdel Monem El Sharkawy, *Civil and Commercial Procedures*, No. 464, 633; Abou Zaid Radwan, *General Principles of International Commercial Arbitration* (Dar El Fikr El Arabi 1981), No. 21, 34; Ismail, *International Construction Contracts Arbitration*, 356–8. The Egyptian Supreme Constitutional Court, Case No (104) of Judicial year (20), session 3/7/1999. In French doctrine, for instance, see M. de Boisséson, *Le droit Français de l'arbitrage* (Gide Loyrette Novel, 2nd edn, 1990), No 324, 283; Samir El Sharkawy; and in international doctrine see: Lew, Mistelis and Kröll; Redfern and Hunter, 1991, 1999; Blackaby and Partasides with Redfern and Hunter, 2009.

17 Mohamed A.M. Ismail, International Construction Contracts Arbitration.

18 For instance, Egyptian Civil Code, Article 374; Syrian Civil Code, Article 375.

19 Ismail, *Globalization and New International Public Works Agreements*, 172–3; www.crcica.org; www.diac.ae and www.bcdr-aaa.org/en

restricted to infrastructure; they also include energy projects for power stations and gas projects for Liquefied National Gas (LNG).[20] A private foreign entity would resort to arbitration out of fear that governments of project-owning states may exercise pressure on their national courts or fear that failure to resort to arbitration may force a situation of state sovereignty to prevail. States sometimes prefer arbitration to avoid resorting to courts of other states.[21]

International commercial arbitration has a long dramatic history in Arab countries; it was rejected by the Arab world legislation and litigation decades ago. From the Middle Eastern perspective, the *Pyramids* case is clear evidence of this.[22]

Arab countries became sensitive to any kind of dispute settlement mechanisms in disputes arising between private entities or states on the one hand and private foreign entities on the other. Statistics show that during the period from 1989 to 1999, 11,143 disputing parties were involved in arbitration cases before the International Chamber of Commerce (ICC) in Paris. Out of these, 2,531 (approximately 23 per cent) were from developing countries, of which 1,073 (42 per cent) were claimants. Out of 873 arbitrations with African, Asian, Latin American and Middle Eastern nationalities at the ICC in Paris, 20 per cent were appointed by the ICC and not by disputing parties. During the period from 1989 to 1999, about 323 arbitration cases took place in no less than 40 developing countries within Africa, Asia, Latin America and the Middle East (60 in Singapore, 27 in Mexico, 13 in Egypt and 9 in Tunisia).[23]

Advantages and Disadvantages of the Arbitral Process: 'The Middle East Perspective'

Arbitration in the Middle East has various advantages as the process is, in most cases, expeditious and cost effective. In light of delays and the workload of the judiciary in many Arab countries, arbitration is therefore of vital importance. Delays by the judiciary, whether in state contracts or in civil and commercial contracts, are threatening the inflow of FDI to some Arab countries. Nowadays arbitration is significant, particularly as it offers rapid and flexible proceedings. The latter aspect applies to international commercial arbitration disputes, in particular those disputes which are of a certain type of complexity such as multi-party arbitration in international construction contracts and in international public works agreement disputes. Further, the arbitral tribunal in complex disputes may issue an interim or partial award. Arbitration as a flexible process can take place in any country, in any language, and the appointed arbitrators can be of any nationality. The disputing parties are free to select a specialized arbitrator in a particular dispute, as is the case in disputes regarding construction, oil and gas, wireless telecommunications, and many other international business transactions. The choice of a specialized arbitrator who is experienced and familiar with the nature of the dispute, whether legal or commercial, is of fundamental importance. In some disputes, state procurement law and knowledge of engineering may be of significance in the process and in the qualifications required in the arbitrator. The whole process is subject to the party autonomy principle, as currently most Arab arbitration acts use the UNCITRAL Model Law. The process is also subject to disputing parties' consent. International commercial arbitration

20 Liquefied Natural Gas (LNG) projects involve the processing and liquefaction of gas, which is then most likely exported by the gas-producing countries. There are some LNG projects in Arab countries such as Qatar, Oman and Egypt.

21 Craig, Park and Paulsson, 661.

22 *Pyramids* case in the Arab doctrine. See Ismail, *International Construction Contracts Arbitration.*

23 In Arab doctrine see Ismail, *International Construction Contracts Arbitration* and Craig, Park and Paulsson.

can be tailored to the particular needs of the dispute, its characteristics and its special nature in the international sphere. Unlike procedures in litigation, pleadings are submitted at or close to the appointment of the arbitrators, which enables the arbitral tribunal to start with the case and to keep in close contact with both sides, allowing the tribunal to be acquainted with the parties from different cultures, languages and legal and commercial backgrounds. It is possible, for instance, to arrange for an arbitral tribunal to inspect the site in construction disputes.[24] Arbitration has other advantages as it maintains confidentiality. Some Arab arbitration acts stipulate that arbitration is confidential unless otherwise agreed by the parties.[25] Thus, it is a private process that avoids the disclosure of commercially sensitive data and trade secrets.[26]

Arbitration in the MENA region as a process avoids many unpredictable outcomes which may occur if the parties choose litigation, where courts of at least two different jurisdictions may play overlapping roles with consequential difficulties in the enforcement of foreign judgments. International commercial arbitration avoids various problems which litigation may have, such as the recognition and enforcement of foreign awards. The arbitral award is enforceable in light of the 1958 New York Convention which has been ratified by all Arab countries. An international treaty which has been ratified by parliaments of Arab Middle Eastern countries is a part of the legal system as it becomes valid legislation after ratification.[27] The New York Convention has been identified as the single most important pillar in the recognition and enforcement of arbitral awards worldwide. It is reported that an estimated 98 per cent of awards in international arbitration are generally successfully enforced.[28]

Arbitration in the MENA region is the most efficient ADR mechanism as it leads to a final, binding and enforceable award. This is the main characteristic of arbitration, which distinguishes the arbitral process from other ADR mechanisms, such as mediation. This final award is not subject to appeal in most Arab jurisdictions. In extensive lists, stipulated in Arab arbitration legislations, the arbitral awards can be challenged on grounds of misconduct by the arbitrators.[29] These lists are not subject to analogy as the disputing parties cannot bring additional cases to challenge arbitral awards. This legislative concept in Arab countries confirms the finality of the award.

In many Arab countries, international commercial disputes brought before national courts may take years to resolve, costing litigants more than the total cost of arbitration expenses and arbitrators' fees put together. Further, delayed resolution jeopardizes the rights of litigants, especially if such resolution comes long after anticipated, when economic changes and currency depreciation may have occurred.

Socialists in Arab countries have argued that arbitration is a mechanism for capitalist systems to seize control over developing countries and to secure their dependence by enforcing the

---

24 Bunni, *The FIDIC Forms of Contracts*, 388; Ismail, *Globalization and New International Public Works Agreements*, 166.

25 Egyptian Arbitration Act, art. 44; Jordanian Arbitration Act art. 42; Omani Arbitration Act, art. 44.

26 Ismail, *Globalization and New International Public Works Agreements*, 165.

27 Ibid, 166; The Egyptian constitution, Article 151 and all Arab constitutions have the same provisions, such as the constitution of Kuwait, Libya, Syria, Lebanese, the UAE and Oman.

28 Ismail, *Globalization and New International Public Works Agreements*, 166; Fouchard, Gaillard and Goldman; Bunni, 388–9.

29 Egyptian Arbitration Act, Article 53; Jordanian Arbitration Act 2001, Articles 49–51; Omani Arbitration Act, Articles 53–54; Kuwaiti Code of Civil Procedures, Article 187; Emirates Code of Civil Procedures, Article 216; Lebanese Code of Civil Procedures, Articles 816–19. Ismail, *Globalization and New International Public Works Agreements*, 166; Lew, Mistelis and Kröll, 65; Redfern and Hunter 1991; Blackaby and Partasides with Redfern and Hunter, 2009, 66.

developed nations' substantive laws instead of those of the developing countries. The presence of an experienced Arab arbitrator, well-acquainted with the arbitral spectrum and directed away from its disadvantages, will lead to the pooling of long-awaited national interests.

Intervention by the national judiciary in Arab legislations will maintain the presence of witnesses during proceedings.

The arbitral tribunal may refer a no-show witness to the competent national court to be fined, should the latter, in accordance with the recommendations of the tribunal, consider such action to be relevant. The Arab national judiciary may intervene in certain strict circumstances to regulate the arbitration process and its relevant proceedings.[30] Further, multi-party disputes may be solved by a consolidation of procedures to achieve a single award. Indeed, multi-party arbitration came into being for this reason. Arab countries began to conceptualize, understand and deal with the arbitration system, as well as to integrate it into their legislation. Consequently, if a developing country enters into a dispute under any of its international contracts, arbitration will be the effective mechanism to protect its rights and interests.

Domestic and International Commercial Arbitration: 'The International Criterion'

As arbitration in the MENA countries is an international phenomenon, the question is: when is arbitration international, and how do we distinguish between domestic and international arbitration? Scholarly opinion points to the arbitrator's nationality or to the place where the head office or place of business of the disputing party is located. Are there procedures which are subject to the national law, so consequently, would the process be domestic arbitration? Further, if the arbitration procedures are subject to a foreign law, is it then an international commercial arbitration? Others point out that the place of issue of the arbitral award is the criterion for determining the nature of arbitration and whether it is domestic or international.[31] 'International' or 'national' had meaning in earlier jurisdictions and legal systems. The term 'international' was used to draw the line between arbitration which was domestic and/or in some way had an international dimension. In international arbitration, the parties usually have no connection with the seat of arbitration. In some states, it is permitted for states or state entities to enter into international arbitration and not only into domestic arbitration.[32]

The UNCITRAL Model Law defines arbitration as international arbitration if:

a) The parties to an arbitration agreement have their places of business in different states at the time of the conclusion of that agreement; or
b) One of the following places is situated outside the state in which the parties have their places of business:
    i) The place of arbitration if determined in or pursuant to the arbitration agreement.
    ii) Any place where a substantial part of the obligations of the commercial relationship is to be performed or the place with which the subject matter of the dispute is most closely connected; or

30 Ismail, *Globalization and New International Public Works Agreements*; see also Ismail, *International Construction Contracts Arbitration.*

31 Samir El Sharkawy, 36–7; and in the international sphere see Lew, Mistelis and Kröll; Redfern and Hunter, 1991; Blackaby and Partasides with Redfern and Hunter, 2009; Fouchard, Gaillard and Goldman.

32 Ismail, *Globalization and New International Public Works Agreements*, 171.

c) The parties have expressly agreed that the subject matter of the arbitration agreement relates to more than one party.[33]
d) A substantial part of an obligation on the commercial relationship is to be performed or the place with which the subject matter of the dispute is most closely connected, or
e) if the parties have expressly agreed that the subject matter of the arbitration agreement relates to more than one party.

The definition establishes criteria: the first relating to parties which have places of business in different states and this is a clear example of internationality when related to the parties. The second criterion on the internationality of the dispute is, when, for instance, the place with which the subject matter of the dispute is most closely connected. Further, the parties may choose a foreign place for arbitration, or they may have expressly agreed that the subject matter of the arbitration relates to more than one country, meaning that the subject matter has an international dimension.

The Egyptian Arbitration Act 1994 points to the same criterion as the UNCITRAL Model Law. The Egyptian legislation adds the point that if the parties to arbitration agree to refer the dispute to a permanent arbitral institution or arbitration centre it could be either inside the Arab Republic of Egypt or outside.[34]

It is recommended that the definition of the arbitration process should be international if it includes an international element which reflects the transitional character of the dispute.

The meaning of 'commercial' usually refers to a subject matter of a commercial nature. In Arab legal systems, trade legislation enumerates commercial transactions which have such a nature and makes a distinction between commercial transactions and civil transactions. The significance of this distinction is that commercial transactions are subject to simple rules in evidence law and are of short period in prescription.[35]

International Commercial Arbitration and Domestic (National) Arbitration

The term 'transnational' or 'international' has various meanings in different jurisdictions and legal systems. Consequently, the meaning of international commercial arbitration differs from one jurisdiction to another. The term 'international' is used to draw the line between arbitrations which are domestic and those which in some way have international elements. In international commercial arbitration, the parties usually have no connection with the seat of arbitration; further, monetary awards in international arbitration are greater than the sums in domestic arbitrations. The UNCITRAL Model law defines an arbitration to be an international arbitration if:

a) The parties to an arbitration agreement have their places of business in different states at the time of the conclusion of the agreement; or

33 UNCITRAL Model Law, Article 1(3); Nigel Blackaby and Constantine Partasides with Redfern and Hunter, 10–12; Fouchard, Gaillard and Goldman; the leading civil legal system, Article 1492 of the French Code of Civil Procedures as amended by Article 1504 on 13 January 2011.

34 Ismail, *Globalization and New International Public Works Agreements*, 171–2; Nigel Blackaby and Constantine Partasides with Redfern and Hunter, 12; UNCITRAL Model Law, Article 13; Article 1504 of the French Code of Civil Procedures as amended 13 January 2011, Egyptian Arbitration Act Article 3.

35 Ismail, *Globalization and New International Public Works Agreements*, 172; for instance, Egyptian Trade Law No. 17 of 1999.

b) One of the following places is situated outside the state in which the parties have their places of business:
   i) the place of arbitration if determined in, or pursuant to the arbitration agreement;
   ii) any place where a substantial part of the obligations arising from the commercial relationship is to be performed or with which the subject matter of the dispute is most closely connected; or
c) The parties have expressly agreed that the subject matter of the arbitration agreement relates to more than one party.[36]

The definition highlights two criteria: the first criterion relates to the parties which have places of business in different states; this is a clear example of internationality when it is related to the parties. The second criterion is the internationalization of the dispute itself when, for instance, the place with which the subject matter of the dispute is most closely connected may be foreign to the parties. Further, the parties may choose a foreign place of arbitration or they may have expressly agreed that the subject matter of the arbitration is related to more than one country, which means that this subject matter has an international dimension.[37]

The French Code of Civil procedures, as amended in January 2011, requires that 'arbitration is international when it involves the interests of international trade';[38] this wide interpretation and legislative policy has been adopted by the French legislature to include transactions that have an international element. The Algerian Code of Civil Procedures 2008 stipulates that arbitration is international if it deals with the international trade of at least two countries, and if one of the disputing parties is domiciled outside of Algeria.[39] The Algerian Code adopts both legal and economic criteria. The new Sudanese Arbitration Act No. 15 of 2005 has adopted UNCITRAL Model Law. This is contrary to the old Sudanese Arbitration Act which was influenced by the English Arbitration Act. The new Arbitration Act No. 15 of 2005 was promulgated pursuant to the Sudanese constitution of 1998. Article 7 of the new arbitration act stipulates that arbitration is international if:

a) the arbitration parties' main place of business is situated in two different countries
b) if the subject matter of the arbitration agreement is connected with more than one country

The Egyptian Arbitration Act 1994 pointed out the same elements as in the UNCITRAL Model Law; the Egyptian legislature added the point that if the arbitration parties agreed to refer the dispute to a permanent arbitral institution or arbitration centre it could be either inside the Arab Republic of Egypt or outside.[40]

Article 4 of the UAE draft Arbitration Act stipulates that:[41]

> Arbitration is international within the scope of this Law, even if conducted in the State, when the subject matter of the dispute relates to international trade and in the following cases:

---

36 UNCITRAL Model Law, Article 1(3).

37 Redfern and Hunter, 12.

38 Article 1492 of the French Code of Civil Procedures as amended by Article 1504 on 13 January 2011; see also Fouchard, Gaillard and Goldman; Blackaby and Partasides with Redfern and Hunter, 2009, 10.

39 Article 1039 of the Algerian Code of Civil Procedures, 2008, Algerian Official Gazette, year 45, 23 April, 2008.

40 Egyptian Arbitration Act, Article 3.

41 El Ahdab (Arabic), 337 and in English (www.kluwerarbitration.com).

- If the parties to an arbitration agreement have their respective head offices in different states at the time of the conclusion of that agreement. If a party has more than one place of business, the place of business is that which has the closest relationship with the subject matter of the arbitration agreement. If a party does not have a place of business, reference is to be made to his habitual residence.
- If the respective head offices of the parties to arbitration are located in the same country at the time of the conclusion of the arbitration agreement, and one of the following places is situated outside the State:

  - the place of arbitration as determined in, or pursuant to, the arbitration agreement;
  - any place where a substantial part of the obligations arising from the commercial relationship is to be performed;
  - the place with which the subject matter of the dispute is most closely connected;
  - if the subject matter of the arbitration agreement relates to more than one country.

Significance of International Arbitration in Arab Legislation

There are several implications for the international dimension of commercial arbitration in Arab legal systems, pursuant to Article 54/2 of the Egyptian Arbitration Act 1994, and other Arab Arbitration Acts.[42] The challenge of an arbitral award in international commercial arbitration is brought before the Cairo Court of Appeal or any other appeal court in Egypt if parties agree to do so. If arbitration is domestic, either party may challenge the arbitral award by appealing to the court which was originally competent to hear the dispute, before going to a second court.

If the arbitral tribunal referred any issue during proceedings to the national courts, it must refer it to the Cairo Court of Appeal and not to the first court, unless the parties agree another court of appeal in Egypt.[43]

It is worth mentioning that Article 39 is applicable only in international commercial arbitration, which stipulates that if the parties agree to apply a particular law of a particular country, the substantive rules are the applicable rules. *Renvoi* is excluded unless otherwise agreed by the disputing parties.[44]

Socialist Decades and Various Constitutional, Political and Economical Ideologies

In the MENA countries, there was considerable debate amongst socialists that arbitration allows the global capitalist system to dominate developing countries as well as ensuring their constant economic dependence on it. Parties to a dispute are free to choose the law they desire the arbitrator to apply; furthermore, the arbitrator himself is free to choose the law to be applied, should there be an absence of choice of substantive law for the parties. It is, therefore, most likely that domestic laws applied in developing countries, whose poor economic conditions almost always make them

42 See Omani Arbitration Act 1997, Article 54; UAE Code of Civil Procedures, Article 216; and Jordanian Arbitration Act 2008, 49–51.

43 For more elaboration see Samir El Sharkawy; Egyptian Arbitration Act, Article 54.

44 See Samir El Sharkawy, 40–41; Ismail, *Globalization and New International Public Works Agreements*. It is worth mentioning that in English case law, if the parties select substantive rules, their choice is valid as it is *bona fide* and legal. It must not be contrary to public policy. *Renvoi* is excluded, see *Vita Food Products v. Unus Shipping*, HL, 1920.

the vulnerable party in a legal relationship, will not be preferred in enforcement.[45] Vulnerability may also emanate from the detriment that may be caused as a result of the enforcement of laws other than domestic ones. Socialist economic and political ideaology was behind the prohibition of states or their public juristic entities to enter into arbitration agreements. Pursuant to the administrative contracts theory, there was debate in Arab doctrine and judiciary regarding the possibility of a state or public juristic entity to be a party to arbitration proceedings.

In Egypt, arbitration was influenced by the socialist concept of governing through planned economy. There was a long debate in the Egyptian Conseil d'Etat on the decisions of the General Assembly for Legal Opinion and Legislation and the Supreme Administrative Court regarding the exclusive competence of the administration judiciary (Le Conseil d'Etat) and arbitration in international administration contracts.[46]

Legal Nature of International Commercial Arbitration in the MENA Region

Legal Nature of International Arbitration

As the task of arbitrators is to resolve a dispute, there has been considerable debate about the legal nature of international arbitration in the MENA region.

Scholars suggest that arbitration is a contractual process and has a judicial nature regarding the final award, which is binding and enforceable for both parties.[47] There are various theories relating to the legal nature of arbitration such as the juridical nature, the contractual theory and the mixed or hybrid theory.[48]

Contract theory is based on party autonomy. It is based on the perspective that consent to arbitration is the consent given by disputing parties to resolve a dispute amicably. Further, it assumes that disputing parties have a common intention of complying with a legal rule, contrary to one that

45 See Ismail, *Globalization and New International Public Works Agreements*, 12, 13. The Law on Arbitration in Civil and Commercial Matters, Explanatory Notes and all Relevant Preparatory Work, Publication of the Department of Legislation, Egyptian Ministry of Justice, 1995. Discussions within the People Assembly concerning the report issued by the committee established jointly between the Committee on Legislative and Constitutional Affairs and the office of the Committee on Economic Affairs concerning a draft law on international commercial arbitration. More precisely, the opinion of Parliament Member Diaa Ed-Din Dawood in his opposition to the Draft Law on International Commercial Arbitration promulgated by Law No. 27 of 1994. Dawood, as a socialist leader, linked arbitration with the concept of foreign western concessions enforced during prior eras, 83; Ismail, *Globalization and New International Public Works Agreements*, 164.

46 Ismail, *Public Economic Law*; and regarding international state transactions see the same author, 'Globalization and New Contractual Regime In International Public Works Agreements in Egypt', *The International Construction Law Review*, 2010.

47 Lew, Mistelis and Kröll; Redfern and Hunter (1991) 8; (1999) 4; Charles Jarrosson, *La Notion d'arbitrage* (Paris: L.G.D.J. 1987), 39; Goldberg, Sanders and Rogers, *Dispute Resolution: Negotiation, Mediation and Other Processes*, Law School Case Book Series (2nd edn, Little, Brown and Company 1992), 223; Jean Robert, *Arbitrage Civil et Commercial* (4th edn, Dalloz 1967) 260, 493. On Arab Middle Eastern doctrine, see Mohsen Shafick, International Commercial Arbitration, lectures for PhD students, Cairo University (1973/1974) 10, 73; Samia Rashed, 70–71; Abou Zaid Radwan, 20; Mahmoud Hashem, *General Theory on Arbitration in Civil and Commercial Provisions, Part I: Arbitration Agreement, A Comparative Study Between Empirical Laws and Islamic Jurisprudence* (Dar El Fikr El Arabi 1990) 216.

48 For an analytical perspective, see Lew, Mistelis and Kröll, 71–83; Redfern and Hunter (1991), 8; Fouchard, Gaillard and Goldman, 12.

solely protects the interests of the other party. The judicial system in Arab countries aims at achieving justice, whereas arbitration aims at achieving specific parties' interests. When parties agree to refer a dispute to arbitration, they implicitly agree to drop any recourse to national courts and to vest in the arbitrator an authority emanating from their own free will.[49] It has been argued that mixed arbitration and hybrid arbitration[50] are considered a compromise to the resolution of the problem.

International commercial arbitration starts as a contractual process pursuant to agreement by the parties; however, in the end, it is a judicial process as it leads to a binding, final and enforceable award. Accordingly, arbitration is considered in MENA countries to be of mixed nature based on the fact that both the contractual and the judicial theories each have an aspect of validity to them. Both theories are integrated and considered as dual arbitration: Contractual and Judicial.[51, 52] It is clear that under Arab doctrine and jurisprudence, arbitration is considered more judicial as it is another form of judiciary.

Arbitration in the MENA countries is an optional process to which parties can refer, with their consent. Further, it has a judicial nature. In MENA doctrine, there were controversial views regarding the contractual and judicial nature. The main feature of arbitration is that parties agree that they will not have recourse to the judicial system but that they will refer the dispute to an arbitral tribunal. Arab arbitration acts stipulate that the parties agree to the arbitration agreement; the national courts are prohibited from hearing the dispute.[53, 54] The jurisdictional theory refers to the state power.

The substance of the jurisdictional theory is that the arbitrator, like the judge, draws his power and authority from the local law; hence the arbitrator is considered a judge. The only difference between judge and arbitrator is that the former derives his nomination and authority directly from the sovereign, whilst the latter derives his authority from the sovereign but his nomination is a matter for the parties.[55, 56] The judicial nature of arbitration which leads to a final, binding

49 The variation in these phases with the variation of the applicable law; Rashed, 70–71; Abou Zaid Radwan, 20; Mahmoud Hashem, 216. See details of the following: Fathy Waly, *Civil Procedures Law* (Dar El Nahda El Arabia 1987) 39; See details of the judicial nature of arbitration: Al-Tihyewi, *Arbitration Agreement and its Stipulations in Civil Procedures and Arbitration Act No. 27 of 1994* (Dar Al Nahda El Arabia, 1994); Rashed, 75; Lew, 51; Redfern and Hunter (1991) 8, and (1999) 4; Jarrosson, 39.

50 Redfern and Hunter (1991) 8, and (1999) 4; Jarrosson, 39; Goldberg, Sanders and Rogers, *Dispute Resolution*, 223; Jean Robert, 493, 260. In Arab jurisprudence: Mohsen Shafik, International Commercial Arbitration, lessons for PhD students on the typewriter, Faculty of Law, Cairo University (1973/1974), 10, 73. Shafik states that 'arbitration in reality does not simply involve a mere process of seeking agreement or judiciary, rather, it is a system that involves a number of phases, in which each phase has its own traits and characteristics. The initial phase is agreement, the middle phase is proceedings and the final phase is an award.'

51 Ismail, *Globalization and New International Public Works Agreements*; Ismail, *International Construction Contracts Arbitration*.

52 See arguments advocating the judicial nature of arbitration: Fathi Waly, *El Wassit in Civil Law Procedures*, 40ff.; Abdel Monem El Sharkawy, 633; Ahmed Abou El Wafa, *The Theory of Sentences in the Code of Procedures* (1965).

53 Lew, 51; Redfern and Hunter (1991) 8 and (1999) 4; Jarrosson, 39. For Arab doctrine, see Fathi Waly, *El Wassit in Civil Law Procedures* 39–40; Rashed, 7.

54 Egyptian Arbitration Act 1994, Article 13; Jordanian Arbitration Act 2001, Article 12; Omani Arbitration Act, Article 13; UAE Code of Civil Procedures, Article 203/5.

55 Lew, para.66. 66; Lew, Mistelis and Kröll, 75; Fouchard, Gaillard and Goldman, 12–13; Redfern and Hunter (1991) 8.

56 Ismail, *Globalization and New International Public Works Agreements.* Lew, Mistelis and Kröll, 77.

and enforceable award distinguishes the arbitral process from other ADR mechanisms, such as mediation.

Party autonomy plays a significant role in the contractual nature. Consequently, arbitration has its origins, existence and continuity in the parties' agreement, indeed it can be argued that arbitration was created by the consent of the parties. The contractual theory was created by the consent of the parties. It denies the control of the state over the arbitral process. The origin of each arbitration is the arbitration agreement. The parties nominate arbitrators who select the rules of procedures, the procedural law, the substantive law and the language of Arbitration.[57]

It is argued worldwide that the party autonomy principle has diminished in practice as international commercial arbitration owes its success to the permanent arbitral institutional role. This concept applies to Arab countries, as the CRCICA since the early 1980s and currently the DIAC play a fundamental role in the institutionalization of international arbitration in the Middle East.[58] However, the role of the international and regional arbitral institutions should be seen as positive, as it increases the efficiency of arbitral proceedings. In most cases it maintains effective procedures in the constitution of the arbitral tribunal, whether nominated by the parties or by the institution as an appointing authority. It also maintains harmonization and a systematic regulatory framework of proceedings within the institutional context.

The institutionalization of the arbitral process is strongly recommended in international infrastructure agreements for complex disputes, particularly multi-party arbitration disputes which are common in infrastructure arbitration.

In international investment arbitration, it is suggested that arbitration can be practised without contractual relationships. This is clear in the 1965 ICSID Convention, Bilateral Investment Treaties (BITs), the 1992 North American Free Trade Agreement (NAFTA) and the Energy Charter Treaty signed in Lisbon on 17 December 1994.[59]

The Mixed (Hybrid) Theory

The mixed or hybrid theory aims to reconcile the contractual and jurisdictional theories. The arbitrators are exercising a judicial function without being members of the judicial power of the state or sitting at the state national courts as state judge. Their function is equivalent to that of the state judge. Moreover, the whole process depends mainly upon party autonomy and the parties' agreement to select the arbitrators constituting the arbitral tribunal and follow the procedures until the final award. This private justice institution represented by the arbitral tribunal selected by the parties or the appointing authority chosen by the parties, has its basis in the contractual

57 The French New Code of Civil Procedure, Article 1494, stating the possibility of applying law chosen by the parties to arbitration proceedings, and Article 1496 leave open the possibility to choose the law applying to the merits of the case. In Switzerland, the Federal Private International Law enacted in 1987, which includes liberal provisions, is favourable to the theory. In Egyptian Law, see Article 39; Omani Arbitration Act, Article 39; Jordanian Arbitration Act of 2001, Article 36.

58 Fouchard, Gaillard and Goldman, 31. In examining the phenomenon of the institutionalization of international arbitration, see particularly 33–35, where it is pointed out that the Iran–United Sates Claims Tribunal, which was established by the Algiers Accords of 19 January 1981, is created by an international treaty, and its jurisdiction is compulsory for disputes between parties from Iran and the United States. It is argued that this mechanism weakens the contractual theory of arbitration. For more elaboration see Ismail, *Globalization and New International Public Works Agreements*.

59 Lew, Mistelis and Kröll, 78; Blackaby and Partasides with Redfern and Hunter, 2009, 467–9; Fouchard, Gaillard and Goldman, 29–35.

arrangements.[60] It leads to an award similar to judicial awards which are final, binding and enforceable.

Most Arab arbitration acts were influenced, to a great extent, by the UNCITRAL Model Law. It is clear that there is harmonization between the contractual approach which respects party autonomy, as in French law, and the jurisdictional approach, as in international instruments such as the New York Convention. In Arab arbitration acts it was emphasized that party autonomy is a fundamental principle in the arbitral process.[61] As the New York Convention is the fundamental pillar to enforcement of arbitration awards, it confirms the judicial nature of arbitration.

It is clear from most arbitration acts made in the MENA region, that Arab legal systems rely upon the national judicial system to control and regulate the arbitral process which takes place within its jurisdictions. This is the judiciary parallel role in assisting the arbitral process in the Middle East.[62]

This parallel role of the national courts in Arab countries supporting the arbitral process is seen as a safeguard for Foreign Direct Investments (FDI) in developing states and encourages the increase of Inward of Foreign Direct Investments (IFDI).[63]

In Arab arbitration acts the arbitral award is final, which means that there are no appeal mechanisms to the arbitral award.[64]

It is appropriate to refer to many conferences which were held at the Cairo Regional Centre (CRCICA) during recent decades concerning the role of the national courts in assisting the arbitral process in Arab Middle Eastern jurisdictions.[65] Nevertheless, by agreeing to start arbitration as an alternative to litigation, parties waive their constitutional rights to have their dispute heard by national courts. The right of litigation is a constitutional right in most Arab jurisdictions.[66] Most Arab countries' arbitration acts include the right of the national court to reject any dispute if there

60 Ismail, *Globalization and New International Public Works Agreements*.

61 Egyptian Arbitration Act, Article 10; Omani Arbitration Act Article 10; Jordanian Arbitration Act 2001, Article 9; and Syrian Code of Civil Procedures, Article 506. The same provisions exist in the Kuwaiti Code of Civil Procedures, the Moroccan Arbitration Act, the Saudi Arbitration Act, the UAE Code of Civil Procedures, the Lebanese Code of Civil Procedures and the Tunisian Arbitration Act.

62 For instance, to enforce an arbitral award in the Tunisian Arbitration Act, Article 19 by the competent court and to challenge an arbitrator, Article 20, enforcement and challenging of arbitral award, Articles 78/1,80–82; Article 43 of the Jordanian Arbitration Act grants the competent national court the authority in cases of forged documents, challenging an arbitral award, Articles 49–51, arbitral award enforcement, Article 54; the Omani Arbitration Act, Article 37 grants the commercial national court the authority to impose penalties (fines) upon witnesses who do not comply with tribunal orders, challenging an arbitral award, Article 54; the Saudi Arbitration Act, Article 23 grants the competent court the authority to determine arbitrators' fees in case of lack of parties' agreement.

63 Ismail, *Globalization and New International Public Works Agreements*; Bunni, 389.

64 The situation varies from one jurisdiction to another. Most Arab countries' legislations stipulate that there is no appeal mechanism from the arbitration award, such as Egyptian Act, Article 48; Omani Act, Article 52; Emirates Code of Civil Procedures, Article 78. On the other hand, in very few countries, arbitral awards were subject to appeal; old Libyan Code of Civil Procedures, Article 767; Syrian Code of Civil Procedures, Article 532 and Qatar Code of Civil Procedures, Article 205. This right of appeal is applicable unless the parties waived the right and agreed that the arbitral award is final and binding.

65 Many conferences were held at CRCICA during the last two decades concerning the judiciary parallel role in Arab Middle Eastern jurisdictions to assist the arbitral process in cooperation with the Egyptian Ministry of Justice and the judiciary of Arab countries.

66 Article 68 of the Egyptian Constitution. The same provision exists in the constitutions of Syria, Libya, Saudi Arabia, Lebanon, Oman, Kuwait and Jordan.

is an arbitration clause and/or agreement.[67] Finally, the hybrid or mixed nature of arbitration is a refined mixed theory that is formed of a mixture of legal ideologies to enable the arbitral process to meet parties' expectations.

Sources of International Commercial Arbitration Law in the MENA Region

National and International Sources of Arbitration Law

The national sources of arbitration law in the MENA countries' legal systems generally derive from particular sources in Arab civil law jurisdiction such as Arab-written constitutions[68] or legislation such as arbitration acts currently codified by states or Codes of Civil and Commercial Procedures,[69] including certain rules and stipulations applicable to arbitration and state procurement laws.[70]

The international sources of arbitration in the MENA region consist of international rules, conventions and treaties. The most important sources in practice and for academia are the UNCITRAL Model Law (the Model Law) adopted by the United Nations Commission on International Trade Law in June 1985 and amendments as adopted in 2006, and the UNCITRAL arbitration rules (the UNCITRAL Rules) adopted by resolution of the General Assembly of the United Nations in December 1976 and amended in August 2010; the Washington Convention of 1965 on the Settlement of Investment Disputes between States and National or Other States; the Rules of Procedures for Arbitration Proceedings (Arbitration Rules) of the International Centre of Settlement of International Dispute (ICSID). It is appropriate to refer to the New York Convention of 1958 on the Recognition and Enforcement of Foreign Arbitral Awards as the pillar for successful enforcement of international arbitration awards worldwide. The latter convention emphasizes the judicial nature of international arbitration.[71]

The UNCITRAL Model Law was the main factor behind the development of modern arbitration laws in most Arab countries. The concepts of party autonomy and the supportive role of courts in the arbitration process are the basis of the Model Law. The Model Law plays a significant role in the modernization and liberalization of the arbitral process in the Middle East, in both theory and practice, in Arab states that promulgated arbitration legislation. In addition, UNCITRAL Rules, the New York Convention and Washington Convention of 1965, as well as ICSID Arbitration Rules are the key features in the step towards a fully liberalized arbitral process in the Middle East as a

---

67 For instance, Egyptian Act, Article 13; Jordanian Act of 2001, Article 12; Omani Act, Article 13; Emirates Code of Civil Procedures, Article 203 and Kuwaiti Code of Civil Procedures, Article 173. The latter legislation is modernized a step further as the national court is prohibited from hearing the case *ipso facto* in case there is an arbitration clause and/or agreement, without a need to be raised by either party as stipulated in the former countries' legislation.

68 For Arab-written constitutions generally, see the Egyptian Constitution of 1971 as amended in 2007; the new constitutional declaration, 2011; the Constitutions of Lebanon, Kuwait, Jordan, Oman, Syria and Morocco. See Ismail, *Globalization and New International Public Works Agreements*.

69 Currently codified arbitration acts such as Egyptian Act of 1994; Omani Arbitration Act 1997; Jordanian Arbitration Act of 2001; Saudi Arbitration Act of 2012 and the Code of Civil Procedures of United Arab Emirates, Qatar, Kuwait, Algeria.

70 Egyptian State Procurement Law promulgated by Law 89 of 1998, and its executive regulations issued by the Minister of Finance decree No. 1367 of 1989.

71 For instance, see www.uncitral.org and https://icsid.worldbank.org.

direct result of legal globalization and towards maintaining the protection of a fair mechanism for dispute settlement to private foreign investments.

The party autonomy principle, which is the arbitration agreement, is the source of law for arbitral proceedings in international commercial arbitration.

Codifying International Commercial Arbitration in the MENA Countries' Legislations

Internationalization of the Arbitral Process in the Middle East and the Influence of the UNCITRAL Model Law on Arab Legislations

The internationalization of the arbitral process in the Middle East is currently recognized through the codification of Arab arbitration acts. This codification adopts the UNCITRAL Model Law. This is evident in the Egyptian Arbitration Act, 1994, the Omani Arbitration Act, 1997, the Jordanian Arbitration Act, 2001, the Bahrain Arbitration Act, 1994, the Libyan Conciliation and Arbitration Act, 2010 and in some other arbitration acts which followed the French law such as the Algerian Arbitration Act, 2008, and the Sudanese Arbitration Act, 2005. This phenomenon in the MENA countries is a considerable step towards the modernization, liberalization and internationalization of the arbitral process. Adopting the same procedural rules maintains the unification of procedures until the final award and will not violate the expectations of foreign investors in the Middle East. Foreign investors are generally from developed countries and expect a modernized legislative system in the MENA countries to manage dispute settlements. The harmonization of arbitral proceedings in the region maintains flexibility in the process and encourages an increase in Foreign Direct Investments (FDI) in the region. The harmonization and unification of the arbitration legislation in the MENA region is a sign of civilization in legislations whether related to international commercial arbitration or international investment arbitration.

Further, Arab state procurement legislations stipulate that the contracting private entity can start arbitration proceedings with certain stipulations. In the Egyptian state procurement law, promulgated by Law No. 89 of 1998, Article 42 stipulates that the contracting entities may start arbitration under certain conditions. These conditions are the consent of the minister concerned and that both parties to the contract must continue to fulfil their own contractual obligation.[72]

The Institutionalization of International Commercial Arbitration in the Middle East

The United Nations Commission on International Trade Law (UNCITRAL)

In 1966, the United Nations General Assembly established the United Nations Commission on International Trade Law (UNCITRAL). Its goal was to promote a standardized set of regulations to govern international trade. The UNCITRAL is structured to ensure that the various geographic regions and the principal economic and legal systems of the world are represented. The General Assembly elects members for terms of six years; every three years the terms of half of the members expire. The UNCITRAL Arbitration Rules were originally adopted on April 28, 1976 with a revised

72 Egyptian State Procurement Law No. 89 of 1998, Article 42.

set released in 2010. The rules contain various other aspects of arbitration proceedings that may arise.[73]

UNCITRAL is the core legal body of the United Nations system in the field of international trade law. UNCITRAL's business is to maintain the modernization and harmonization of rules on international business.

New opportunities through commerce were created by the UNCITRAL:

> In order to increase these opportunities worldwide, UNCITRAL is formulating modern, fair and harmonized rules on commercial transactions. These include:
>
> - Conventions, model laws and rules which are acceptable worldwide
> - Legal and legislative guides and recommendations of great practical value
> - Updated information on case law and enactments of uniform commercial law
> - Technical assistance in law reform projects
> - Regional and national seminars on uniform commercial law.[74]

UNCITRAL plays an important role in developing that framework in pursuance of its mandate to further progress harmonization and modernization of the law of international trade by preparing and promoting the use and adoption of legislative and non-legislative instruments in a number of key areas of commercial law. Those areas include dispute resolution, international contract practices, transport, insolvency, electronic commerce, international payments, secured transactions, procurement and sale of goods.[75, 76]

UNCITRAL played a pivotal role decades ago in the institutionalization of the arbitral process; since 1976 the UNCITRAL Rules have been the fundamental set of arbitration rules in practice whether in a*d hoc* or institutional arbitration. Arbitration is subject to party autonomy and parties' choice plays a significant role in selecting the procedural and substantive framework of the dispute, particularly the arbitral proceedings. UNCITRAL was well known in the MENA region decades ago. The Cairo Regional Centre for International Commercial Arbitration (CRCICA) was adapting the UNCITRAL Rules 1976, with minor modifications, until CRCICA amended its arbitration rules in 1998. CRCICA is the oldest arbitral institution in the MENA region, having been active for several decades, thus the UNCITRAL Rules have been well institutionalized in the region since the early 1980s.

---

73 www.uncitral.org. last accessed 24 December 2011.

74 www.uncitral.org.

75 www.uncitral.org

76 For details concerning the mandate for the progressive development of the law of international trade, see the report of the Secretary-General contained in document A/6396 (Official Records of the General Assembly, Twenty-first Session, Annexes, agenda item 88, document A/6396, reproduced in UNCITRAL Yearbook, vol. I: 1968–1970, part one, chap. II, sect. B); the report of the Fifth Committee of the General Assembly at its twenty-first session on the relevant agenda item (Official Records of the General Assembly, Twenty-first Session, Annexes, agenda item 88, document A/6594, reproduced in UNCITRAL Yearbook, vol. I: 1968–1970, part one, chap. II, sect. D); and the relevant summary records of the proceedings of the Sixth Committee, which are contained in the Official Records of the General Assembly, Twenty-first Session, Sixth Committee, 947th–955th meetings and from which excerpts are reproduced in the UNCITRAL Yearbook, vol. I: 1968–1970, part one, chap. II, sect. C. See www.uncitral.org, last accessed 24 December 2011.

ICC Arbitration Rules and its Influence in the Middle East

The International Chamber of Commerce was founded in 1919 to serve world business by promoting trade and investment, open markets for goods and services and the free flow of capital. The ICC International Court of Arbitration was created in 1923.

After the deterioration of communism in Eastern Europe and the former Soviet Union, ICC faced fresh challenges as the free market system won wider acceptance than ever before and countries that had relied on state intervention switched to privatization and economic liberalization. As the world entered the twenty-first century, ICC began to build a stronger presence in the Middle East as did the emerging economies of other regions such as Eastern and Central Europe.[77]

ICC's activities cover a broad spectrum, from arbitration and dispute resolution to making the case for open trade and the market economy system, business self-regulation and fighting corruption. ICC has direct access to national governments all over the world through its national committees.[78]

The Court is currently receiving new cases at a rate of more than 500 a year. Arbitration under the rules of the ICC International Court of Arbitration is on the increase. Since 1999, the ICC's Uniform Customs and Practice for Documentary Credits (UCP 600) have been the rules which banks apply to finance billions of dollars worth of world trade every year. ICC has developed incoterms which are standard international trade definitions used every day in thousands of contracts in the Middle East and Arab countries. ICC supports government efforts to make a success of the Doha trade round and provides world business recommendations to the World Trade Organization. ICC is the main business partner of the United Nations and its agencies.[79]

Together with the United Nations Conference on Trade and Development (UNCTAD), ICC helps some of the world's poorest countries to attract FDI. In partnership with UNCTAD, ICC has set up an Investment Advisory Council for the least developed countries. Regular ICC regional conferences focus on the concerns of business in Africa, Asia, the Arab World and Latin America.[80] ICC arbitration was well known in the Middle East before establishing regional centres such as the CRCICA in Egypt, the DIAC in Dubai and the BCDR-AAA in Bahrain. Most Arab countries were involved in international commercial arbitration at the ICC with private foreign entities before the rise of international commercial arbitration in the Middle East and international investment law worldwide.

LCIA Arbitration Rules in the Middle East

The LCIA (London Court of International Commercial Arbitration) is one of the leading international institutions for commercial dispute resolution. Its organization, operation, outlook and services are offered worldwide in the fields of arbitration, mediation and other forms of ADR. The LCIA's dispute resolution services are available to all contracting parties, without any membership requirements. The LCIA aims to make its administrative services cost-effective, basing its charges principally on the hourly rates of its neutrals and of its administrative staff, without reference to the sums in issue.[81]

---

77 www.iccwbo.org, last accessed 24 December 2011.

78 www.iccwbo.org, last accessed 24 December 2011.

79 www.iccwbo.org, last accessed 24 December 2011.

80 www.iccwbo.org, last accessed 24 December 2011.

81 www.lcia.org, last accessed 24 December 2011.

The Dubai International Financial Centre (DIFC) was established in 2004. The DIFC LCIA Arbitration Centre is founded on a strategic partnership between two institutions whose individual and complementary sets of strengths add great value to their association. The mission of this partnership is to promote more effective resolutions of international business disputes through arbitration and mediation worldwide. The LCIA is one of the longest established international institutions for commercial dispute resolution and it plays a significant part in the development of arbitration practice.[82]

The history of the LCIA can be traced back to 1883, when the Court of Common Council of the City of London set up a committee to draw up proposals for the establishment of a tribunal for the arbitration of trans-national commercial disputes. The institution was formally inaugurated in 1892 as the London Chamber of Arbitration, and was renamed in 1981 as the London Court of International Arbitration to reflect the international nature of its work.

The Dubai International Financial Centre was established in 2004 as a financial centre to serve the region between Western Europe and East Asia. The centre has a unique location at the crossroads of the major international capital markets worldwide. The DIFC is now ranked as the world's fastest growing international financial centre and continues to attract international investors from around the world. The DIFC is one of the main factors in creating an environment for progress and economic development in the UAE and in the MENA region.

The Cairo Regional Centre for International Commercial Arbitration

The Cairo Regional Centre for International Commercial Arbitration (the CRCICA or the 'Centre') is an independent non-profit international organization established in 1979 under the auspices of the Asian-African Legal Consultative Organization (AALCO), in pursuance of AALCO's decision taken at the Doha Session in 1978 to establish regional centres for international commercial arbitration in Asia and Africa.

In 1979, an agreement was reached between AALCO and the Egyptian Government over the establishment of CRCICA for an experimental period of three years. In 1983, another agreement was reached between AALCO and the Egyptian Government granting permanent status to CRCICA. CRCICA is an independent arbitral institution with a unique status in the Middle East and worldwide.

Pursuant to the Headquarters Agreement reached in December 1987 between AALCO and the Egyptian Government, CRCICA's status as an international organization was recognized. This organization is headquartered in New Delhi, India and was established in 1956 as an outcome of the Bandung Conference, which took place in 1955 in Bandung, Indonesia. It was formerly known as the Asian-African Legal Consultative Committee (AALCC) until June 2001 when it changed its name to the Asian-African Legal Consultative Organization (AALCO). AALCO presently has 47 member countries, comprising almost all of the major states from Asia and Africa.[83]

These states are: Arab Republic of Egypt; Bahrain; Bangladesh; Brunei Darussalam; Botswana; Cameroon; Cyprus; Democratic People's Republic of Korea; Gambia; Ghana; India; Indonesia; Iraq; Islamic Republic of Iran; Japan; Jordan; Kenya; Kuwait; Lebanon; Libya; Malaysia; Mauritius; Mongolia; Myanmar; Nepal; Nigeria; Oman; Pakistan; People's Republic of China; Qatar; Republic of Korea; Saudi Arabia; Sierra Leone; Senegal; Singapore; Somalia; South Africa, Sri Lanka; Palestine; Sudan; Syria; Tanzania; Thailand; Turkey; Uganda; United Arab Emirates;

82 www.lcia.org, last accessed 24 December 2011.

83 www.crcica.org.eg, last accessed 22 December 2011.

and Republic of Yemen. This reflects the international character of the regional centre as well as its independence from any state influence as an independent and international centre. CRCICA is the oldest arbitral organization in the Middle East and is composed of a Board of Trustees, the Director of the Centre and an Advisory Committee, composed of members of the Board in addition to other eminent legal experts.

Since its establishment, CRCICA has adopted, with minor modifications, the Arbitration Rules of the United Nations Commission on International Trade Law (UNCITRAL), approved by the General Assembly of the United Nations by Resolution No. 31/98 on 15 December, 1976. CRCICA amended its Arbitration Rules in 1998, 2000, 2002 and 2007 to ensure best practice in the field of international institutional arbitration. The present CRCICA Arbitration Rules are based upon the new UNCITRAL Arbitration Rules.[84] These amendments became effective as of 1 January 1998, 1 October 2000, 1 November 2002 and 1 June 2007, respectively. The last amended version of 2007 was revised in 2010, with minor modifications emanating mainly from the Centre's role as an arbitral institution and an appointing authority.[85]

The scope of services offered by CRCICA encompass the following:

1. Administering domestic and international arbitrations as well as ADR techniques under its auspices;
2. Provision of institutional arbitration services according to its Rules or any other rules agreed upon by the parties;
3. Providing advice to the disputants;
4. Promotion of arbitration and other ADR techniques in the Afro-Asian region through the organization of international conferences and seminars as well as the publication of research serving both the business and legal communities;
5. Preparation of international arbitrators and legal scholars from the Afro-Asian region by organizing training programs and workshops in cooperation with other institutions and organizations;
6. Coordination with and provision of assistance to other arbitral institutions particularly those existing within the region;
7. Providing ad hoc arbitration with necessary technical and administrative assistance at the request of the parties;
8. Providing advice and assistance for the enforcement and translation of arbitral awards;
9. Conducting academic and practical researches and studies; and
10. Establishing a comprehensive library specializing in Arbitration and ADR. Branches and Institutions were established under the auspices of CRCICA in July 1990, the Institute of Arbitration and Investment was established under the auspices of CRCICA. In January 1991, the Society of Arab and African Arbitrators was established under the auspices of CRCICA. In October 1992, CRCICA inaugurated its Maritime Arbitration Branch in Alexandria. In November 1997, the Arab Union of International Arbitration (AUIA) was established under the auspices of CRCICA at its offices. In February 1999, the Cairo branch of the Chartered Institute of Arbitrators (CIArb) was established under

84 For more information about this Agreement, CRCICA and its activities, visit www.crcica.org.eg. The last amended version of 2007 is available at: http://www.crcica.org.eg/publication/arbitration_rules/pdf/

85 www.crcica.org.eg

the auspices of CRCICA. In June 2001, CRCICA inaugurated its branch, the Alexandria Centre for International Arbitration (ACIA). In August 2001, The Mediation and ADR Centre was inaugurated as a branch of CRCICA.

11. In February 2003, the ILI- Cairo Middle East Development Law Institute (MEDLI) was established under the auspices of CRCICA. In February 2004, CRCICA inaugurated its commercial and maritime branch in Port Said.[86]

Panel of International Arbitrators and Experts

The panel of international arbitrators and experts maintained by the Centre includes eminent personalities from all over the world. Various specializations are represented in the Centre's panel, which allows the parties a wide choice in selecting their arbitrators or experts according to the nature of the dispute. The parties are not obliged to appoint their arbitrators or experts from amongst this panel. However, the Centre is bound to appoint from amongst this panel when exercising its role as an appointing authority under the rules. CRCICA is the oldest arbitral centre in the Middle East region with an international reputation of credibility, accountability and independence.

The independence and impartiality of CRCICA from Arab governments and public juristic entities in the MENA region has been acknowledged over the decades.

The Dubai International Arbitration Centre (DIAC)

Dubai International Arbitration Centre is rapidly becoming a leading arbitration centre in the Middle East region and worldwide. The DIAC assists businessmen in resolving their commercial disputes through arbitration and conciliation proceedings. Arbitration is the primary choice when it comes to settling business disputes in an impartial, cost-efficient and confidential manner. The DIAC employs an international team of arbitration-trained lawyers and business people, who closely supervise every case according to its specifics. DIAC provides appropriate workshops, information sessions and general case assessment.[87] Statistics show that DIAC is a very fast growing arbitral institution not only in the MENA region but worldwide. DIAC is recognized as having an international reputation for independence, credibility and reliability.

Bahrain BCDR-AAA

The Bahrain Chamber for Dispute Resolution (BCDR-AAA), in partnership with the American Arbitration Association (AAA), provides international and regional businesses and governments contracting in the Gulf and beyond with an objective to build Alternative Dispute Resolution (ADR) solutions for the rapid, effective and binding resolution of commercial disputes.

Cases before the BCDR-AAA are divided between:

- Section One: Statutory ADR Tribunals; and
- Section Two: Mediation and Arbitration services.[88]

86 www.crcica.org.eg

87 Visit: http://www.diac.ae/idias/resource/photo/diac_biannual.pdf, last accessed 24 December 2011.

88 Visit: http://www.bcdr-aaa.org/en/why-bcdr-aaa.html, last accessed 24 December 2011.

BI-ANNUAL STATISTICS 2010[1]

NATIONALITIES OF THE APPOINTED ARBITRATORS	
GCC	15
EUROPE	9
NORTH-AMERICA	3
ASIA	2
TOTAL	29

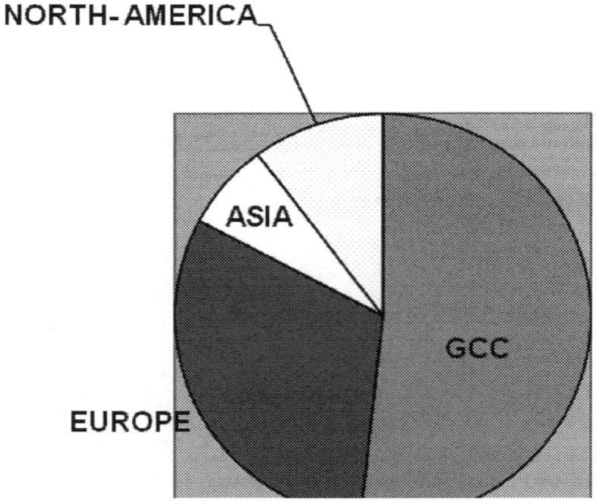

[1] Visit: http://www.diac.ae/idias/resource/photo/diac_biannual.pdf, last accessed 24 December 2011.

2.1 The Dubai International Arbitration Centre, Annual Statistics 2010. Nationality of appointed arbitrators

BI-ANNUAL STATISTICS 2010[1]

NATIONALITIES OF THE CLAIMANT–PARTIES	
GCC	87
EUROPE	39
ASIA	22
NORTH-AMERICA	20
AFRICA	18

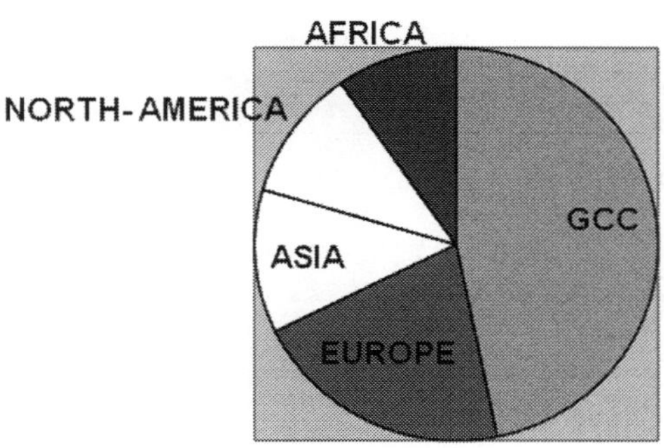

[1] Visit: http://www.diac.ae/idias/resource/photo/diac_biannual.pdf, last accessed 24 December 2011.

2.2 The Dubai International Arbitration Centre, Annual Statistics 2010. Nationality of claimants-parties

BI-ANNUAL STATISTICS 2010[1]

MAIN SUBJECT MATTER OF DISPUTES	
REAL ESTATE	105
CONSTRUCTION	41
OTHERS	40
TOTAL	186

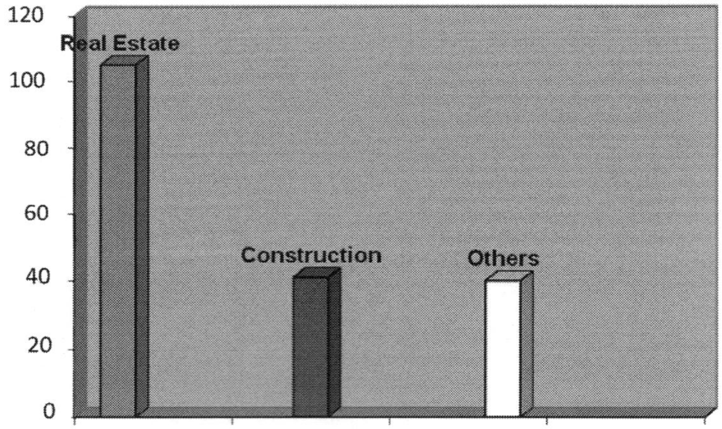

[1] Visit: http://www.diac.ae/idias/resource/photo/diac_biannual.pdf, last accessed 24 December 2011.

2.3 The Dubai International Arbitration Centre, Annual Statistics 2010. Main subject matter of disputes

BI-ANNUAL STATISTICS 2010[1]

LANGUAGE OF ARBITRATION	
ENGLISH	170
ARABIC	16
TOTAL	186

[1] Visit: http://www.diac.ae/idias/resource/photo/diac_biannual.pdf, last accessed 24 December 2011.

2.4 The Dubai International Arbitration Centre, Annual Statistics 2010. Language of arbitrations

The BCDR-AAA has a perspective which prevails over other regional institutions because:

- The Bahrain Chamber for Dispute Resolution (BCDR-AAA) is partnered with the world's leading alternative dispute resolution centre, the American Arbitration Association (AAA), ensuring the highest standards of international best practice;
- BCDR-AAA's 'Free Arbitration Zone' provides business with the jurisdictional and legal certainty to the recognition of arbitration awards without the involvement of the national courts;
- BCDR-AAA provides the very latest in global ADR solutions with high-tech, custom designed facilities;
- BCDR-AAA is entrenched in Bahraini law – providing independence from the government;
- BCDR-AAA offers flexibility, whereby parties may choose their lawyer, the applicable law and the language in which the dispute resolution is carried out;
- BCDR-AAA offers tailor-made solutions for businesses in the shape of pre-emptive dispute resolution clauses which can be inserted into company contracts.[89]

Practitioners recommend BCDR-AAA as it provides an excellent environment for ADR services due to its professional and effective legal system; it is the Middle East's largest and most effectively regulated financial centre, with over 400 licensed financial institutions. It is appropriate to refer to the fact that multinational companies have felt comfortable doing business in Bahrain for decades.

Pursuant to Royal Decree No. (30) of 2009, any dispute whereby the claim exceeds BD 500,000 (approximately USD 1.3 million) and involves either an international commercial dispute or a party

89 Visit: http://www.bcdr-aaa.org/en/why-bcdr-aaa.html, accessed 24 December 2011.

BI-ANNUAL STATISTICS 2010[1]

TOTAL NUMBER OF CASES FILED 2007–2010[2]	
2007	77
2008	100
2009	292
2010	186

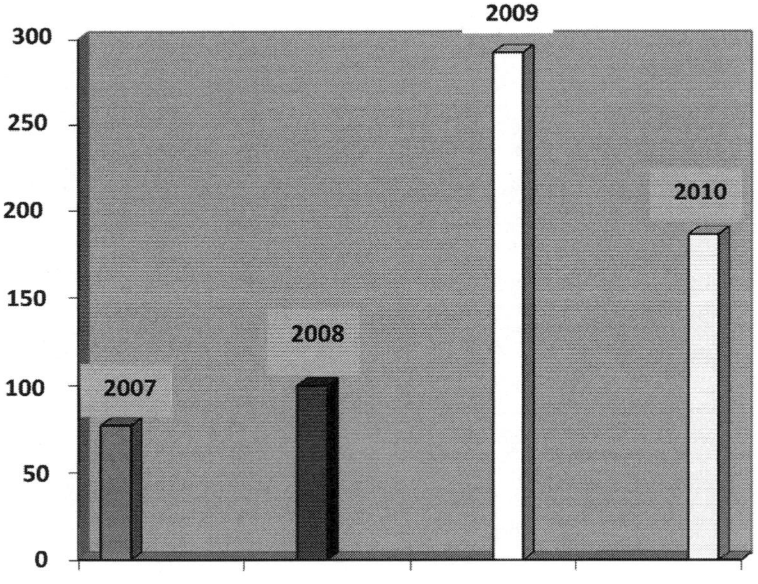

[1] Visit: http://www.diac.ae/idias/resource/photo/diac_biannual.pdf, last accessed 24 December 2011.
[2] The total amount of cases in dispute registered from January to June 2010 was AED 2,383,827,402.

2.5 The Dubai International Arbitration Centre, Annual Statistics 2010. Total number of cases filed from 2007–2010

licensed by the Central Bank of Bahrain (CBB), is referred to the BCDR-AAA. Previously, these cases would have come within the jurisdiction of the courts of Bahrain. Statutory ADR Tribunals have several benefits, which can be summarized as providing faster resolutions than national courts and potentially saving the parties legal fees; benefiting Bahrain's commercial, banking and financial services sectors; offering flexibility to the parties to choose their lawyer and the applicable law; and finally, providing independence from the government.

BCDR-AAA provides ADR services such as mediation and arbitration in the unique 'Free Arbitration Zone' which offers jurisdictional and legal certainty for the recognition of arbitration awards, an essential component of modern day commercial transactions.

The Free Arbitration Zone is a world first, whereby parties to an international dispute are bound to the outcome; the award is guaranteed and is not subject to challenge in Bahrain. The Free Arbitration Zone therefore offers jurisdictional and legal certainty for the recognition of arbitration awards.

Mediation is a confidential process through an independent and neutral third party mediator who assists the disputants to negotiate and reach a mutual decision in their dispute. Trained mediators do not impose a decision upon the parties but assist the disputing parties to achieve their decision.[90]

Mediation has several advantages, as it is through mediation that individuals and organizations are saved from lengthy court battles; there is less risk: mediation settlements are with the agreement of both parties, therefore a settlement is only made when both parties are satisfied with the agreement and, unlike arbitration, it does not violate one of the parties' expectations through an award which is, in some cases, against one of the disputing parties.

Further, mediation maintains privacy and business relations as mediation within BCDR-AAA is confidential, thereby maintaining privacy between the parties and often leading to more satisfactory outcomes for both parties. It can also save costs, by potentially saving on the huge amounts that are spent in legal fees. It also saves time as the majority of disputes are resolved within one working day.[91]

Conversely, arbitration is a dispute resolution process in which the disputing parties present their case to a third party intermediary (or a panel of arbitrators) who examines all the evidence and then make a decision for the parties. Unlike mediation, the arbitrator determines the verdict.

From the BCDR-AAA perspective, the advantages of arbitration are:

- Arbitration it is more flexible than the court process;
- Arbitration as a route to resolve a legal dispute has become ever more attractive due to lower fees and faster processing than traditional litigation;
- With the BCDR-AAA, disputants can choose their own arbitrator, who can be an expert in the topic in dispute, unlike the judge for litigation;
- Arbitration is usually much quicker than litigation, especially since the result is binding and not open to appeal as is litigation;
- Arbitration is private, avoiding the disclosure of trade secrets and potentially embarrassing information;
- Arbitration provides the ability to retain greater control over the process including the selection of applicable law, language and location of the arbitration process;
- Arbitration is generally considered more efficient and fair.[92]

90 Visit: http://www.bcdr-aaa.org/en/why-bcdr-aaa.html, last accessed 24 of December 2011.

91 Visit: http://www.bcdr-aaa.org/en/why-bcdr-aaa.html, accessed 24 December 2011.

92 Visit: http://www.bcdr-aaa.org/en/why-bcdr-aaa.html, accessed 24 December 2011.

BCDR-AAA offers businesses across the region an effective, transparent and fair way to resolve disputes, providing an important part of doing business in the Kingdom of Bahrain and the region more widely, as an alternative to potentially lengthy and costly proceedings in the national courts.

In conclusion, mediation and arbitration services offer international companies a more efficient alternative to litigation.

The Bahrain centre stipulates that businesses do not need to wait for a dispute to occur to approach BCDR-AAA; pre-emptive action can be taken in the form of dispute clauses inserted into contracts that are tailored to the parties' needs. By entering into formal ADR/mediation agreements and establishing mediation services or schemes employers can manage conflict efficiently and control risk factors in litigation.

Inserting an ADR clause potentially provides substantial savings in legal and management fees, and most importantly, keeps the dispute out of the public arena.[93]

Arbitration Time Bar in Standard Forms of Contracts[94]

International commercial arbitration has special difficulties such as the legal nature of the time bar provided for in the FIDIC Form of Contracts (Fourth Edition, 1987). This critical issue is clearly apparent in infrastructure projects, whether in international commercial arbitration, or international investment arbitration.

Clause 67 of the FIDIC (fourth edition) provides that in the case where a dispute arises between the contractor and the employer, the injured party shall refer the dispute to the engineer to make a decision thereon within 84 days. In cases where either party to the dispute is dissatisfied with the engineer's decision, or if the engineer fails to issue a decision within 84 days, either the contractor or the employer shall notify the other of his or her desire to initiate arbitration procedures within 70 days.

If neither party notifies the other of a desire to initiate arbitration within the said period, arbitration may not start before 56 days so as to give the parties the opportunity to settle the dispute amicably. After 56 days, the arbitration may be initiated pursuant to the ICC Rules or any other rules to be agreed upon by the parties.

Clause 67(1) states the penalty for breaching these dates; thus, it provides that the engineer's decision is final and binding on both the contractor and the employer.

Clause 20(4) of the 1999 edition provides that in cases where either party is dissatisfied with the (Dispute Adjudication Board) DAB's decision, such party shall, within 28 days from receiving such decision, notify the other party of the dissatisfaction. If the DAB fails to issue its decision within 84 days (or if another time limit is provided) as of the date of receipt of this notification or payment, either party, within 28 days of the aforementioned period, shall notify the other of the dissatisfaction.

In these cases, a notice of dissatisfaction must specify, according to clause 20(4), the grounds for dispute and the reasons for dissatisfaction.

Notwithstanding the aforementioned clauses 20(7) and 20(8), (failure to comply with the DAB's decision) starting arbitration must be pursuant to clause 20(4).

The DAB's decision shall be final and binding should either party fail to report its dissatisfaction within 28 days.

---

93 Visit: http://www.bcdr-aaa.org/en/why-bcdr-aaa.html, accessed 24 December 2011.

94 Ismail, *Globalization and New International Public Works Agreements*, 203–6.

Clause 20(5) provides that in the case of dissatisfaction and sending a notice thereof under clause 20(4), the parties shall settle the dispute amicably prior to initiating arbitration. Accordingly, unless otherwise agreed by the parties, the arbitration shall start within or after 56 days from the day following the expression of dissatisfaction, even if no attempt is made towards an amicable dispute settlement.

Pursuant to these provisions, if the time bars lapse, the dispute shall not be referred to arbitration.

Questions arise: Are the time bars provided in these articles considered organizational or prescribed dates that cause the lapse of the substantive right? What are the consequences?

An eminent commentator pointed out[95] that the 70-day period as per the provision of clause 67 of the FIDIC agreement is an organizational, procedural period for the following reasons:

1. The Egyptian Arbitration Act promulgated in 1994 provides in Article 13(1) that 'A court seized with a dispute in respect of which an arbitral agreement exists must rule the case non admissible if the respondent invokes a plea of non admissibility before raising any request or defence in the case'.
2. It is incumbent that in the case where a dispute in respect of which an arbitral agreement exists is filed in a court, the court shall dismiss the case, and such dismissal shall apply to the procedural formal aspects only without applying in any way whatsoever to the substantive right itself.
3. The dates provided for in the arbitration clause shall be binding for the arbitral tribunal, rather than the competent national court, especially if the arbitration starts after the lapse of these dates; the competent arbitral tribunal shall decide its non-jurisdiction without tackling the substantive right. The matter here is related to defence of procedural rather than of a substantive nature.
4. Prescription periods have a different nature under Egyptian law. The lapse of the period does not preclude the hearing of the case as per Articles 374 to 388 of the Egyptian Civil Code. Prescription periods only impact the substantive right, whereby the person entitled to the right may not claim same by way of court. In other words, when the national court in Egypt decides not to hear a case because of the lapse of the period specified, it should initially verify that it has jurisdiction to consider the case. Prescription based defence shall not influence the jurisdiction of a national court, because it is a defence relating to the subject matter of the case that impacts the substantive right, and if it is adopted, the right shall lapse by way of a court ruling.
5. In consideration of the foregoing, in a case where the defence is based on a specific period for prescription under the governing law and before the arbitral tribunal, this defence shall not impact the jurisdiction of the arbitral tribunal. Indeed, a defence based on prescription of a case will only be decided after verifying the jurisdiction of the arbitral tribunal as this defence relates to the substance and not the procedural issues or jurisdiction.
6. The time bar provided for in clause 67 is not of a prescribed nature, therefore it does not contradict any provision based on prescription in the Arab legislation.
7. Further, the period provided for in clause 67 relates to the right to resort to arbitration whereas the prescription period relates to the right to resort to litigation before national courts

95 El-Geddawy Ahmed, 1996, 'The Time Limit for Commencing Arbitration under FIDIC Rules Relating to Construction Contracts: Its nature and Effect in light of Egyptian law', Paper Presented in the International Commercial Arbitration Conference Organized by CRCICA, Nile Hilton Hotel, Cairo, June 1996.

8. Dr Geddawy quotes Dr Mahmoud Hashem's view in Arab doctrine, stating: 'The right to resort to arbitration is a legal privilege in favour of the parties to the dispute, as they might have agreed to refer any dispute to arbitration instead of the national competent courts'.
9. Eventually, the right to resort to arbitration differs from the right to resort to national courts. The latter right is a legal privilege for one person who claims entitlement to a right or a legal position. This privilege, when exercised, allows the plaintiff to obtain a ruling from the competent national court on the subject matter of the case.
10. Claims of rights or legal positions do not provide sufficient grounds for resorting to arbitration; this rather takes place if both parties are satisfied with resorting to arbitration, i.e. they are satisfied to refer the dispute to a selected person instead of referring same to the national court.
11. In cases where either party fails to obtain the satisfaction of the other to resort to arbitration, such party shall not be able, solely, to refer the dispute to arbitration. In cases where such party wishes to obtain his or her right, the court will be the only option, by following the procedures prescribed for a court case and verifying the conditions required for filing same.[96]
12. After the right to arbitration and the right to resort to national courts have been considered, it becomes apparent that the legal provisions of prescription in the Arab legislation only relate to the right to take judicial proceedings before the national court rather than arbitration.
13. On the other hand, the reference to 'the lapse of time limits' is to the period during which the national court is precluded from hearing the case, and the substantive right is protected by the judicial case. All legal provisions dealing with prescription are explicit in this regard.

Based on the foregoing, the right to resort to arbitration does not fall within the scope of these provisions as it is a right of a procedural nature which has been established by virtue of a joint agreement with the individuals.

The procedural nature of the right to resort to arbitration is not controversial. Indeed, the right, which was created by the consent of both parties, directly impacts the judicial case and the litigation procedures before the national court. Furthermore, this would preclude the national court from hearing the case, the subject of the arbitration agreement.

To summarize, Dr El-Geddawy[97] is of the view that the prescription periods provided for in Egyptian and Arab laws relate to the right to resort to a judicial procedure and the impact of the lapse of the time bar on the substantive right, whereas the periods in Article 67 relate to the right to resort to arbitration and the impact of the lapse of the time bar thereupon without affecting the substantive right.

The question arises: Does the lapse of the time bar provided for in clause 67 cause the prescription of the right to resort to a competent national court?

It is axiomatic that the lapse of this time bar would deprive the arbitral tribunal of its jurisdiction and the award thereof would be liable to challenge.

English commentators[98] have analysed the same issue in depth. The English doctrine also views that the wording of Article 67 of the FIDIC agreements, using 'final and binding' is decisive, and

96 Mahmoud Hashem, *The General Theory of Arbitration in Civil and Commercial Provisions, Part I: Arbitration Agreement, a Comparative Study Between Empirical Laws and Islamic Jurisprudence* (1990) 58–9.

97 El Geddawy.

98 Ian Duncan Wallace, *Construction Contracts, Principles and Policies in Tort and Contract* (Sweet & Maxwell 1986) 280.

does not imply any doubt regarding the construction of solving the issue at stake to the support of the previous opinion.[99]

In the Egyptian jurisprudence it is viewed by some[100] that arbitration is the exception to the general rule as disputes are settled by national courts;[101] if there is an arbitration agreement, this shall prevent national courts from considering the dispute so long as the said agreement continues to be in force. If, however, this agreement is revoked for any reason, jurisdiction shall be restored by the national courts (Article 13 of the Arbitration Act). The right of litigation before the national courts is a constitutional right. The same vision applies to all Arab jurisdictions.[102]

It is the view of commentators that if the time limits provided for in clause 67 of the FIDIC agreement, relating to arbitration in construction contracts, lapse without arbitration taking place, they cause the prescription of the parties' right to take the dispute to arbitration. The provisions relating to prescription in the Egyptian Civil Code, however, deal with the substantive right, where the case serves as a method whereby the person entitled to the right protects his or her right; thus the right remains with no case to protect it.[103]

It is noticeable that the end sought by the 84-day period specified for the engineer's decision and a period for the parties to resort to arbitration within 70 days is to settle the disputes arising from public works contracts rapidly. In cases where such periods lapse without resorting to arbitration, the only channel for dispute settlement would be blocked. Nevertheless, this does not entail the lapse of the parties' right to resort to the national competent courts to claim their rights so long as the prescription period has not been duly exhausted. In terms of clause 20 of the FIDIC agreement (the new edition 1999), the same abovementioned concept applies.

The right to litigation and to resort to the national courts is a constitutional right duly established by Article 68 of the previous Constitution of the Arab Republic of Egypt promulgated in 1971, the constitutional declaration of March, 2011 and in all Arab constitutions.[104]Article 172 of the 1971 Egyptian Constitution and Article 48 of the constitutional declaration, March 2011, entrust the State Council with deciding on all other administrative disputes. Accordingly, the State Council has jurisdiction to decide on all administrative disputes; therefore, if the parties fail to resort to arbitration, it is incumbent on them to resort to their natural judge in operation of the two constitutional principles, namely that the right to litigation is secured for all, and that the State Council is the body having fundamental jurisdiction to decide on administrative disputes. This general fundamental principle is provided for by the Constitution and the State Council Law promulgated by virtue of Article 10 in Law 47/1972 that provides for the jurisdiction of the State Council to consider administrative contracts disputes. This fundamental principle renders the State Council the body with jurisdiction to consider disputes relating to international commercial transactions upon the lapse of the periods prescribed for arbitration, pursuant to Article 67 of the FIDIC agreement, fourth edition, and Article 20 thereof in the 1999 edition.[105]

It is suggested, however, that party autonomy is fundamental as the contracting parties primarily agreed to refer the dispute to arbitration. Thus, if the time bar expires, there is no possibility to start

99 Ibid.

100 El-Geddawy.

101 Egyptian Court of Cassation, Case 1579 of 49, dated 10/2/1986.

102 The same concept applies to Arab jurisdictions as they are all civil law countries, and all Arab civil codes and arbitration acts were directly influenced by the Egyptian legal system.

103 El-Geddawy.

104 Ismail, *International Construction Contracts Arbitration*, 504; and Arab constitutions such as those of Libya, Lebanon, Jordan, Kuwait, Oman, Morocco and Syria.

105 Ismail, *Globalization and New International Public Works Agreements*, 203–206.

litigation proceedings before the national courts of Arab countries. This vision is supported by the party autonomy principle which is adopted by Arab Arbitration legislations, whether those which are directly influenced by UNCITRAL Model Law, or others which follow French Arbitration legislation. As both legal systems supersede the party autonomy principle, it is suggested that the right approach, in Arab countries, is that there is no possibility of recourse to the national courts if the time bar stipulated in the FIDIC form of contract to start arbitration has expired.

The Increase of Inflow of Foreign Direct Investments (FDI) as a Direct Result of Recognition, Institutionalization and Internationalization of Arbitration in the Middle East

Most private foreign entities which have huge investments in the Middle East and North Africa are investors from developed countries. These investments are generally in infrastructure, telecommunications, oil and gas, energy sectors and tourism etc. Statistics show that the total value of projects in the Middle East region is USD 2.288 billion. It also shows that other projects may not be disclosed.[106]

The fact is that the World Bank and other international investment institutions, whether academic or in practice, consider to a great extent the encouragement of investments when ranking Arab countries, as international commercial arbitration is well recognized as a dispute settlement mechanism in the region.[107] It is true that adopting UNCITRAL Model Law, BITs in Arab legislation and the role of regional arbitral institutions in the region such as CRCICA, DIAC and BCDR-AAA are significant. Arab legislation and the institutionalization of international commercial arbitration are fundamental to increasing FDI in various economic sectors to the MENA region. As mentioned previously, the enforcement of arbitral awards through the 1958 New York Convention is a fundamental pillar for the enforcement of arbitral awards worldwide. These factors are of vital importance to the success of the arbitral process in the MENA region and consequently, the increase of FDI in various economic sectors.

106 www.zawya.com, accessed 1 November 2011.

107 For instance, see United States Conference on Trade and Development (UNCTAD), World Investment Report, 2009, and for FDI statistics visit www.unctad.org/fdistatistics and for World Investment Report visit www.unctad.org/wir. For the most eminent academic institution worldwide visit: Vale Columbia Center at Columbia Law School, Columbia University, USA, at: www.vcc@law.columbia.edu

Chapter 3

Harmonizing International Arbitration and *'Le Contrat Administratif'*[1] Constraints in the MENA Region with Special Reference to Egypt (Egyptian Case Study)

Introduction – The Arbitration Clause in Administrative Contracts

The significance of the administrative contracts' *'Le Contrat Administratif'* is clear as all investor–state disputes are based on administrative contracts in the MENA region.

Arbitration in administrative contracts has only recently become highly controversial. The point of contention was initially over the administrative contract and the competent judicial authority, given the fact that as per the State Council Law, administrative contract disputes fall within the jurisdiction of the State Council courts. The State Council Law, providing for the jurisdiction thereof to decide on disputes arising from administrative contracts, intends to differentiate between the jurisdiction of ordinary courts and that of administrative courts; yet, it remains silent in terms of prohibition of resorting to arbitration in administrative contract related disputes.

As legal research proceeded into this question, a legal opinion, *fatwa*, was issued by the General Assembly for the *Fatwa* and Legislation Departments at the State Council, considering the subjective nature of this contract, which confines the disputes thereof to the national administrative judiciary. This legal opinion was issued on 18 December 1996 following the enactment of Law 27/1994, which eventually entailed the issuance of a legislative amendment to decide on the matter.

The Legislative Status and Jurisprudent Discord Regarding the Legitimacy and Constitutionality of the Arbitration Clause before the Promulgation of the Arbitration Law 27/1994 amended by Law 9/1997

Law 27/1994 amended by Law 9/1997 has resolved this matter in Article 1 thereof,[2] notwithstanding the jurisprudent and judicial debate currently in place regarding the provisions of this law in relation to this problem. This eventually entailed the issuance of a legislative amendment promulgated

1 See the leading authority on administrative contracts in the civil law legal culture from several decades ago: André de Laubadère, Franck Moderne and Pierre Delvolvé, *Traité des contrats administratifs* (Paris: LGDJ, 1983), Tome I, 210ff., and Tome II; and Laurent Richer, *Droits des Contrats Administratifs* (LGDJ 1995) 85ff. In Arab doctrine, see Soliman El Tamawy, *General Principles of Administrative Contracts* (5th edn, Dar El Fikr El Araby 1991).

2 Art.1: 'Without prejudice to the provisions of the international conventions in force in the Arab Republic of Egypt, the provisions hereof shall apply to every arbitration between parties of the public law or private law persons, notwithstanding the nature of the legal relation subject of dispute, in case such arbitration

by Law 9/1997, which explicitly provides for the permissibility of arbitration in administrative contracts.

Jurisprudent and Judicial Debate on the Arbitrability in Administrative Contracts

Prior to the enactment of the Law of Arbitration in Civil and Commercial Articles, the permissibility of arbitration in administrative contracts has stimulated two different opinions. The first maintains the impermissibility of arbitration in administrative contracts, whereas the second maintains the permissibility thereof.

Impermissibility of Arbitration in Administrative Contracts

One opinion in Egyptian jurisprudence maintains that the key characteristic of states per se lies in their sovereignty, which is the essence of the legal personality of the state.

The basic characteristic in the arbitration clause provided for in contracts is the element of acceptance; however, jurisprudence, in part, views that this might clash with the integrity of the state and its higher interest which supersedes the soundness of the law. Moreover, arbitration might impair certain political considerations (such as sovereignty) thereof.

It was suggested that the essence of the problem lies in how permissible it is to treat the state as individuals when it simulates those individuals in their economic and commercial activities, and whether the state could be party to an international commercial arbitration agreement.[3]

The Situation in Egypt

In Egypt some maintain[4] that the attitude adopted by the Supreme Administrative Court manifests itself in its verdict issued in the hearing of 20 February 1990, in which it effectively denies administrative bodies access to arbitration to settle disputes, so far as arbitration is not explicitly permitted by the legislature, which is the decision of the Administrative Court in its verdict issued in the hearing of 9 December 1990.[5] The court stated in its justification of this verdict that Article 10 of the State Council Law 47/1972 provides that the state council courts shall be exclusively competent to decide on the following matters:

> First … Eleventh: Disputes pertaining to concession contracts, or public works, or supply, or any other administrative contract.

---

is taking place in Egypt, or if same is an international commercial arbitration taking place abroad where the parties thereof agree to subject same to the provisions hereof.'

3 See: article by Al-Sayed Al-Habib Maloush, member to the International Arbitration Committee at the International Chamber of Commerce, entitled 'The Latest Developments in the Field of International Arbitration in Tunisia', submitted to the Cairo and Alexandria Conference on International Arbitration held in Cairo, 11–15 October 1992; Dr Mohammed Maged Mahmoud, *Arbitrability in Administrative Contracts* (Kuwait Conference for International Commercial Arbitration 1997) 129; Dr Samia Rashed *Arbitration in Private International Relations*, 330.

4 Dr Mohammed Kamal Mounir, 'Arbitration in Administrative Contracts', *Administrative Sciences Law Journal*, 1991, 33:1, 337.

5 Case 5837/44j.

The purport of the foregoing is that it is the State Council courts which have jurisdiction to hear administrative contract-related disputes. This is provided for in a legislative provision, and may not be disputed by legislation of lower rank in the hierarchy of legal rules, which may be called the principle of parallelism of legal rules, i.e. a piece of legislation may only be superseded by another piece of legislation of an equal degree and rank.

It is manifest that the position adopted by the Administrative Court and the Supreme Administrative Court before the new Arbitration Law promulgated by Law 27/1994 is in agreement with the opinion of jurisprudence and judiciary in France. It was concluded by some[6] that the resolution passed by the General Assembly of the *Fatwa* and Legislation Departments at the State Council to the effect of permitting arbitration in administrative contracts is questionable for the following reasons:

First, the legislature elicited in the Civil and Commercial Procedures Law is that the general rule in settling disputes is to resort to the judiciary and that the exception is arbitration. In administrative disputes, resolution takes place in two methods, the first through the State Council courts and the second through the General Assembly of *Fatwa* and Legislation Departments at the State Council to resolve these disputes by a binding opinion. Those are the disputes that arise between ministries or between public authorities and public bodies or between public institutions or between local authorities or in-between these bodies (Article 66/d of the State Council Law promulgated by Law 47/1972).

Based on the foregoing, since the legal system enacted by the legislature in the Civil and Commercial Procedures Law is independent of the legal system enacted by the State Council Law regarding administrative dispute resolution, which are two separate systems, the voluntary arbitration system provided for in the Procedures Law as a means of dispute settlement in administrative contracts may not be borrowed. It is thus understood by way of contraries that in administrative management, contracts subject to the Civil and Commercial Procedures Law may resort to voluntary arbitration as provided for in Article 501 of the Procedures Law to settle disputes arising therefrom. The foregoing is not impaired by the provisions of Article 3 of the Presidential Resolution number 47/1972 promulgating the State Council Law which reads as follows: 'The procedures provided for in this law shall be applied, as well as the provisions of the Procedures Law where this law is silent, until a law is promulgated in relation to the procedures pertinent to the judicial department'.

The State Council court has maintained that the provisions of the Procedures Law are not applicable to administrative disputes, if those provisions contravene any of the provisions or the spirit of the State Council Law, whether in the procedures or foundations of the judicial system at the State Council.

The author is of the view that the foregoing is corroborated by the fact that the State Council Law is a private law that restricts the Procedures Law on the grounds that the private restricts the public. Indeed the borrowing by the State Council judiciary of the voluntary arbitration system from the Procedures Law and applying it to administrative disputes runs counter to the foundations of the judicial system at the State Council.

Second, Article 501 of the Procedures Law does not permit administrative bodies to resort to arbitration to resolve disputes arising from their administrative contracts. Therefore, given the fact that dispute resolution between litigants by way of arbitration is exceptional, arbitration should be accessed only upon the explicit and decisive will of the legislature which leaves no room for conclusion or extrapolation.

6 Mounir, *Arbitration in Administrative Contracts*, 339ff.

Third, Article 58 of the State Council Law finds its true interpretation in the fact that in cases where the legislature authorizes administrative bodies to resort to arbitration, the relevant arbitration agreement may only be concluded by virtue of the opinion of the competent *Fatwa* department at the State Council.[7] Therefore, it was opined prior to the promulgation of the Arbitration Law that arbitration is not permissible in public law contracts in Egypt.

Permissibility of Arbitration in Administrative Contracts

Scholarly opinions are that the situation in Egyptian law does not cast any doubt over the permissibility of the state or any of its bodies being party to an arbitration agreement. In Egyptian law, however, given certain provisions of the law[8] and the accession by Egypt to international conventions, the settlement of disputes is permissible if arising in relation to investment before the World Bank International Centre for Settlement of Investment Disputes (ICSID) by virtue of Law 70/1971, which is part of the ICSID internal legislation of the state. In terms of private international transactions, states may not argue that they have their own internal legislative provisions and that the state and other public law persons are not eligible to conclude arbitration agreements, as this runs counter to contemporary international life requirements,[9] and states' international undertakings.

Furthermore, scholars maintain that the refusal of arbitration in administrative contracts according to the Supreme Administrative Court does not match modern economic life; investment and development in Egypt require that the considerations of national sovereignty be overlooked, as far as this sovereignty is intact, especially as today's world does not differentiate, as far as the economy is concerned, between intervention by states in the international trade market and intervention by individuals.

This view also maintains that developed countries such as France and Belgium permitted international arbitration in administrative contracts, which is not the case with internal arbitration, as the aforementioned states based their stance on their accession to a number of international UN conventions.[10]

This same opinion adds that the accession by Egypt to UN conventions and the Arab Convention for Arbitration as well as the conventions pertaining to the execution of foreign verdicts are considered private laws in this regard. Furthermore, these conventions have been promulgated by virtue of private laws in Egypt and acquired the power of laws which are said to limit judicial jurisdiction exclusively to the judiciary of the state. Finally, the General Assembly for the *Fatwa* and Legislation Departments of the Egyptian Conseil d'Etat opined that arbitration in general is permissible, stating no difference between domestic arbitration and international arbitration. It favours the permission of arbitration in administrative contracts in general, and predicated in this regard Article 58 of the State Council Law which permits the Assembly to consider arbitration in administrative contracts as elicited from the mandatory referral to the competent *Fatwa* department for the execution of the arbitrators' award. Given the absence of an external legislation regulating arbitration in contract disputes, where the administrative body is a civil or administrative party, it is imperative to refer to the general conditions and procedures for arbitration provided for in the Procedures Law which do not contradict the nature of administrative links. Advocates of this

7 For elaboration of the previous three arguments, see ibid.

8 Law 143/1974 on Arab and Foreign Fund Investment and Free Zones, in its eighth article, as it involved four options of arbitration, three of which are abroad and the fourth is domestic.

9 Rashed, 331.

10 Dr Mohammed Maged Mahmoud, 'Administrative Contracts and the International Arbitration Clause', *Administrative Sciences Law Journal*, 1993, 35:1.

opinion view that it is fundamental to find some sort of distinction between domestic arbitration and international arbitration in state contracts, as internal contracts may not include an arbitration clause. Yet, it is permissible to include an arbitration clause in international contracts to ensure that the state exercises its rights satisfactorily; legislative intervention is required to create such a distinction, thus precipitating the liberalization of the national economy and keeping abreast with modern developments in this regard.[11]

The ICC in Paris has recently passed verdicts that corroborate the arbitrability in administrative contracts, in addition to Article 10/11 of the State Council Law 47/1972 and Article 172 of the Egyptian Constitution. One verdict referred to the opinion (*fatwa*) of the General Assembly of the *Fatwa* and Legislation Departments at the State Council issued on 11 July 1989, which permits arbitration in administrative contracts. The verdict rejected the defence, effectively submitting the impermissibility of arbitration in administrative contracts.[12]

In the United Kingdom, major reference books in administrative law and state contracts were silent about tackling the problem of arbitration in administrative contracts.[13]

Approaches of the Judiciary and Legislation in Egypt Regarding the Permissibility of Arbitration in Administrative Contracts

Opinion of the General Assembly for the Fatwa and Legislation Departments at the State Council

The issue was initially raised when a contract was concluded between the Ministry of Construction and Urban Communities (The Research and Studies Fund) and the Construction and Planning Group. Article 10 of the contract in question provides that the parties have agreed that disputes arising from the execution of the contract or the interpretation of the provisions thereof shall be resolved by an arbitration tribunal. Because of its significance and generality, the second committee of the *Fatwa* Department decided to refer the subject to the General Assembly, with regard to how it relates to the principle of permissibility of agreeing on arbitration in administrative contracts.

Upon scrutinizing the subject, the Assembly reviewed the provisions of Articles 167 and 172 of the permanent constitution of Egypt issued in 1971,[14]Articles 501, 502, 506 and 509 of the Civil and Commercial Procedures Law 13/1968,[15] and certain articles of the State Council Law 47/1972.

11 Mahmoud, 'Administrative Contracts'.

12 Jean-Jacques Arnaldez, Yves Derains and Dominique Hascher, *Collection of ICC Arbitral Awards, 1996–2000,* vol. 3 (ICC 2002) 75, case no. 6162 of 1990.

13 J.F. Garner and B.L. Jones, *Garner's Administrative Law* (6th edn, Butterworths 1985); B.L Jones, *Garner's Administrative Law* (7th edn, Butterworths 1989); D.C.M. Yardley, *Principals of Administrative Law* (Butterworths 1981); Colin C. Turpin, *Government Contracts* (Penguin 1972); Alan Redfern and Martin Hunter, *Law and Practice of International Commercial Arbitration*, 1991, 1999, and Blackaby and Partasides with Redfern and Hunter, *Redfern and Hunter on International Commercial Arbitration*, 2009; Laurence Craig, William W. Park and Jan Paulsson, *International Chamber of Commerce Arbitration* (ICC 1985).

14 The law shall determine judiciary authorities and their functions, organize the way of their formation, define conditions and procedures for the appointment and transfer of their members. Article 172 provides for the following: 'The State Council shall be an independent judiciary body and shall have the competence to decide in administrative disputes, and disciplinary actions. The law shall determine its other competencies.'

15 Arbitration may be agreed in a dispute specified by a special document. Arbitration may also be agreed in disputes that arise from the execution of a given contract. Arbitration may only be proven by way of writing. The subject of dispute should be specified in the arbitration document or during the hearing if the arbitrator is authorized to effect reconciliation. Otherwise arbitration shall be null and void. Arbitration may

The General Assembly defined arbitration as an agreement to refer a dispute to one or more arbitrator(s) – instead of the competent court – by virtue of an award that is binding to the parties. The Assembly added that the agreement may be mentioned in the text of the contract establishing the legal relation, and it is thus considered an arbitration clause. The parties may not agree on arbitration in the original contract, but rather, after the dispute arises between them they may conclude a special arbitration to decide on the dispute. This agreement is called arbitration agreement. The Assembly maintains that arbitration is based on two foundations, namely the will of the litigants and the legislature's recognition[16] of this will, as this constitutes an exception to the general principle in legislation. Henceforth, no person may be forced into adopting a certain behaviour, or be denied recourse to the judiciary unless this is performed willingly and voluntarily. Moreover, the litigants' will does not exclusively suffice to rule on their disputes by way of arbitration, as this should take place within the rules set by the legislature to regulate arbitration and its procedures.

The General Assembly's opinion was guided by the articles of the Civil and Commercial Procedures Law and Article 58 of the State Council Law which permits the administration body to resort to arbitration in its contractual disputes (administrative or civil). The third clause of the said article provides for the fact that any ministry or general body or state authority is bound not to conclude or accept or permit any contract or reconciliation or arbitration or execute the arbitral award in a matter exceeding EGP 5,000 in value without consulting the competent *Fatwa* Department at the State Council. If the administrative body was prohibited from agreeing on arbitration, the legislature would not have required it initially to submit this agreement or execute

---

not be applied in matters where reconciliation is impermissible. Arbitration is only valid for parties who may act on their rights.

Article 502 of the same law provides for the following: 'An arbitrator may not be a minor or interdicted or deprived of his civil rights on the ground of a criminal penalty or bankruptcy unless rehabilitated. In case of multiple arbitrators, it is imperative in all events that their number be odd, otherwise the arbitration is null and void. Without prejudice to the provisions of private laws, the persons of arbitrators should be specified in the arbitration agreement or in a separate agreement.'

Article 506 of the said law: 'Arbitrators shall issue their award on the grounds of law, unless they are authorized to effect reconciliation.'

Article 509 provides that 'The court ruling is only applicable by virtue of an order to be issued by the execution judge at the court in the clerks' bureau of which the original award was lodged, based on the request of any of the parties concerned, after duly reviewing the award and the arbitration document and after verifying the absence of any obstruction to the execution thereof. The said judge shall have jurisdiction over all that is related to the court ruling.'

The State Council courts shall have exclusive jurisdiction to rule over the following questions: '… (Eleventh) Disputes pertaining to concession agreements or public works contracts or supply agreements or any other administrative agreement …'

Article 58 of the same law provides that 'the *Fatwa* Department is constituted of competent departments for the presidency of the republic, the council of ministers, the ministries and the general authorities.

The aforementioned departments are competent to opine on matters where opinion is requested mentioned in the first paragraph and shall examine administrative grievances. No ministry or general authority or any of the bodies of the state may conclude or accept or permit any contract or reconciliation or arbitration or the execution of an arbitral award in an article which exceeds EGP 5,000 in value without consulting the competent *Fatwa* department.'

16 In this regard, see an earlier opinion of the assembly no. 96 dated 15/1/1970, *Administrative Encyclopedia*, vol. 10, p. 152 and cassation 2, appeal 194/37j, the hearing of 15/2/1972, p. 168 the *Golden Encyclopedia*, vol. 4, p. 565.

the arbitral award to the State Council for review. However, given the absence of legislative text regulating arbitration in contractual disputes where an administrative body is a party, whether civil or administrative, it is fundamental to refer to the general conditions of arbitration and the procedures thereof set out in the Procedures Law, which do not contradict with the nature of the administrative relations. Meanwhile, this does not add up to say that the State Council courts are competent to decide exclusively on administrative contracts disputes, pursuant to Article 10 of the State Council Law. Therefore, agreement on resolving such disputes by way of arbitration leads eventually to stripping the administrative judiciary of its exclusive jurisdiction in this regard. The purport of Article 10 is to determine the demarcation line between the jurisdiction decided for the State Council courts and that of the ordinary courts. The legislature's intention in this regard may not be exceeded and it may not be interpreted as to falsely mean the prohibition of arbitration in administrative contracts.[17]

It is thus clear that the Assembly saw that the provision of Article 10 of the State Council Law should not be overloaded with unintended meanings, and should restrain the legislature's intention to demonstrate the demarcation line between the jurisdiction of the State Council courts and ordinary courts.

The second *fatwa* of the Assembly was issued after opinion was sought on the permissibility of agreement on arbitration in administrative contracts disputes. This came following the second committee review of the contract concluded between the Awqaf Ministry and Al-Ahram Center for Organization and Microfilming affiliated with the Al-Ahram Institution, as the contract included a provision to the effect of resorting to arbitration to resolve disputes arising from the contract. The committee decided, in its hearing held on 16 September 1991, to submit the issue to the General Assembly.

Article 16 of the contract provides that the parties may resort to arbitration in case a dispute arises during the execution of the contract.[18]

The General Assembly reviewed the previous opinion referred to in the hearing of 17 May 1989 pertaining to the permissibility of resorting to arbitration in administrative disputes, where it opined in favour of arbitration on the grounds that arbitration is 'an agreement to submit the dispute before one or more arbitrator(s) to decide thereupon instead of the competent court' by virtue of a ruling that is binding on the parties.

The General Assembly concluded that the correct *fatwa* is to permit agreement on resorting to arbitration in administrative contracts in this case and concluded the same reasons set out in the aforementioned *fatwa*.

This trend adopted by the General Assembly for the Legal Opinion and Legislation Departments demonstrates that it has admitted arbitration in administrative contracts on the basis of the provisions of the Procedures Law and finally Article 10 of the State Council Law 47/1972 which renders the State Council the sole body responsible for public jurisdiction over disputes arising from administrative contracts. The Assembly's interpretation of the provision

---

17 The *Fatwa* of the General Assembly for *Fatwa* and Legislation Departments at the State Council, file number 54/1/265, hearing of 17/5/1989.

18 Clause 16 of the contract provides the following: 'The Parties agreed that any dispute or disagreement that arises during the execution of this contract shall be resolved amicably. In case it becomes impossible to settle it amicably, the Parties shall resort to arbitration, where each Party appoints two arbitrators, and notifies the other Party of their names; provided the four arbitrators select a casting arbitrator … the arbitral award shall be binding and final for both Parties. In case it is impossible for the court to meet or to select a casting arbitrator within fifteen days as of the date of the expression by either Party of his/her desire to resort to arbitration, same shall resort to the judiciary.'

is that it draws a demarcation line between the jurisdiction of the administrative judiciary and that of the ordinary judiciary regarding the consideration of disputes arising from administrative contracts. This positively proves that the Assembly is inclined not to overload the legislative provision with unintended meanings and not to over-interpret its provisions, thus exceeding the requirements of legislative interpretation and the practical alignment to decide on disputes arising from administrative contracts; in particular the General Assembly decided not to exclude disputes referred to the arbitral tribunal from the operation of the substantive legal rules applicable to administrative contracts.[19]

Approach of the State Council Judiciary in this Regard (The Administrative Court and the Supreme Administrative Court)

The matter was first submitted to the Administrative Court (The Contracts and Compensation Circuit) in a case[20] filed by the Egyptian Joint Stock Company for Development and Tourist Constructions against the Minister of Housing and Utilities and others.

The Plaintiff requested that the Ministry of Housing appoint an arbitrator on its behalf to resolve the outstanding disagreements between the Plaintiff and the government pursuant to the provisions of the Moqattam Plateau Concession Agreement.

The Court ruled in this well-known case in favour of the Company in operation of Article 5 of the agreement annexed to the exploitation agreement of Al-Montazah Palace area and the reclamation and development of Al-Moqattam Hill area concluded on 9 November 1954, given that this annexed agreement was concluded on 14 April 1955.

Nevertheless, the State Lawsuits Authority appealed against the ruling before the Supreme Administrative Court by virtue of the appeal number 3049/32j. The Supreme Administrative Court's discretion regarding this ruling, which has become material for many studies and comments, is that the legislature is immune to omission and error, thus it is mandatory to interpret Article 5 of the aforementioned agreement in a manner that does not undermine the characteristics of the administrative contract, and the jurisdiction of the State Council should consider the disputes pertinent to that contract.

The jurisdiction of the State Council is provided for in a substantive law, i.e. as a general rule, whereas granting concession of public utilities is considered an administrative task and falls within the jurisdiction of the legislative authority as a kind of patronizing authority over the executive authority. These acts are not laws in terms of substance, although they take the form of a law. The foregoing entails that such administrative acts may not contradict the provisions of law, notwithstanding the fact that they are issued by the same authority: an established rule of public law provides that authority may not lay down a general rule and may not contravene the same by way of individual acts, yet it may amend it by virtue of another general rule.

The Supreme Administrative Court corroborated the reasons in Article 501 as to why the Procedures Law does not apply to administrative contracts, as it only permits arbitration in civil law contracts. Meanwhile, the minister may not extend a contract concluded on the basis of a private law unless another law that permits this is promulgated.

In its hearing of 20 February 1990 the Supreme Administrative Court vacated the appealed ruling passed by the Administrative Court in the aforementioned lawsuit.

19 The formal legal opinion issued in the hearing of 10/3/1993.

20 Case no. 486/38 judicial year.

Provision of the Arbitration Law in Civil and Commercial Articles Promulgated by Law 27/1994.

Article 1 of the above law promulgated by Law 27/1994 provides for the following:

> Without prejudice to the provisions of the international agreements applicable in the Arab Republic of Egypt, the provisions of the present law shall apply to each arbitration between parties of the public law or the private law, notwithstanding the nature of the legal relation subject of dispute, in case such arbitration is conducted in Egypt or if same is an international commercial arbitration conducted abroad, where the parties thereof agree to apply the present law thereto.

This text raises a number of points, the most significant of which follows.

The Concordance of Article 172 of the Previous Permanent Constitution of the Arab Republic of Egypt with the State Council Law 47/1972

Article 172 of the previous permanent constitution[21] of the Arab Republic of Egypt of 1972 reads as follows:

> The State Council shall be an independent judiciary body, and shall have the competence to decide in administrative disputes and disciplinary actions. The law shall determine its other competencies.

The purport of the foregoing is that the constitutional legislature assigned the State Council to consider all administrative and disciplinary disputes, leaving all its other competencies to be specified by law, given that the law is the instrument required by the legislature to regulate the competencies of judiciary bodies in Egypt (Article 167 of the permanent constitution of the Arab Republic of Egypt).

In application of the above, the State Council Law 47/1972 was enacted and provides in Article 10 thereof for the following:

> The State Council courts shall be exclusively competent to decide in the following actions:
>
> ...
>
> 'Eleventh' Disputes pertinent to concession or supply contracts or any other administrative contract.

The General Assembly interpreted in its two previous legal opinions the intent of the legislature of this article and that it has been enacted to differentiate between the competencies of the administrative and the ordinary judiciary, which maintains that this article does not contradict the provision of the constitution, as it is mentioned in the application of the constitution and was interpreted by the Assembly in alignment with the practical considerations required by the nature of the new administrative contracts and the relevant ramified economic transactions and several variables that require quick resolution of these disputes by way of arbitration.

21 The same article exists in the constitutional declaration of March 2011, after the Egyptian Revolution in January 2011.

The provision of Article 1 of the new Arbitration Law, the instrument which permits arbitration in public law contracts, in operation of the provision of Article 167 of the permanent Constitution of Egypt, reads as follows:

> The law shall determine judiciary authorities and their functions, organize the way of their formation, define conditions and procedures for the appointment and transfer of their members.

It is true that the legislature resorted to the above in order to avoid any problems pertaining to constitutionality if arbitration is permitted by virtue of an instrument of lesser degree than the law; this could be considered an intervention in the jurisdiction of a judiciary body by way of amendment in a manner that disagrees with the provision of the aforementioned article of the constitution.

In Article 1 of the Arbitration Law, the legislature has attempted to decisively resolve the disagreement regarding arbitrability in administrative contracts: how far has the legislature succeeded in this regard?

The Formal Legal Opinion of the General Assembly for the *Fatwa* and Legislation Departments on 18 December 1996 to the Effect of the Prohibition of Arbitration in Administrative Contracts

The General Assembly arrived at the decision that parties may resort to arbitration in administrative contracts before the enactment of the new Egyptian Arbitration Law, on the grounds that Article 10 of the State Council Law was provided for in order to draw a demarcation line between the jurisdiction of the civil judiciary and that of the administrative judiciary, and that the legislature's intent should be restricted to this provision and not to overload the Article 10 with unintended meanings, so long as the article is not excluded when considering the dispute in operation of the substantive legal rules applicable to administrative contracts.

The Supreme Administrative Court in its ruling referred to earlier establishes the antithesis of the two aforementioned legal opinions issued by the General Assembly and decided the arbitrability in administrative contracts. The Supreme Administrative Court based this ruling as the interpretation of Article 5 of the addendum to exploit the area of Al-Montazah Palace and Al-Moqattam Hill concluded on 14 April 1955 in the aforementioned lawsuit and annexed to the original contract provided that the legislature is immune to omission and error, and Article 5 of the above agreement should be interpreted, provided this does not undermine the characteristics of administrative contracts and without stripping the State Council of its jurisdiction to consider disputes related to such contracts. Such jurisdiction has been provided for in a substantive law as a general rule, whereas granting concessions of public utilities is considered an administrative work performed by the legislative authority as a kind of patronizing authority over the executive authority. The legislative authority's acts in this regard are not considered laws in terms of substance, although they take the shape of a law. This means that such administrative work should not contradict the provisions of law. Meanwhile, the court referred to Article 105 of the Code of Civil Procedures, which only permits arbitration in civil contracts, and the minister may not extend a contract concluded on the basis of a private law unless another law is enacted in lieu of this.

This matter was resubmitted to the General Assembly on another occasion, when the draft contract intended to be concluded between the Supreme Council for Antiquities and the British company Glitzer Silver Knight regarding complementary works to the coordination works of the Nubian Antiquities Museum landscape in Aswan, and the contract intended to be concluded between them in relation to completing the works of the said museum, were submitted to the second committee of the *Fatwa* Department for review.

Upon reviewing the contract, the Second Committee of the *Fatwa* Department at the State Council was in favour of omitting the 16th article from the first contract, and the 22nd article from the second contract, as they included a provision effectively resolving any disputes that might arise from the two contracts by way of arbitration before Cairo Regional Centre for International Commercial Arbitration on the grounds that jurisdiction falls with the State Council courts exclusively in relation to resolving the disputes that arise from administrative contracts.

The Second Committee was inclined to agree with the two rulings issued by the Supreme Administrative Court on 20 February and 13 March 1990. However, this opinion disagrees with that reached by the General Assembly for the *Fatwa* and Legislation Departments in its legal opinion issued in the hearings of 17 May 1989 and 7 February 1993, where it concluded that it was permissible to agree to resort to arbitration in administrative contracts, and in particular that a new law has been promulgated in relation to arbitration in civil and commercial articles.

In operation of the provision of Article 66/2 of the State Council Law promulgated by virtue of decree 47/1972, the committee shall refer the matter to the Assembly for jurisdiction in cases where it discovers a disagreement with a previous legal opinion issued by the assembly.

The issue was submitted to the General Assembly for the *Fatwa* and Legislation Departments in its hearing held on 18 December 1996. The Assembly rejected arbitrability in administrative contracts.

The Opinion of the Cairo Court of Appeals[22] Regarding the Present Subject

The subject was submitted to the Cairo Court of Appeals (commercial circuit 63) when the Supreme Council for Antiquities filed a lawsuit on 12 November 1996 against Glitzer Silver Knight requesting the following: to immediately stay the execution of the arbitral award number 66/1995 passed in the hearing of 20 October 1992; the nullification of the appealed arbitral award and to consider it as null and void with all the effects entailed thereby; and to bind the defendant to pay the expenses and fees. The foregoing claims were based on the grounds that when the State Council legal opinion was issued against the company, it filed arbitral case number 66/1995, whose award was subject to appeal, requesting the disbursement of an amount of EGP 545,166 in consideration of the insulation works that took place and to enable the company to execute the remaining contracted jobs for the value of EGP 950.38 per metre as well as damages in the amount of EGP 500,000 for the injury sustained thereby.

The arbitral tribunal decided to bind the Supreme Council for Antiquities to charge the company on the basis of EGP 943.65 per metre for a surface area of 503.63m^2 for a total amount of EGP 474,452 to be deducted from the amount duly paid, and further to charge the company for the distance of 70 metres of insulation works the amount of EGP 659.26 on the basis of EGP 9.418 per metre and annual delay fees of 5 per cent for the amounts delayed as from 8 November 1995 until completion of payment.

The Supreme Council for Antiquities filed the above lawsuit requesting the aforementioned claims which were not satisfied by the aforementioned ruling.

22 See Cairo Court of Appeals (circuit 63 commercial) in the appeal number 64/113judicial year (unpublished).

The Council predicated two reasons, the first being the fact that the appealed ruling bound it to pay legal fees under the pretext that it had delayed performance of its obligations in relation to the insulation works duly executed. The applicant had not requested interest to be ruled in favour thereof and the delay in disbursing the ruled amounts was attributed to the infringement by the company of the specifications. Moreover, those amounts were not specified when the lawsuit was filed. The ruling was, thus, passed in matters not included in the arbitration agreement and the Council had, thus, exceeded its limits.

The second reason for claiming the nullification of the arbitration clause was that the contract subject of dispute was an administrative contract and may not be subject to arbitration as per the provision of Article 10 of the State Council Law. Meanwhile, arbitration may not be resorted to in administrative contracts pursuant to Article 11 of the Arbitration Law, where reconciliation is ruled out.

The court rejected the lawsuit and bound the plaintiff to pay the expenses and fees and an amount of EGP 20 in consideration of legal fees. The court alluded in its counterargument to the second reason for the nullification of the arbitration clause, by maintaining that the contract subject of dispute is an administrative contract and thus may not be subject to arbitration as Article 1 of the new Arbitration Law (before amendment) provides that

> … the provisions of the present law shall apply to every arbitration between parties of the public law or private law notwithstanding the nature of the legal relations subject of dispute in case such arbitration is taking place in Egypt or if it is an international commercial arbitration taking place abroad, where the parties thereof agree on the present law as the governing law.

The Court invoked the rule 'no discretion in the existence of text' to maintain that the significance of this text is conclusive and clear in the fact that the legislature permits agreement on arbitration even if a party thereto is a public legal person and notwithstanding the nature of the legal relation subject of dispute.

The court corroborated its opinion in the provisions of the explanatory notes, as it maintained the scope specified for the application of the bill's provisions as set out in Article 1 after giving priority to the provisions of the conventions in force in Egypt, whereby such provisions apply to every international commercial arbitration taking place in Egypt, whether one of its parties is a public or private legal person. The legislature thus resolved the doubts cast over how far certain kinds of contract where one of the parties is a public legal person are subject to arbitration, and provided that all disputes arising from these contracts shall be subject to the provisions of this bill, notwithstanding the nature of the disputed legal relation.

The court alluded to the report of the joint committee made up of the Constitutional and Legislative Affairs Committee and the Bureau of the Economic Affairs Committee at the People's Assembly (Parliament) about the arbitration bill which is clearer and more conclusive in disclosing the legislature's intention from the phrases of Article 1 of the Arbitration Law. It stated that the Committee amended Article 1 to encompass wider scope than the scope of enforceability of the bill provisions, as having given preponderance to the provisions of the conventions in force in Egypt, the Committee regulated the enforceability of the provisions of the bill on every arbitration conducted in Egypt whether any of its parties is a public or a private law person and notwithstanding the relation subject of dispute. The purport intended by this phrase is the enforceability of this law on administrative contracts, so that its provision would codify the opinion reached by the State Council in this regard.[23]

The court deduced from the foregoing that the legislature intended conclusively and categorically to permit arbitration in administrative contracts.

The court pointed out that the above is in agreement with the legislative motive for the Arbitration Law, namely to cope with the magnanimous efforts exerted by the state to create a conducive environment for investment and to attract investing capital (FDI) and restore confidence to businessmen and investors – whether Arabs or foreigners – by regulating arbitration provisions in a manner that accommodates commercial disputes of the state and the requirements of resolving disputes, especially after the laws enacted in the field of investment proved insufficient on their own to realize the goal of increasing investment. Meanwhile it is meaningless to argue that the provision of Article 10 of the State Council Law 47/1972 has vested the State Council with the authority to resolve disputes arising from administrative contracts, because the intended objective is to draw a demarcation line between the jurisdiction of the state council courts on the one hand and that of the ordinary courts on the other, and not to prohibit resorting to arbitration in administrative contracts-related disputes. Moreover, Article 58 of the State Council law provides that no ministry or public authority or state authority may conclude or accept or permit any contract or reconciliation or arbitration or execute the arbitrators' award on any case with a value exceeding EGP 5,000 without consulting the competent *fatwa* department at the State Council.

The court added that, notwithstanding the viewpoint in interpreting Article 10 of the State Council Law, Article 3 of the promulgation articles of the Arbitration Law provides for vacating any ruling which contravenes the provisions of the later law. The court also maintained that there are no grounds to make a challenge by claiming that Article 172 of the permanent Constitution of Egypt might be effectively interpreted as arbitrability in administrative contracts, as this Article aims to elicit the functions of the State Council as one of the authorities constituting the judicial authority to distinguish it from ordinary courts having general jurisdiction as provided for by Article 165 of the Constitution.

During the arbitration hearing, no argument was made to the effect of nullifying the arbitration clause in administrative contracts; yet, that same argument was later articulated by the Supreme Council for Antiquities, which runs counter to the mandatory implementation of obligations in good faith, which is a general principle in civil and administrative contracts alike.

The Court has, rightly, reached its aforementioned ruling, and its decision is viewed as sound regarding its dismissal of the argument submitted by the Supreme Council for Antiquities to the effect of the impermissibility of arbitration.

Conclusions on the Opinion of the *Fatwa* Department at the State Council and Cairo Court of Appeals

(1) The General Assembly for the *Fatwa* and Legislation Departments at the State Council mixed capacity with guardianship/patronizing authority (as the same concept exists in Sharia'a Law), and compared the public person to the guardian or custodian of a minor as mentioned in several occasions in the legal opinion. This elicits that the Assembly addressed the subject from the perspective of guardianship, which it attributes to the public person, rather than the perspective

23 This means the two previous legal opinions (*Fatwas*) of the General Assembly which corroborated the permissibility of arbitration in administrative contracts.

of capacity. The *fatwa* concluded that this public guardianship is only valid through legislative action that permits the public person to conclude arbitration stipulation under the argument that it is concluded regarding a party other than itself, and property other than its own, because originally speaking – in the case of absence of a provision – any act undertaken by a person regarding the affairs or property of another is invalid.

It is suggested[24] that a public person upon concluding an arbitration agreement is not concluding it on the basis of a general mandate which is established by virtue of a legislative act, but rather on the basis of his proven competency in this regard, due to being a legal entity pursuant to the provisions of the Civil Code (Article 253/d of the Civil Code). The capacity to perform is established for public legal entities, whether they are authorities or local persons. Natural persons (i.e. human beings) serve as the means for a legal entity to express itself and its intentions.

A legal person, whether public or private, enjoys the capacity to make a contract via its representative and members, from whom it is inseparable. That is justified by the establishment of personal and direct responsibility for the errors committed thereby, given that these errors are attributed to the legal person itself.

Admittedly, an arbitration agreement is a contract, therefore, the capacity to conclude this agreement is per se the capacity required to conclude the contract.

(2) The legal opinion issued by the General Assembly for the *Fatwa* and Legislation Departments on 18 December 1996, even if it was based on the substantive nature of the administrative contract, which may not be subject to arbitration and is repulsive therewith, could be counter-argued by the fact that the legislature permitted arbitration in administrative contracts by virtue of an explicit legislative text duly corroborated by the explanatory notes of the law alluded to by the Court of Appeals in its ruling and by the Assembly itself in its earlier legal opinion, where it permitted arbitration in administrative contracts without infringing the substantive framework of the theory of the administrative contract which was a compromising and sound solution at the time.[25]

The concept of the administrative contract finds its origin in French jurisprudence, yet the French legislature has permitted arbitration in administrative contracts of an international nature. However, in internal administrative contracts, this was permitted in case a law is enacted permitting arbitration.

(3) The Supreme Council for Antiquities argued that conciliation is impermissible in matters where arbitration is not permitted as per Article 11 of the Arbitration Law 27/1994. The ruling was silent regarding this argument; it should have pointed out that it is misplaced to argue that the arbitration agreement in one of its aspects means conciliation, which is only permissible for those who are entitled to act on the property of the administrative body. Therefore, this contradicts the well-established principles of the administrative law which do not permit the employees at the administrative body to waive the property thereof in any way whatsoever whether by way of assignment or conciliation, as arbitration does not represent an assignment or conciliation as much as it represents an attempt to settle the dispute which is as per our discretion a right secured for the administrative body. The constitutional legislature also secured its right to litigation, as the right of litigation may, during the practising thereof, cause the administrative body to gain funds. On the

24 Dr Habib Ibrahim Al-Khalili, 'Permissibility of Arbitration in Administrative Contracts – comment on the legal opinion of the General Assembly for the *Fatwa* and Legislation Departments at the State Council issued in its meeting held on December 18, 1996 to the effect of the invalidity of the arbitration clause in administrative contracts', *The Judgments Journal* (1997) vol. 7, 153.

25 The aforementioned legal opinion of the General Assembly issued on 17 May 1989 and 7 February 1993.

other hand, the administrative body may lose money or assign rights in return for compensation, which resembles the same arbitration philosophy in state contracts.

(4) The idea which serves as grounds for the *fatwa* (legal opinion) that no delegation may be authorized over another delegation to support the arbitrability could be averted by arguing that the legislature permitted arbitration by a conclusive legislative provision that abolishes all differences that might arise regarding the permissibility of arbitration.

(5) The Assembly's assumption that Article 1 was general in its wording and that general terms are inconclusive in their significance, could also be rebutted by arguing that the legislative text is corroborated with the explanatory notes of the law and the report of the joint committee made up of the Constitutional and Legislative Affairs Committee and the Economic Affairs Committee Bureau at the People's Assembly about the Arbitration Law (both alluded to in the ruling) in relation to the intention of the legislature in permitting arbitration in administrative contracts, which was explicitly mentioned in the latest report. This eventually elicits the legislature's intention in this regard, thus leaving no room for interpretation or construction.

(6) The aforementioned ruling applied the fundamental rule which provides that no discretion may be performed when a text is present. It also predicated the explanatory notes and the aforementioned committee report, and avoided overloading the matter with unintended meanings, as it operated the sound legal logic upon reading the provision of the said article and the explanations thereof in each of the aforementioned notes and report.

(7) The Administrative Court in a recent ruling[26] implicitly acknowledged arbitration in public works contracts. That ruling was passed upon submitting to the court a dispute claiming to discharge an arbitrator and the court ruled upon that claim to the effect that it inevitably acknowledges the principle of arbitration in administrative contracts.

Based on the above, the legislature considered it proper to intervene by a legislative amendment which explicitly provides for the permissibility of arbitration in administrative contracts.

Legislative Amendment of Article 1 of the Arbitration Act and Permissibility of Arbitration in Administrative Contracts

There was discrepancy in opinions regarding the arbitrability in administrative contracts, after the General Assembly opined on 18 December 1996 that arbitration is impermissible in this regard. The Cairo Court of Appeals 'Commercial Circuit' passed a ruling which runs counter both to the opinion of the General Assembly and that of the third committee for *Fatwa* Department at the State Council. It states that public persons may not agree on settling disputes arising from administrative contracts concluded between them by way of arbitration and that jurisdiction falls with the General Assembly; the legislature preferred to intervene to settle the disagreement that arose regarding this problem.

New Legislation Amending Certain Arbitration Law Provisions

The aforementioned legislative amendment and the provision of Article 1 states that a second clause should be added to Article 1 of the Arbitration Act 27/1994 reading as follows:

26 The ruling of the Administrative Court, the Contracts and Compensation Circuit, no. 4760/49judicial year, unpublished.

> In all events it is permissible to agree on arbitration in disputes arising from administrative contracts upon the approval of the competent minister or his pro tempore involving public legal persons and no delegation is permissible in this regard.

Article 2 provides that the present law be published in the *Egyptian Gazette*, provided it enters into force as of the day following the date of publication.

The explanatory notes pointed out that the legal relations of economic nature have expanded in scope with the wide strides taken by the country towards growth and reform. States and other public legal persons take part in the establishment of those considerations so as to encourage investment and give impetus to the economic development process and to assist it in achieving its goals, amongst which is the conclusion of administrative contracts closely related to public utilities with local and foreign parties.

Resorting to arbitration is an agreement to settle disputes arising from these contracts, and a means of settlement which is of particular use in resolving issues and disputes related to investment and commerce on national and international levels; henceforth, it was viewed as proper to include an amendment in addition to this article to explicitly provide for the permissibility of agreeing on arbitration in disputes arising from administrative contracts, and to specify the competent authority which permits such agreement. This aims to adjust the use of this licence, and to guarantee the satisfaction of the arbitration agreement without prejudice to public interest.

Assessment of the Arbitration Act in Civil and Commercial Matters Promulgated by Law 27/1994 Regarding the Permissibility of Arbitration in Administrative Contracts

There are legislative loopholes in the provisions of this law resulting from the incongruity between certain articles of this law and the nature of administrative contracts. These loopholes can be summed up as follows:

(1) Article 1 permits arbitration in administrative contracts, and Article 39 of the same law provides that:

a. The arbitral tribunal shall apply the rules agreed upon by the parties to arbitration to the subject of dispute. In case it is agreed to apply the law of a specific state, the substantive rules thereof shall be applied exclusive of the rules pertinent to the conflict of laws, unless otherwise agreed.
b. In case the parties fail to agree on the governing legal rules to be applied to the subject of dispute, the arbitral tribunal shall apply the substantive rules in the law, viewed thereby as the most closely linked to the dispute.
c. The arbitral tribunal shall, upon deciding on the subject of dispute, observe the terms and conditions of the contract subject of dispute as well as the applicable use and practice in this kind of transaction.
d. The arbitral tribunal may, in case the parties to arbitration explicitly agree to delegate same to affect conciliation, decide on the subject of dispute on the basis of the prerequisites of the rules of justice and equity without being limited by the provisions of law.

It could be inferred from the provision of the foregoing article that the governing law applicable to the subject of dispute is elected by the disputants and the arbitral tribunal applies the substantive rules independent of the rules pertinent to conflict of laws, unless agreed otherwise. The article then specifies the modus operandi of designating the applicable rules in case the parties fail to agree on specifying same, either in the text of the contract or in a separate arbitration agreement. This eventually gives rise to the likelihood of applying a law other than the national law when hearing a dispute where a party thereto is a public legal person.

In some scholarly opinions, this is a violation of *Le Contrat Administratif* theory.

In addition to the foregoing, this law may involve rules that run counter to the nature and terms and conditions of administrative contracts, as the idea of administrative contract is not reflected in several legislations in foreign countries. This proves that when the legislature permitted arbitration in public law contracts, it was not clear on the legal opinion of the General Assembly for the *Fatwa* and Legislation Departments at the State Council stating that arbitration does not exclude the application of the substantive legal rules applicable to administrative contracts. This eventually requires legislative amendment to avoid this manifest contradiction between permitting arbitration in administrative contracts and vesting the parties to the contract with the power to select a law to be applied to the subject of dispute, other than the national law or the application by the arbitral tribunal of the rules satisfactory thereto, in case the parties fail to choose, which might be in conflict with the nature of public law contracts.[27]

(2) The provisions of law seem to involve another contradiction. Whereas Article 1 permits arbitration in administrative contracts, Article 11 of the same law provides for the following:

> Arbitration may only be agreed by a natural or legal person who is entitled to act on its rights, and arbitration may not be conducted in issues where conciliation is prohibited.

It is suggested that it may not be argued that agreement on arbitration means reconciliation in one of its aspects which is only permissible for those who are entitled to act on the property of the administrative authority. Therefore, it contradicts the well-established principles of the Administrative Law which do not permit the workers at any given administrative authority to assign or waive its property in any way whatsoever, whether by way of assignment or reconciliation. This rests on the fact that arbitration does not represent an assignment or reconciliation as much as it represents an attempt to settle the dispute, which is, as per our discretion, a right secured to the administrative body. Besides, the constitutional legislature secured thereto the right to litigation. As the right of litigation is practised, the administrative body may gain or lose money, or may waive its right in return for compensation, which echoes the arbitration philosophy in the state contracts.

These contradictions require a rapid legislative amendment to be aligned with the requirements of arbitration in administrative contracts. Legislation can thus be adapted to the administrative contracts of international nature, and some flexibility can be imparted to the provisions of the Administrative Law to keep pace with the recent variables imposed on the legal and economic arena, and the cross-impact of each arena on the other in the modern age.

Legislative Amendment of Article 1 of the Arbitration Law and the Permissibility of Arbitration in Administrative Contracts

After the General Assembly had passed its famous legal opinion on 18 December 1996 to the effect of arbitrability in administrative contracts, and out of the legislature's will to settle the case by a

27 The legal opinion of the General Assembly for *Fatwa* and Legislation Departments previously mentioned in the hearing of 10 March 1993.

legal provision to put an end to all discretions, the legislative amendment was introduced by virtue of Law 9/1997 which provides in Article 1 thereof for the following:

> In all cases arbitration may be agreed in disputes arising from administrative contracts upon the approval of the competent minister or the acting minister regarding public legal persons, and no delegation may be made in this regard.

It is true that the prerequisite of the minister's approval or the approval of the person acting in lieu thereof regarding public legal persons, coupled with the impermissibility of delegation in this regard, is an unfair condition that renders the legislative permissibility of arbitration in administrative contracts void. It renders resorting to arbitration an option conditional upon the will of the contracting administrative body to either operate it, or refrain from applying same. This eventually highlights the pressing need for abolishing the condition of the competent minister's approval of arbitration in administrative contracts which could be abused, and thus the discretionary power vested in the administrative body in this regard would deviate. It is self-evident that this is an intended defect[28] that must be proven before the Administrative Court. When the minister grants his approval of arbitration in a given contract, but refrains from granting approval in another similar contract, this could be considered an abuse of the discretionary power granted to him and justifies resorting to the administrative judiciary in this regard.

The added clause concluded by referring to the impermissibility of delegation of this function vested in the competent minister or the person acting in his stead. This prohibition of delegation is a prohibition to delegate the authority to any other entity or person. This indicates that the legislature was later adopted by the latest legal opinion issued by the General Assembly[29] where it opined that no delegation may be granted on another delegation, as public legal persons are delegated to in managing public utilities. Henceforth, they may not delegate this authority to others. This is in accordance with the well-established jurisprudent rule which indicates that a delegated authority may not be re-delegated to another party.

Small wonder that it is useless to get involved in all such contradictions which prolong dispute proceedings and cause the reason for resorting to arbitration to collapse. A main feature of globalization is the encouragement of foreign direct investment (FDI), provided such investments flow into developing countries, mainly to secure effective, efficient, specialized and neutral means to settle disputes, so as to culminate in a binding and enforceable ruling. No doubt that investment in infrastructure and the incoming of foreign contractors to undertake infrastructure projects, coupled with the growth of investments in construction in the private sector, require a safe and sound climate for settling disputes as mentioned earlier. This is one of the factors cited by international institutions such as the World Bank when ranking investment-attracting countries (rankings for doing business) in terms of their legislation and whether foreign investors may resort to arbitration and if there are any legislative impediments to this end. Moreover, there are plenty of international conventions to which Egypt is bound, due to its being a signatory to a number of bilateral investment treaties and multilateral investment treaties which have become part and parcel of the internal Egyptian legislation after ratification. As per these conventions, Egypt undertakes to

28 See the established principles in the administrative judiciary in Egypt: Supreme Administrative Court in the appeal number 1129/37judicial year, hearing of 15 February 1994, The Technical Office Group year (39), and the ruling of the Supreme Administrative Court in the appeal number 462/36judicial year, hearing of 9 October 1994, The Technical Office, year (40).

29 See the legal opinion of the Assembly on 18 December 1996.

protect foreign investors who are nationals of states contracting therewith and undertakes to settle disputes arising from their investment activities in Egypt by way of arbitration.

Admittedly, the condition of the competent minister's approval stipulated by Law 9/1997 for arbitration in administrative contracts is a legislative limitation on foreign investors for whom Egypt has secured protection by virtue of international treaties and conventions. Therefore Law 9/1997 contravenes all conventions and limits them, as the said conventions have become, after ratification and endorsement, internal enforceable legislation, which eventually discredits Egypt as an investment-attracting country, not only at the international level for foreign investors, individuals and companies, but with monetary and economic international institutions in charge of ranking investment-attracting countries (rankings for doing business) as well.[30]

Permitting arbitration in an administrative body's contracts, even with the aforementioned legislative limitation, is an inevitable and natural outcome of the phenomenon of globalization. Egypt is a state governed by the civil law legal culture, which is the same legal culture as that of Arab countries. The influence of common law legal culture, where arbitration is permissible in administrative contracts, is a natural result of this amalgamation of discrepant legal cultures. The integration of the Egyptian legal system into the global legal system marks the dawn of a new legal culture, a global legal culture based on new concepts of international norms that in essence are natural outcomes of globalization. Those norms have grown to regulate international commercial transactions, amongst which are: documentary credits, international sales, various banking transactions; different kinds of international contracts that encompass public works international contracts and arbitration therein; infrastructure contracts implemented by foreign contractors and foreign giant companies (whether one company or a consortium of companies) with hi-tech competence, significant financial credibility and international goodwill and reputation in infrastructure. These encompass the underground metro, airports, aqueducts, railway lines and other infrastructure projects. The transactions between private persons and states at the international level cover energy contracts and concession agreements to exploit natural resources of oil and gas.

All such international transactions which are the subject of international business law, and which are mainly concerned with international business transaction, have become fertile soil for applying the so-called new legal culture which distinguishes civil law legal culture from the Anglo-American legal culture. Both cultures are fused in one crucible due to the particular motives dictated by economic considerations which necessitate new, unified and common special provisions for these international contracts including the settlement of disputes by way of arbitration[31] and other alternative means which play a critical role as a branch of international business law. The role of mediation has recently become evident in a way which might appear in the short run to be of greater benefit, less costly, more rapid and more efficient than international commercial arbitration, notwithstanding its various advantages. In support of the foregoing, the prevailing approach in the USA and Europe is currently in support of intermediation to resolve disputes and to reach a satisfactory settlement for the parties concerned to protect them from resorting to arbitration and save them the costs thereof.

This kind of thinking has started to permeate into developing countries, in spite of the fact that it is not visible at the practical application level. Nevertheless, the integration between cultures in

30 See criticism of this stipulation by Mohammed A.M. Ismail, *Public Economic Law and New International Administrative Contracts* (Beirut: El Halabi 2010); the book was awarded the State's Prize in Legal Research in the Arab Republic of Egypt 2011/2012.

31 Most legislation in countries worldwide has been greatly influenced by the UNCITRAL Model Law as amended 2006. No doubt this secures rigorous harmony between arbitration laws all over the world as a trans-cultural universal phenomenon.

the latest contracts is expected to expand the base of its application into developing countries and the Arab countries very shortly. Added to this is the internationalization witnessed by traditional workings of administrative contracts and the way they are throwing off the limitations in which they used to be imprisoned for long decades. Since the inception of the Egyptian State Council and until very recently, they were very much enshrined in rigid fundamental thinking which assumed, until the present time, that the parties to a contract are not on an equal level, and lay down exorbitant clauses (*Les Clauses Exorbitants*) that do not exist in private law contracts concluded by contracting parties on the basis of contractual justice between the contractors.

A crucial question arises here: Are PPP and BOT/ BOOT contracts, in this sense, subject to the limitations and legislative stipulations enacted in Law 9/1997, such as the requirement of the competent minister's approval before resorting to arbitration?

It is certain that after the promulgation of the PPP Law in 2010, this kind of contract is no longer considered an administrative contract, whether it is purely commercial or of a hybrid nature. It is true that certain arbitration provisions pertinent to administrative contracts have been issued by the Cairo Regional Centre for International Commercial Arbitration asserting that the legislative discourse at this very point requires the competent minister's approval as enacted by Law 9/1997, amending Arbitration Law 27/1994. This legislative discourse is addressed to the administrative body as it is obliged to obtain the competent minister's approval and not the private legal entity contracting therewith. In light of the foregoing, and a fortiori in interpretation approaches, this becomes easier in civil and commercial contracts and hybrid contracts which are mainly limited to PPP, BOT and BOOT contracts of all forms, where the requirement for the competent minister's approval becomes a misplaced regulation check in contracts concluded by the state, and which are deemed private law contracts. Therefore, it is unquestionable that the contracting administrative body should enter into civil and commercial contracts as much as administrative contracts; this general principle was established long ago in jurisprudence and public law judiciary.

In brief, BOT, BOOT and PPP contracts are not administrative contracts, whether these contracts are commercial or of a hybrid nature, due to the emergence of certain manifestations of public authority. Nevertheless, even though BOT and PPP contracts are not administrative, and given the fact that in certain administrative contracts the approval of the competent minister is not required by arbitration tribunals to be obtained by the private legal person contracting with the state, and that the administrative body's abstention from obtaining such approval is considered *mala fide*, arbitration tribunals decided their competence to hear disputes notwithstanding the dissociation of arbitration clause from the competent minister's approval. This is due to the fact that the refraining by the administrative body from obtaining this approval is not tolerated by the contracting private person, rather, the administrative body shall be held liable for the foregoing on the account that the administrative body is the addressee by the provisions of Law 9/1997 requiring the approval of the competent minister and prohibiting delegation in this matter. This eventually decisively negates the requirement of the competent minister's approval in contracts concluded by the administrative body, which are not covered by the administrative contracts. These include BOT contracts and a priori PPP contracts as per the provision of Article 1 of the promulgation provisions of the PPP Law (Law 67/2010), which provides, as mentioned earlier, that PPP contracts are not subject to the State Procurement Law 89/1998 and its executive regulations and the Public Utilities Concession Law 129/1947 and the Natural Resources Concession Law 61/1958. This new legal nature of PPP contracts, changed pursuant to Article 1 of the aforementioned promulgation articles, is no longer a traditional administrative contract.

It could be concluded from the foregoing that the condition of the competent minister's approval mentioned in the legislative amendment of Article 1 of Law 9/1997 should be abolished on the account that administrative bodies recurrently abuse that condition. It goes without saying that in administrative contracts the link between the administrative body and the party contracting therewith is a contractual relation created upon the conformity of two wills and causes the creation of individual and subjective legal centres with the contract concluded between them. Moreover, in relation to the conclusion of administrative contracts, the administrative body is the entity in charge of undertaking the contracting procedures, together with notifications required by these procedures and obtaining prior approvals and procuring financial credits and all other procedures required by the law to conclude administrative contracts. Therefore, this body is exclusively in charge of completing such procedures, so that if it overlooks any of those stipulated procedures, intentionally or unintentionally, it shall exclusively be held liable particularly if the other party plays no role in satisfying those procedures. This is only logical and finds its grounds in the fact that the link between the other party and the administrative body is a contractual link, not a public organizational one. Therefore, that other party ought to be protected and confidence in the administrative body should not be shaken, especially if the other party is incapable of knowing in advance whether the administrative body had satisfied the necessary administrative procedures or obtained the required approvals. Based on the foregoing, Article 1 of Law 27/1994 amended by Law 9/1997, which requires the competent minister's approval of the arbitration clause in administrative contract related disputes, addresses the administrative body exclusively. For it is inconceivable that the other party would play any role in this regard, especially if the arbitration clause is mentioned in the administrative contract itself or any of the addenda thereto. The legislative discourse in this regard is addressed to the administrative body on the predicate that it is the body that has the dominance over the contracting procedures and that is in charge of verifying the soundness and validity of those procedures undertaken, apart from the will of the other party. Under such circumstances, it is impossible to apply nullification as a penalty for failing to obtain the approval of the minister of the arbitration clause. Otherwise, the party in default may benefit from its mistake at the expense of the other party which runs counter to the most basic principles of justice. Moreover, nullification is basically only applicable by virtue of a provision.

The legislature in Article 1 of the Arbitration Law has not provided for nullification as penalty for failing to obtain the approval of the minister of the arbitration clause. All results of such procedure shall, in this case, be considered as operation of the administrative and disciplinary rules against any of the workers at the administrative body who prove to be liable for not satisfying this procedure.[32]

In addition, the Egyptian legal system urgently needs an integrated legislative regulation of public utilities concessions and partnership by the private sector (PPP) in financing, operating and owning public utilities and turning them back to the state by the BOT/BOOT system, instead of dispersed partial pieces of legislation (Law 100/1996, Law 229/1996, Law 3/1997 and law 22/1998). It is mandatory to adopt an integrated legislative policy that accommodates all such contractual patterns, in addition to any new contractual forms that might develop or be imported from the Anglo-American legal culture, or common law legal culture. Laws promulgated in the mid-twentieth century (129/1947 and 61/1958) have become incompatible with recent developments as they tackle variable and developed dynamic contractual relations rather than static relations which are characterized by sluggishness and rigidity.

If the minister's jurisdiction in this regard is observant of the aforementioned regulations with the aim to align interests conflicting with the interest of the contracting state and the foreign contractor, it is thus mandatory, provided it strictly observes the foregoing regulations. However,

32 See the *ad hoc* arbitration case enrolled under number 464/2006 at CRCICA, hearing of 2 July 2006.

the said jurisdiction still lacks the specification of the minister's powers, framework and the regulations of applying it to strike the necessary balance.

It is true that the minister's power in this regard is subject to the control of administrative judiciary in case the administrative body abuses the discretionary authority vested therein. It goes without saying that in the State Council judiciary,[33] this last defect is considered a deliberate defect that should be established before the administrative court. In cases where the minister chooses to grant his approval of one contract and withhold it regarding another similar contract, such an act could be considered an abuse of the discretionary power vested in him and justifies recourse to the administrative judiciary.

The Position of the French Conseil d'Etat before the New Millennium of Arbitration as a Means to Resolve Administrative Contract Disputes

The French State Council conducted a report (a study) including certain proposals regarding arbitration as a means to resolve disputes arising from administrative contracts.[34]

The French State Council suggested that arbitration is mandatory in certain administrative contracts, exclusive of other contracts with special reference to public works contracts.

The State Council then presented its proposals in this regard and concluded by stating the regulation and procedures of the arbitral process.

A crucial issue arises whether a state's consent to arbitration in a BIT is overridden by an arbitration clause in a related investment contract. Tribunals have generally held that, as long as the arbitration claims allege a cause of action under the BIT, they are not subject to the contractually elected jurisdiction.[35]

In the *Vivendi* case, Argentina argued that the dispute resolution clause of the concession contract, Article 16.4, establishing the jurisdiction of the local courts for the purpose of interpretation and application of the contract, precluded jurisdiction under the French treaty. Rejecting this argument, an ICSID Annulment Committee held:

> ... where 'the fundamental basis of a claim' is a treaty laying down an independent standard by which the conduct of the parties is to be judged, the existence of an exclusive jurisdiction clause in the contract between the Claimant and the respondent state or one of its subdivisions cannot operate as a bar to the application of the treaty standard.[36]

---

33 The Supreme Administrative Court, Appeal 1129/37judicial year, hearing of 15 February 1994, the Technical Office in the year (39), and the Supreme Administrative Court, Appeal 462/36judicial year, hearing of 9 October 1994, the Technical Office in the year (40).

34 *Régler Autrement des Conflits, Conciliation, Transaction, Arbitrage, en Matière Administrative*, Conseil D'Etat, Section du Rapport et des Etudes, 1993, titre III, 'L'arbitrage'.

35 Blackaby and Partasides, with Redfern and Hunter, 2009, 481; 'In *Lanco v Argentina*, for example, the contract contained an exclusive jurisdiction clause in favor of the Argentine courts. Argentina argued that this clause applied and that the dispute was not within the jurisdiction of the ICSID Tribunal. The Tribunal rejected this argument, holding that the exclusive jurisdiction clause in the contract could not exclude the jurisdiction of the ICSID Tribunal in relation to the BIT claim.'

36 Blackaby and Partasides with Redfern and Hunter, 2009, 481.

Chapter 4
International Investment Arbitration in the MENA Region

An Overview

The international legal framework governing foreign investments consists of unique treaty mechanisms, vast networks of international investment agreements (IIAs) and the general rules of international law. These international instruments have been recognized in the MENA countries in recent decades. Although other international treaties interact with the above mentioned networks in important ways, IIAs are the primary public international law instruments governing the promotion and protection of foreign investment. IIA texts generally differ in many important respects, but most IIAs combine similar or identical treaty-based standards of promotion and protection for foreign investments. Protection through the investor–state arbitration mechanism exists as it allows foreign investors to enforce these standards on the MENA hosting states. The network of IIAs provides foreign investors with a powerful and dynamic method of international treaty enforcement. This is the real dynamics of international investment law. A comprehensive explanation of the substantive standards of treatment that MENA states grant to foreign investors and investment under IIAs are provided in the following chapters.[1]

One eminent scholarly opinion points out that:

> The uniqueness of the current IIA network is a product of an historical evolution going as far back as the Middle Ages. Prior to the twentieth century, international standards of foreign investment and investor protection developed primarily through the related processes of diplomatic protection and claims commissions. In the late nineteenth and early twentieth centuries, as the world economy became increasingly internationalized, the limits of the diplomatic protection model became apparent, particularly as controversies arose between capital exporting and importing states regarding the customary international law minimum standard of treatment to be accorded to foreign investors and investments. In the aftermath of the Second World War (WWII), the process of international economic integration was rekindled, leading to the emergence of the contemporary investment treaty framework. It is crucial to consider this historical development in order to better understand current debates and contentious issues in investment treaty law.[2]

In 1927, the 1924 Committee of Experts for the Progressive Codification of International Law, which was established by the League of Nations, reported some recommendations that seven subjects were ripe for codification. On 27 September 1927, the Eighth Assembly of the League of Nations resolved to submit three topics to the First Conference for the Codification of International Law (the 1930 Codification Conference), including the 'Responsibility of States for Damage done

---

1 Andrew Newcombe and Lluis Paradell, *Historical Development of Investment Treaty Law, Law and Practice of Investment Treaties: Standards of Treatment* (Kluwer Law International 2009) 1–2.

2 Newcombe and Paradell, 1–2.

in their Territory to the Person or Property of Foreigners'. In anticipation of the 1930 Codification Conference, a number of organizations, including the Institute of International Law, Association de Droit International du Japon, the American Institute of International Law and the International Commission of Jurists instituted research projects on rules of international responsibility relating to injuries to foreigners. The Harvard Law School undertook a programme of research in international law for the purpose of preparing a draft international convention on each of the three topics to be discussed at the 1930 Codification Conference. The reporter for the responsibility of states, Edwin Borchard, prepared a *Draft Convention on Responsibility of States for Damage done in their Territory to the Person or Property of Foreigners* (1929 Harvard Draft).[3]

The 1930 Hague Conference, during its proceedings on codifying customary international law rules, drafted the '*Responsibility of States for Damage Caused in their Territories to the Persons and Properties of Foreigners*'. Article 10 of the draft codification provides as follows:

> As regards damage caused to the person or property of foreigners by a private person, the State is only responsible if the damage sustained by the foreigner results from the fact that the State has failed to take the measures which may reasonably be expected of it in the circumstances in order to prevent, remedy or inflict punishment for the damage.

Opinions were divided on standards of treatment. In voting on the article, 17 states (mainly capital importing states) maintained the position that foreign nationals were only entitled to equality of treatment with nationals, while 21 states, including the capital exporting states, maintained the existence of a minimum standard of treatment. Divided opinion on the issue of the minimum standard was a significant factor in the breakdown of the conference's codification efforts in the area of state responsibility. The final version of the codification was not adopted because it failed to receive the requisite support of two-thirds of the states at the conference.[4]

Much of the expansion of international investment in the eighteenth, nineteenth and twentieth centuries occurred within colonial, political and legal regimes. Consequently, there was no need for colonists to have recourse to international law processes since colonial political and military powers protected colonists and their property from local governmental interference. In addition, extraterritorial jurisdiction, which allowed foreign powers to apply their laws to their nationals in foreign states, was exercised under treaties. In some cases, these regimes were imposed by force through treaties of capitulation. Extraterritorial jurisdiction in one form or another existed in Egypt, Morocco, Turkey and other parts of the Ottoman Empire as well as in China, Japan, Thailand, and Iran.[5] The existence of extraterritorial jurisdiction was evident in the MENA region before decolonization.

Post-WWII developments were significant to international investment law dynamics and practice. Decolonization and nationalization played a considerable role in establishing new rules for international investment law practice.

> Disputes over the treatment of foreign investment increased and intensified after WWII as the process of decolonization resulted in colonial territories becoming states. Many of these newly independent states, along with the Eastern European communist states, adopted socialist economic policies, including large scale nationalizations of key sectors of their economies. Notable examples

3 Ibid., 14–15.
4 Ibid., 15–16.
5 Ibid., 10–11.

> include the nationalizations of major industries in Eastern European states, China, Cuba, and Latin America (Argentina, Bolivia, Brazil, Chile, Guatemala and Peru); the Indonesian nationalization of Dutch properties; the Egyptian nationalization of the Suez Canal and the nationalizations of the oil industry throughout the Middle East and Northern Africa (Algeria, Iran, Iraq, Libya, Kuwait and Saudi Arabia). The foreign investment disputes that ensued focused on two principal issues: the extent to which acquired rights, including natural resource concessions granted by colonial powers, were to be respected and the standard of compensation for the expropriation of those acquired rights. In a series of cases, newly independent and developing states asserted that, upon independence, states were entitled to review concession agreements that had been granted by colonial powers, and, furthermore, maintained that compensation for the expropriation of property would be based on national laws.[6]

International investment law in the MENA region is emerging from the dynamics of direct investor–state arbitration. International investment law has to be understood as a process with its own culture and dynamics. It has specific culture, style and dynamics which relate to the nature, history and establishment of international investment arbitration, whether in the Middle East or elsewhere.

The first ICSID cases such as *SPP v. Egypt* established the foundational role of the ICSID convention,[7] meanwhile, modern international investment law was created by the 'founding fathers', conceived of investment protection treaties, both multilateral and bilateral, such as the 1958 New York Convention on enforcement of arbitral awards which may not have focused directly on investment protection. Major contract based arbitral awards, now seen as dealing with investment disputes, were issued before and at that time and enforceability against government must have been an investment protection aspect.[8]

> Investment arbitration is, firstly, not made by a permanent court. There is therefore less pressure within the arbitral tribunal towards internal consistency as would or should exist within a standing international court where institutional or personal relations are established and where the court (and its support staff) has developed its own culture, traditions and conventions. Arbitral tribunals, with their set up based on commercial rules and practices, tend to consist of two arbitrators appointed by the parties and a president, normally appointed by the appointed institution. Their personal dynamics can be quite different from a standing court.[9]

It is unlikely that tribunal presidents who have acted in a way that is not liked by the appointing authority would be re-appointed.

Arbitration is not determined by specific national legal cultures. In practice, arbitration tends to lean more towards party control, moderated and monitored by the tribunal such as in the common law system. This is because the tribunal is mainly appointed by the parties; meanwhile, the ICSID appointing authority injects an element of international justice that is not under exclusive party control. The parties cannot control the tribunal's composition despite the fact they still pay its fees, nor can they control exclusively the tribunal's composition except in the unlikely case they completely agree.

6 Ibid., 17–19.

7 Thomas W. Wälde, *New Aspects of International Investment Law*, ed. Philippe Khan and Thomas W. Wälde (The Hague Academy of International Law 2007, Martinus Nijhoff Publishers) 69.

8 Ibid., 70.

9 Ibid., 71–72.

The parties under the ICSID rule can agree on the president but that would appear to be rare. As they are likely not to agree, the appointing authority (e.g. ICSID) appoints the tribunal, but always after some informal sounding out of the parties. That gives each party – in particular influential ones – a *de facto* veto right and adds to the other asymmetrical advantage of states parties in the ICSID and even more so the NAFTA system.[10]

The Minimum Standard of Treatment

Each country is bound to give to nationals of another country in its territory the benefit of the same laws, the same administration, the same protection which it gives to its own citizens, neither more nor less, provided that the protection which the country gives to its own citizens conforms to the established standard of civilization.

There is a standard of justice, simple and fundamental, and of such general acceptance by all civilized countries as to form part of the international law of the world. This minimum standard is essentially similar to standards of justice and treatment accepted by 'civilized states/ nations', including the European states and the US. Developments in African and Middle Eastern countries were significant, as many African and Middle Eastern states were early signatories to BITs. As already noted, these early BITs were generally based on model agreements prepared by capital exporting states. In the early 1980s, the Asian-African Legal Consultative Organization (AALCO) published three draft BITs, which provided different models of investment liberalization and protection. In 1980, the United Treaties Agreement for the Investment of Arab Capital in the Arab States was signed creating an Arab Investment Court. A number of other regional investments have been concluded in the Middle East and Africa.[11]

The Sources of International Investment Law in the MENA Region

In international investment disputes, non-state actors such as industrial entities, professions, NGOs and civil society institutions, have acquired novel rights against states enforceable directly by investment arbitration initiated at the option of the investor. *L'arbitrage unilateral transnational*, which is direct investor–state arbitration, is a full individual subjective right held only by the investor. There are arguments to eliminate the differences in treatment between foreign investors (treaty protected) and domestic investors (not protected).[12] There is an asymmetric relationship, legal, political and factual, at issue between state and foreign investor. The applicable law may include domestic law (e.g. Article 42 of the ICSID convention), but international law is invariably present, either co-existing with and normally considered to be 'controlling' domestic law or as the exclusivity cited or in practice applied source of law. The primary source of applicable law is the relevant treaty at issue. The most modern BITs play a considerable role in codifying the international investment treaty in the Middle East. Before that, and until the present day, the 1958 New York Convention and the 1965 Washington Convention were and still are the fundamental international sources for international investment law. International customs are generally evidence of a general practice accepted as law. In addition, 'the general principles of law recognized by civilized nations'

10 Ibid., 74.
11 Newcombe and Paradell, 11–12.
12 Wälde, 122.

are considered a fundamental source. State practice is of great significance as it is sufficiently widespread and is generally seen as a source for customary international law. Investment disputes are, however, in the main not about commercial contract disputes but disciplining governmental conduct *vis-à-vis* foreign investors. That function is not directly comparable either to inter-state disputes or to commercial disputes between parties who have equal bargaining powers and similar status. More comparable are the administrative courts or general courts, which exercise powers of judicial review of governmental acts on the level of general regulations of administrative conduct. The comparative law of civil and administrative procedure is a very important source. Investment arbitration is a form of international judicial review of governmental conduct and, in the absence of an international investment law court, uses for that purpose the procedures, conventions and legal culture of international commercial arbitration which are of fundamental importance in providing a threshold of protection to foreign investors.[13]

Conclusions

In conclusion, the introduction of treaty based direct investor–state arbitration following the creation of ICSID in 1965, the spread of bilateral treaties in the Middle East and earlier experience with investment arbitration based on contracts, have introduced a significant discontinuity into a system that was based on investor–state arbitration, after the establishment of arbitral jurisdiction in a specific, individualized agreement between the state and investor.[14] International investment law, in its hybrid/mixed form, involves states and private foreign investors and is now taking its own development path. Protection of foreign investors has a secondary, indirect good governance effect from which domestic investors also benefit. However, it would be more logical if the international treaty protection could extend to also cover domestic investors, as domestic investors have a lower threshold of protection. Access to international arbitration by domestic investors on the basis of a contractual system of investment arbitration was attempted in Argentina in recent awards, which recognize that domestic investors can obtain investment arbitration protection by setting up an investment vehicle in another member state. Article 25/2 of the ICSID Convention may be read to encourage further movements towards this direction.[15]

Conversely, a domestic investor in the MENA region has a lower threshold of protection as he or she is not covered by BITs, as are foreign investors.

State Sovereignty and International Arbitration[16]

Historical Background

At times, states tend to invoke immunity against international commercial arbitration; nevertheless, the existence of an arbitration clause under a contract can usually mean that a country has waived such immunity. In other words, if a country consents to arbitration by signing an arbitration clause and later retracts its consent, arbitration still prevails.

13 Ibid., 122–32.

14 Ibid., 151.

15 Ibid., 153; on the same reference see *Tokios Tokeles v. Ukraine*.

16 Mohamed A.M. Ismail, *Globalization and New International Public Works Agreements in Developing Countries* (Ashgate Publishing 2011) 156–60.

In the case of *Liamco v. Libya*, the US oil company tried to execute an arbitration award against the Libyan government after the latter had nationalized the company's rights stated under an oil concession agreement. With the refusal of Libya to take part in the relevant proceedings, an award was issued in Geneva in 1977 granting USD 8 million in favour of the company. Liamco tried to have the arbitration award recognized in the state of Colombia; nonetheless, although the Colombian judge admitted competence to take cognizance of the dispute, he refused to exercise his competence for a law issued in a contracting state applying the concept of nationalization. For the judge to avoid having to contend the said arbitration award, he referred in his judgment to Article 5/2/a of the New York Convention stating that 'recognition and enforcement of an arbitral award may also be refused if the competent authority in the country where recognition and enforcement is sought finds that the subject matter of the difference is not capable of settlement by arbitration under the law of that country'. Accordingly, with respect to the opinion of the judge, the action taken by the country was not grounds for arbitration.

Liamco attempted attachment against Libyan assets in France, Sweden and Switzerland. In France, attachment was recognized by the French government, and Liamco attached some 29 Libyan assets. The French courts granted Liamco the right to ascertain that none of the assets were exempt from state immunity.

In Sweden, the Court of Appeal decided that the Libyan government had waived the right to invoke immunity by having accepted the arbitration clause. By doing so, the court made no distinction between immunities against jurisdiction and immunities against execution.

In Switzerland, the Federal Court annulled the judgment of the Court of Zurich to attach Libyan assets in six Swiss banks. The Federal Court did not reject the judgment but rather found that the Court of Zurich had no jurisdiction to attach Libyan assets on the grounds of absence of a 'sufficient domestic relationship', which must be proved by the existence of some activities reflecting Swiss jurisdiction.[17]

To that extent, Liamco was nothing short of being the primary cause behind the 1998 changes to the US legislation. The Foreign Sovereign Immunities Act (FSIA) was amended to allow the execution of arbitration awards against commercial properties and assets owned by foreign countries. Whether or not such assets were grounds for arbitration was not a matter of concern.[18]

The core importance attached to this case gave effect to many legislative amendments in numerous countries all around the world. Application and execution of arbitral awards, as well as attachment of foreign country assets, have become increasingly recognized over time.

Generally, there is a distinction between acts of a private nature, whether civil or commercial, and state activities, which are public. States are expected to be immune from legal proceedings in a foreign court in relation to their sovereign activities, while no immunity exists for activities of a purely commercial or private nature.[19]

State immunity can be from jurisdiction or execution. It has been settled in international doctrine that the existence of a valid arbitration agreement prevents reliance on sovereign immunity by the state.[20] The arbitration agreement is generally considered to be an implied waiver of immunity

17 Ibid., 672–3.

18 For details, see Lew, Mistelis and Kröll, *Comparative International Commercial Arbitration* (Kluwer Law International 2003) 759; *Libyan American Oil Company (LIAMCO) v. Socialist People's Libyan Arab Jamahiriya, 482, F Supp 1175 (DDC 1980).*

19 Lew, Mistelis and Kröll, 744–5.

20 For an overview, see ibid., 746; Nigel Blackaby and Constantine Partasides, with Redfern and Hunter, *Redfern and Hunter on International Commercial Arbitration* (Oxford University Press 2009); Fouchard, Gaillard and Goldman, *International Commercial Arbitration* (Kluwer Law International, 1999).

in relation to the arbitral tribunal itself. If the state agrees to arbitration, it cannot at a later stage oppose the jurisdiction of the tribunal and thereby defeat the agreement it entered into. However, in some Middle Eastern jurisdictions,[21] the administration's consent is compulsory to start arbitration proceedings against the government. The concerned minister's consent is obligatory for foreign or domestic investors to start arbitration.

Arbitration Agreement and State Sovereignty

A fundamental question arises as to the binding effect of an arbitration agreement signed by a public juristic entity and its occasional contradictions with state immunity.

Is a provision for arbitration necessary for a contracting country to be obliged to abide by it?

Conceptually, contracting parties come to an agreement with regard to international arbitration so that it eventually becomes a part of the contract between them, either in the form of an arbitration clause or an arbitration agreement. However, in the event of parties failing to agree to resort to arbitration, can the contracting country be pressured into doing so?

There has certainly been a rising trend to grant a foreign party the right to resort to international arbitration against a contracting country even if that country has not signed an arbitration agreement.

In the *Pyramids* case,[22] the claimant built his argument on a provision stated under the Egyptian Investment Law of 1974 stating that investment disputes may be resolved by virtue of the Convention on the Settlement of International Disputes between States and Nationals of Other States (Washington Convention), which Egypt ratified under Law No. 90 of 1971.

The Egyptian Government made a defence, claiming that the provision did not suffice to establish jurisdiction of the arbitral tribunal. The defence was based on the fact that the provision included two sentences which stated 'within the framework of the convention' and 'where it applies', where each necessitated the acquisition of a special approval to resort to the International Centre for the Settlement of Investment Disputes (ICSID) in order to settle a dispute through arbitration.

The arbitral tribunal denied all pretexts invoked by the Egyptian Government.

In the *Pyramids* case, the ICC arbitral tribunal rendered an award in favour of SPP, a Hong Kongbased company, against the Egyptian General Organization for Tourism and Hotels (EGOTH), an Egyptian public juristic entity, taking into consideration the words of the Minister of Tourism, who 'approved, agreed and ratified' the cancellation of the project by the Egyptian government. The arbitrators assumed jurisdiction and found that the government was a party to the arbitration agreement and consequently bound by the agreement. Egypt applied to the French courts for annulment of the award.[23] The *Cour d'appel de Paris* invalidated the award and upon appeal by SPP, the *Cour de Cassation* upheld the decision. The words 'approved, agreed and ratified' must be interpreted in light of the Egyptian legal system and the contracting parties' declaration. The ratification was not justification for the minister to become a party to the joint venture agreement.

In the *Westland* case, a joint venture between the English company Westland Helicopters and the Arab Organization for Industrialization (AOI), an international organization set up in 1975 by the Arab Republic of Egypt, the Kingdom of Saudi Arabia, the United Arab Emirates and Qatar, AOI was dissolved by three member states for political reasons. Westland started arbitral proceedings against AOI and all four states based on the arbitration clause that was included in

21 Egyptian Arbitration Act, 1994, S.1 as amended by Law No. 9 of 1997.

22 *Southern Pacific Properties v. Arab Republic of Egypt*, referred to in Craig, Park and Paulsson, *International Chamber of Commerce Arbitration* (ICC 1985) 664–5.

23 See Redfern and Hunter, *Law and Practice of International Commercial Arbitration*, 2nd edn (1991) and Blackaby and Partasides, with Redfern and Hunter (2009); Lew, Mistelis and Kröll, 740–41.

the shareholders' agreements concluded between AOI and Westland for setting up a joint venture company. Egypt denied being bound by the arbitration agreement and none of the three Arab states participated in the arbitration proceedings. The arbitral tribunal rendered an award on jurisdiction and held that 'The tribunal had to examine the founding documents of the AOI which does not exclude liability of the state. If there are any national rules excluding liability, it is not applicable regarding the transnational nature of AOI. The tribunal decided that states were bound by the arbitration agreement entered into by AOI.'

Egypt applied to the Swiss courts, and the *Tribunal Fédéral* annulled the award in relation to Egypt for lack of jurisdiction. The Swiss court held that an arbitration clause cannot be opposed by a party which did not sign it unless this party was bound by the signature of an entity or a third party empowered to act on behalf of the first party, on the basis of an act granting to that entity or third party the power to refer a dispute to arbitration. The court elaborated that AOI's autonomy ruled out the possibility that its contracts with third parties, and more particularly the arbitration clause signed by it, might be considered as contracts concluded by a representative or any agency. The predominant roles played by these states in AOI and AOI's highest authority, a committee consisting of ministers, could not affect AOI's independence and legal personality, nor could it lead to the conclusion that AOI be bound by the founding states when dealing with third parties.[24] Moreover, the Geneva court of appeal and the *Tribunal Fédéral* also rejected the equity argument, as equity could not apply to this case. The court stated that there was no denial of justice as Westland could start litigation proceedings against Egypt in the Egyptian courts.

In another dispute between Manufacturers Hanover Trust Company and the Arab Republic of Egypt (General Authority for Investment and Free Zones – GAFI), the claimant company built its defence on the fact that the Egyptian government had shown legislative consent to the jurisdiction of the ICSID; however, the dispute was resolved before an arbitration award on jurisdiction was issued.[25]

The same rules apply if the question arises in the enforcement stage.[26] Enforcement of awards against Arab Middle Eastern states can face some difficulties regarding attaching state-owned property to a public juristic entity, with a separate legal personality, through national courts.

The above mentioned perspectives are well illustrated by the United States courts in the case of *S & Davis International Inc. v. The Republic of Yemen*.[27] United States courts held that ministerial intervention was the reason behind enforcement of the award against a public juristic entity owned by the state (property of a state-owned entity).

In conclusion, accession of countries to international treaties or conventions involving their legislative consent to arbitration only obliges them to accept such arbitration. International conventions function as domestic legislation in some countries whereas in others they transcend it. Accordingly, accession of a country to a convention necessitates its comprehensive abidance by its provisions. If a contracting country breaches its legislative obligations and chooses to deny arbitration, this acts as grounds for application of the fundamental rule stating that recanting a consented action is grounds for invalidation of the abjuration.

---

24 For an analytical perspective, see Lew, Mistelis and Kröll, 741–3; Blackaby and Partasides with Redfern and Hunter (2009), 465; Fouchard, Gaillard and Goldman, *International Commercial Arbitration* (Kluwer Law International, 1999).

25 *Manufacturers Hanover Trust Company v. Arab Republic of Egypt and General Authority for Investment and Free Zones*, ICSID Cases, 31 March 1994, 27.

26 Lew, Mistelis and Kröll, 743.

27 218 F 3d 1292, XXVI YBCA 978 (2001) 980 (11 Cir, 2000). For details, see Lew, Mistelis and Kröll, 743.

Great importance is undoubtedly attached to the application of Bilateral Investment Treaties (BITs).[28] In the France/Paraguay BIT of 1978, Article 8 states that an investor may resort to the ICSID for arbitration. Further, Article 10 of the agreement concluded by and between France and Yugoslavia in 1990 states that an investor may, in accordance with the UNCITRAL rules, resort to the ICSID or to arbitration if the state party to the dispute is not a member of the World Bank-affiliated ICSID. The 1989 BIT between France and Poland states under Article 8 that in expropriation disputes, an investor is entitled to resort to *ad hoc* arbitration in the event that no satisfactory response is received within a six-month period from the date of filing a complaint.

In this context, reference should also be made to the Franco-Moroccan Agreement concluded in 1975 which states under Article 10 that an investor may seek ICSID arbitration on the proviso that the subject matter of the dispute is related to productive investment matters, having been approved by the host state and guaranteed by the state of the investor, and that the matter is of a legal nature and has not been dealt with satisfactorily by internal recourse within a two-year period.

These international agreements furnish investors with an opportunity to resort to arbitration for the resolution of their disputes. Accordingly, the provision of an arbitration clause or an arbitration agreement is not necessarily elemental in this case; instead, the accession of a state to such a treaty will suffice. Once a contracting state has acceded to and ratified an international treaty, it has implicitly consented to the arbitrational jurisdiction of the ICSID or any other arbitration mechanism provided under the treaty. In this event, the arbitration clause or arbitration agreement stipulated under each individual contract will not need to provide reference to arbitration; rather, the general rule concerning a contracting state resorting to arbitration would already have been established. The rule allows the state to be subject to arbitration, with a view to warding off any breach of international obligations and to divesting any *mala fide* (bad faith). As such, there is no room for breach of obligations when a state feels an urge to reject the arbitration clause; it automatically becomes liable to the previously mentioned rule stating that recantation of a consented action is grounds for invalidation of the abjuration.

Perhaps multilateral treaties assume a vital role in approving arbitration as a mechanism for the settlement of disputes, which can never be denied by a host country. A significant example of this is the North American Free Trade Agreement (NAFTA), in which the contracting states have agreed to arbitration as a mechanism for settling disputes.[29]

International Investment Law in the MENA Region

As international investment law has emerged from the dynamics of direct investor–state arbitration, it has been widely applied in the MENA region in recent decades. The Middle East has recognized investor–state arbitration between a private investor and a host state since the ratification of the 1965 Washington Convention. In the twentieth century, the relevant investor–state cases influencing the evolution of international investment were mainly 'claims commissions' set up by bilateral treaties.[30]

Claims commissions continue, such as in the Iran/United States Claims Tribunal, but investor–state arbitration, usually by an ex-ante agreement in 'investment contracts', has taken on a life of

28 Craig, Park and Paulsson, 665; also arbitration award issued by ICSID, concerning *Asian Agricultural Products LTD v. Republic of Sri Lanka*.

29 Ismail, *Globalization and New International Public Works Agreements*, 156–60.

30 Wälde.

its own, with a good number of cases in the period between the two world wars. Decolonization in the 1950s and 1960s and the new international economic order era in the 1970s dealt mostly with concession-type agreements in the petroleum industry, often subsequent to nationalization.[31] Investment treaty law may provide a jurisdictional basis, the major concepts in starting and categorizing the necessary more detailed line of enquiry, but the way treaty language develops into operative law is now mainly a matter of emerging case law, for instance, through the principles and rules governing the way tribunals decide.[32]

The normal methodology for law development comes through collecting and restating evolved case law.[33] International investment legislations in the MENA region developed significantly, adopting the same methodology in recent decades. The codification of the 1965 Washington Convention and making many bilateral investment treaties part of the internal legislation of Arab countries, after ratification, is a fundamental step towards broadly liberalizing investment legislation in Arab countries. Further, national instruments, such as national legislations for investment incentives and guarantees, provided a legislative and regulatory framework for protection.

Most Arab legal systems contain investment legislations which provide guarantees for investments, whether local or international, such as the prohibition of nationalization, and various incentives, such as tax exemptions for certain periods of time upon fulfilling particular requirements; in some cases this may be customs duty exemption or the choice of the foreign investor to establish their project as a private free zone joint stock company.[34]

In conclusion, international investment legislation in the Middle East has developed from the codification of the 1965 Washington Convention, the codification of bilateral investment treaties and, after ratification of these international treaties, the promulgation of an incentive-based legislative and regulatory framework for investments in Arab countries.

The Washington Convention and bilateral investment treaties provide procedural rules which offer a minimum threshold of protection, whilst Arab national legislations provide substantive and procedural rules for a widely liberalized climate for investments and an incentive-based legal framework, whether legislative or regulatory.

Legal Framework of International Investment Law

International investment law in the MENA countries is considerable for both the foreign investor and the Arab hosting state. To create a safe climate for foreign investors and to increase the FDI in the Middle Eastern Countries, both developed and Arab states have entered into a large number of bilateral investment treaties. Further, international organizations have been established and have been engaged in promoting international treaties to provide a stable and a widely liberalized legal framework of investments in an effort to create a minimum threshold for the protection of foreign investment. There are a number of bilateral treaties which aim to promote foreign investment through providing harmonized instruments for protection. The international community has played a significant role in codifying the legislative framework for international investments in the MENA region.

31 Wälde, 65.
32 Wälde, 66.
33 Wälde, 67.
34 See Egyptian Law No. 7 of 1997 on investment guarantees and incentives.

International Instruments

The most significant instrument that provides a coherent legal framework for international protection of foreign investments is the Washington Convention for the settlement of investment disputes between contracting states and nationals of other states. ICSID was established by the 1965 Washington Convention. The Convention was established under the auspices of the World Bank to provide a special mechanism for the settlement of investment disputes in order to encourage foreign investment. ICSID created the 'Additional Facility' in 1978 to cover cases which fall outside the scope of the ICSID convention, particularly where one of the parties is not from a contracting state.[35] In addition, there are many bilateral investment protection treaties providing arbitration under ICSID. Consequently, there has been a considerable increase in the number of cases filed each year. Involvement of Arab states in ICSID arbitration is clear evidence of the internationalization, liberalization and delocalization of arbitration as a process which can be governed by international rules and not submitted to the provisions of any one national arbitration legislation.[36] An ICSID award is not submitted to national courts for annulment or enforcement.

It is considered a waiver of sovereign immunity if a dispute is submitted to ICSID arbitration for any jurisdictional question. By contrast, Article 55 stipulates that such waiver does not extend to issues of execution where the national rules are relevant and are not affected by the ICSID rules. A clear example of this would be if the execution violated a mandatory rule, in any Arab country, as mandatory rules are considered a part of public policy.

If there is an arbitration clause/agreement to submit the dispute to ICSID arbitration, most Arab national courts are prohibited from hearing the case. Pursuant to most Arab arbitration acts,[37] if there is an arbitration clause/agreement made by and between the disputing parties, and either party started litigation before the national courts, the other party may contend before the latter court that there is an arbitration clause/agreement.

If there is a contention before the national court that there is an arbitration clause/agreement, the National Judge is obliged to dismiss the case. It is of great significance to Arab legislature to supersede the party autonomy principle which prevails by national arbitration acts in Arab countries. This scenario applies if the parties submit the case to ICSID arbitration, but in some Arab legislations the foreign investor has to fulfil certain procedural steps before starting arbitration against an Arab state or a public juristic entity in an Arab state if the dispute concerns an administrative contract *Le Contrat Administratif.*

Article 25(1) of the ICSID convention defines the scope of the convention as:

> The Jurisdiction of the Centre shall extend to any legal dispute arising directly out of an investment, between a Contracting State (or any constituent subdivision or agency of a Contracting State designated to the Centre by that state) and a national of another Contracting State, which the parties to the dispute consent in writing to submit to the Centre. When the parties have given their consent, no party may withdraw its consent unilaterally.

In light of the stipulations in Article 25(1), investment disputes fall within the ambit of the ICSID convention if it is a legal dispute, and parties must be between a contracting state or its subdivisions

35 Lew, Mistelis and Kröll, 774.

36 Ibid., 775.

37 Egyptian Arbitration Act, 1994, Art. 13; Omani Arbitration Act, 1997, Art. 13.

and a foreign investor from another contracting state. It must be an investment dispute.[38] If there is a bilateral investment treaty (BIT) between an Arab hosting state and the foreign investor's state, it is a part of the Arab legislation after ratification by the Arab state's parliament. Consequently, an Arab hosting state or any of its public juristic entities cannot contend that there is a lack of arbitration clause/agreement if this Arab hosting state has signed and ratified a BIT with the foreign investor's state. This BIT, when providing an arbitration provision, is a part of the Arab legislative system. Thus, BITs are fundamental instruments which provide a minimum threshold of protection to foreign investors in Arab countries, by providing recourse to arbitration through a legislative clause stipulated at the BIT. This legislative stipulation is recognized in the BITs and codified in Arab legislations after ratification by Arab parliaments.

Constitutional and Legislative Aspects

Arab constitutions stipulate that if an international treaty is signed and ratified by national parliaments, it is part of the internal national legislation.[39] Arab legal systems are civil code systems but do not follow the 1958 French constitution which stipulates that an international treaty after ratification supersedes a national legislation.[40] However, the Arab legal systems recognize an international treaty, whether the Washington Convention or the BITs' part of the national legislation which is obligatory for the states and public juristic entities to start arbitration proceedings.

National Instruments

Arab states have adopted investment protection legislation. The main objectives of national instruments such as national investment laws and regulations is to provide the foreign investor with a friendly environment and to increase the FDI in various economic sectors by guaranteeing a minimum threshold of protection in the MENA countries.

This minimum protection includes national treatment, no expropriation without fair compensation and flexible recourse to arbitration. These national instruments usually provide for arbitration as a means of dispute settlement.[41]

Bilateral investment treaties provide protection for particular investors from specific states which signed and ratified the BIT, meanwhile, unlike BITs, Arab national investment legislations provide protection which extends to all foreign investors. There is no discrimination among foreign investors for any reason in rational investment legislation. Provisions contained in rational investment legislations providing the possibility to arbitrate may, in effect, contain an open offer to arbitrate disputes with foreign investors.[42]

---

38 Lew, Mistelis and Kröll, 775.

39 For example see Egyptian Constitution 1971, Article 151, and Constitutional Declaration by the Military Council, March, 2011; Syrian Constitution, Article 71; UAE constitution, Article 125; Qatar Constitution, Article 68; Bahrain Constitution, Article 37; Omani Constitution, Article 76.; Kuwaiti Constitution, Article 70; Jordanian Constitution, Article 33; Algerian Constitution, Article 132, was influenced by the French Constitution of 1958 and considered an international treaty, after ratification by the Parliament, supersedes legislation; Moroccan Constitution, Article 31; Iraqi Constitution, Article 59; Lebanese Constitution, Article 52.

40 The 1958 French Constitution of the Fifth Republic, Article 55.

41 Egyptian Previous Investment Law No. 43 of 1974.

42 Lew, Mistelis and Kröll, 766; Blackaby and Partasides with Redfern and Hunter, 2009.

As a matter of practice, Arab states have in several cases challenged the jurisdiction of tribunals in arbitration proceedings initiated on the basis of investment protection laws.[43]

An example is provided by *SPP v. Arab Republic of Egypt* (the *Pyramids* case), where arbitration arose out of a project to construct a hotel complex near the pyramids. This is a leading case as one of the parties tried to initiate arbitration on the basis of a provision in the national investment law. Article 8 of the Egyptian Investment Law (Law No. 43 of 1974) provides:

> Investment disputes in respect of the implementation of the provisions of this law shall be settled in a manner to be agreed upon with the investor, or within the framework of the agreement in force between the Arab Republic of Egypt and the investor's home country, or within the framework of the convention for the settlement of Investment Disputes between the state and the nationals of other countries to which Egypt has adhered where it applies.

After the Egyptian Government challenged an ICC arbitral award before the French court and the award which was rendered in SPP's favour had been annulled due to lack of an arbitration agreement, SPP successfully initiated ICSID arbitration proceedings relying on the abovementioned Article 8.

Egypt objected to the jurisdiction of the tribunal for three reasons. Firstly, it submitted that the claimants had not contested the ICSID jurisdictions since it first initiated ICC proceedings. The tribunal held that by sending a request for arbitration and an earlier letter to the minister, the investor consented to ICSID arbitration. Secondly, the Egyptian government denied the applicability of Law No. 43, since the approval for the Pyramids project had been withdrawn before the arbitration proceedings were initiated. Egypt alleged that Law No. 43 of 1974 only extended to investments for which an approval existed. The tribunal held that the relevant question was whether the investment when made was covered by Law No. 43 not whether an approval had subsequently been withdrawn.

The tribunal held that the withdrawal was invalid. Further, the withdrawal of the permission constituted a violation of the protection granted under the investment law in the tribunal's view. The tribunal held that the dispute was covered by Law No. 43. Finally, the Egyptian government argued that, even if Law No. 43 was applicable, Article 8 would not suffice to establish Egypt's consent to ICSID jurisdiction. This contention was rejected by the tribunal as the language of Article 8 was sufficiently broad to create a binding offer for arbitration which covered the case in issue.[44]

The three contentions by the Egyptian government were all rejected by the tribunal.

In conclusion, to allow a state to withdraw an offer to arbitrate contained in an investment law after an investment has been made would deprive the investor of its basic protection. Thus, investment legislation in Arab countries provides basic protection for foreign investors. Further, it includes substantive and procedural rules which provide a widely liberalized environment for foreign investments through incentive based legislative and regulatory framework. The legislative framework generally provides for tax exemptions, customs duty exemptions and several patterns for investments such as private free zone options for projects covered by investment laws.[45]

43 Lew, Mistelis and Kröll, 766.

44 Lew, Mistelis and Kröll, 766–7; visit https://icsid.worldbank.org

45 See Egyptian Investment Law No. 8 of 1997.

The regulatory framework deals with policies and procedural issues such as the establishment of investment companies in a very short duration and other procedural matters.[46]

Special Characteristics of Investment Dispute Arbitration in the MENA Region

Arbitration legislation in the Middle East provides arbitration as a dispute settlement mechanism in civil, commercial and state contracts. The Egyptian Arbitration Act, 1994, in Article 1 provides that arbitration is permitted in state contracts if the concerned minister grants consent to a foreign investor to start arbitration. Without the concerned minister's consent, an arbitration clause/agreement is not considered by the Egyptian judiciary. The Egyptian Appeal Administrative Court upheld that decision as follows.[47]

Regardless of the legal nature of BOT/BOOT agreements and whether they are administrative contracts *Le Contrat Administratif* or commercial transactions, they are subject, in the Egyptian and most Arab legal systems, to the legislative stipulations of arbitration in *Le Contrat Administratif*. The private entity, whether a foreign or domestic investor, has to obtain the concerned minister's consent to start the arbitral process. The Appeal Administrative Court at the Egyptian Conseil d'Etat pointed out one of the leading cases concerning a BOOT agreement for the Ras Sedr airport in Egypt, when the Civil Aviation public corporation (a public juristic entity) announced a public tender for the BOOT for the airport. The foreign private entity made an offer and stated that the capital of the company was GBP 100 million. The public juristic entity discovered that this figure was not correct and was a misrepresentation in Egyptian law. The BOOT agreement included an arbitration clause for any disputes between the contracting parties to be settled through arbitration in the Cairo Regional Centre for International Commercial Arbitration (CRCICA). The procedural and substantive laws of the arbitration are Egyptian law, with the arbitration to be held in Cairo. The public juristic entity issued an administrative decree to rescind the contract (*La Résiliation Administrative*) and to forfeit the performance bond. The latter procedures were taken pursuant to the state procurement law (Article 24). The private foreign entity started arbitration proceedings against the public juristic entity in CRCICA and in accordance with the contractual arbitration clause. The claimant claimed compensation in the sum of USD 508 million, to be paid by the Egyptian government. The public juristic entity alleged before the Appeal Administrative Court that the arbitration clause/agreement is null and void as there is no consent from the concerned minister to start arbitral proceedings. Further, it alleged that the competent court for this dispute is the Administrative Appeal Court at the Egyptian Conseil d'Etat, not arbitration, as this is an administrative contract and it is necessary to obtain the concerned minister's consent for arbitration. The public entity claimed before the court to terminate arbitral proceedings before CRCICA. The court held:[48]

> In the light of Administrative Appeal Court jurisdiction, the agreement is not an international trade law transaction as it is not a transnational transaction for goods and transfers of sums across borders.

---

46 Executive regulations of Egyptian investment law, issued by the Prime Minister's decree.

47 Appeal Administrative Court, *Minister of Civil Aviation v. Mali Corp Co. Ltd*, case No. 18628 of judicial year 59.

48 Appeal Administrative Court, *Minister of Civil Aviation v. Mali Corp Co. Ltd*, case No. 18628 of judicial year 59; see Article 1 of the Egyptian Arbitration Act 1994 as amended by Law No. 9 of 1997. See also the Supreme Administrative Court of the Egyptian Conseil d'Etat, case No. 6268 of judicial year 46, session 31/5/2005.

> The latter transactions, pursuant to comparative international doctrine and judicial precedents, are international commercial transactions meanwhile the BOOT agreement in this case is a concession agreement. It is purely an administrative contract (*Contrat Administratif*) and, consequently, falls within the jurisdiction of this court. The court affirmed that this contract is a concession agreement for public utilities. The concessionaire assumes risks pursuant to this agreement but it also imposes certain tariffs for end users (the public). Pursuant to Article 10 of the Conseil d'Etat Legislation No. 47 of 1972, the competent court for administrative contracts is the Appeal Administrative Court at the Conseil d'Etat. The Cairo Appeal Court (Commercial Circuit) is not the competent court, pursuant to Article 9 of the Egyptian Arbitration Act 1994. The BOOT agreement is not an international trade law agreement; it is an administrative concession agreement.
>
> In addition, Article 13/1 of the Arbitration Act 1994 stipulates that the court must deny the case if there is an arbitration clause/agreement made by and between the disputing parties and either parties reject the national court jurisdiction. Pursuant to party autonomy principles, the arbitration clause/agreement shall prevail, but the situation differs in this case. Further, the principle of *Competence à Competence* (Arbitration Act, Article 22), is not applicable at this stage, as the court jurisdiction is a matter of constitutional issue and the application of Article 10 of the Conseil d'Etat Law is directly related to the constitution and the role of the judiciary pursuant to the constitution which is the real application of the constitutional principle of the supremacy of law. All allegations related to the existence of arbitration clause/ agreements are rejected. Article 1 of the Arbitration Act No. 27 of 1994, and its amendments by Law No. 9 of 1997, stipulates that the arbitration clause/agreement, in state contracts, is not valid as there is no consent to start arbitration from the concerned minister. The latter stipulation is fundamental, in practical reality, and to the application of the arbitration law due to the nature of the administrative contract (*Le Contrat Administratif*). The court pointed out that the French Conseil d'Etat had a long history of rejecting arbitration in the *Contrat Administratif*. The concerned minister in the court's view is the legal entity who can grant the permission (consent) to start arbitration, pursuant to the Arbitration Law 1994 and its amendments of 1997. Without the latter consent, the arbitration clause/agreement is null and void. Consequently, the court concluded that if the arbitral tribunal issued an award, the latter award is not enforceable as the baseline of the arbitral proceedings, which is the arbitration clause/agreement, is null and void. The court held that the arbitration case before CRCICA, No. 382 of 2004, must be terminated as the arbitration clause/agreement is null and void.[49]

Having scrutinized the court's decision, it is clear that the Egyptian Conseil d'Etat considers the executive power's consent (the concerned minister) as a fundamental procedure which cannot be ignored in administrative contracts as it is in state contracts. The court adopted in its analysis a combination of the arbitration law and constitutional principles which directly relate to judiciary competence in administrative disputes. The legislation dealing with judicial competence is a *Loi Organique* in the Arab legal systems. It does not supersede normal legislation, but requires certain procedural steps upon promulgation as it concerns the national court's jurisdiction, which is a matter of constitutional principle. It has to be passed through the two houses of parliament in the Egyptian legal system. The court applied Article 1 of the Arbitration Act 1994 as amended in 1997, in light of the Conseil d'Etat legislation (*Loi Organique*) and the constitutional principles, which are similar in all MENA regions.

---

49 Appeal Administrative Court, *Minister of Civil Aviation v. Mali Corp Co. Ltd*, case No. 18628 of judicial year 59.

Further, when analysing Arab state procurement legislations in state contracts, whether in infrastructure or in other sectors, it is clear that they have currently permitted arbitration in state contracts *Le Contrat Administratif*, with certain legislative stipulations, as previously stated.[50]

International Investment Law and ICSID Disputes in the MENA Region

Disputes in the MENA Region

The MENA region recognized investor–state arbitration from the early 1970s.[51] By then, the ICSID had started its role as a leading institution offering a specific threshold of protection to foreign investors in hosting states through investor–state arbitration. Arab countries began to be involved in investor–state arbitration through the ICSID before the institutionalization of international commercial arbitration in the region in the early 1980s when the Cairo Regional Centre of International Commercial Arbitration (CRCICA) was established.

The fact is that the ratification of the Washington Convention by the Arab states had considerable enhancements in the Middle East in establishing a threshold of protection for foreign investors from developed countries. Arab state countries which have not ratified BITs with developed countries to protect foreign investors in the Middle East are, nevertheless, obliged to provide a minimum threshold of protection through investor–state arbitration in the ICSID pursuant to the Washington Convention. Arab constitutions stipulate that if an international treaty or convention is ratified by the Arab parliament, the treaty/convention is considered an integral part of the internal Arab legislation. It has been obligatory for Arab nations, since the ratification of the Washington Convention, to accept (and be bound by) ICSID arbitration. It is the minimum threshold of protection for foreign investors, which was accepted by Middle Eastern Countries, even before signing and ratifying BITs, with developed nations being the major players in the MENA region in recent decades.

Multilateral Investment Treaties

The North American Free Trade Agreement

Multilateral investment treaties are one of the most significant international instruments worldwide in international investment law practice. The North American Free Trade Agreement (NAFTA) was entered into in 1993 by the United States, Canada and Mexico to provide a liberalized common market between the three countries. The most relevant dispute settlement mechanism is in Chapter 11 of the agreement. NAFTA contains dispute settlement mechanisms in three different chapters. Chapter 11 deals with investments and comprises three parts: Part A sets out the substantive obligations of the contracting states; Part B provides a dispute settlement mechanism and Part C defines the terms used in the chapter.

The three contracting states guarantee certain standards of treatment, e.g. national or most favoured nation treatment (whichever is better for the foreign investor), the right to repatriate profits without restrictions and certain conditions for expropriation. Any dispute arising out of an

---

50 See for example Egyptian State Procurement Law No. 89 of 1998, Article 42.

51 The same meaning see Lew, Mistelis and Kröll, 770.

alleged violation of any duty at the convention, in relation to an investment as defined in Article 1139, is to be settled under the provisions of Part B.[52] The non-mandatory provision of Article 1118 stipulates that the disputing parties shall first try to settle any disputes amicably. If such an attempt fails, the investor from a state party to NAFTA can proceed to arbitration on giving 90 days' notice of an intention to submit a claim, provided six months have elapsed since the events giving rise to the claim (Articles 1119, 1120(a)). The investor has the choice of initiating arbitration under the ICSID convention, the ICSID Additional Facility rules or as an *ad hoc* arbitration under UNCITRAL Rules. Pursuant to Article 1121 the investor when doing so has to submit to arbitration under NAFTA to ensure that any adverse award is also binding on him and to waive the right to continue the same claim before other courts or tribunals.[53]

Party autonomy is significant as the disputing parties have to choose the relevant procedural rules and the method to appoint the arbitral tribunal. Unless otherwise agreed by the disputing parties, the tribunal will consist of three arbitrators, one to be appointed by each party. While the proceedings will generally be governed by the relevant ICSID or UNCITRAL rules, there are particular characteristics of NAFTA arbitrations. The first is the right to exercise the right of consolidation if a controversial state measure affects several investors under Article 1126 of NAFTA. The state party should be protected from having to defend numerous arbitrations for the same subject matter with the unpredictability of inconsistent findings.

The state or an investor may ask the Secretary-General to establish a 'super- tribunal' under UNCITRAL rules for the consolidation of all claims in a single arbitration. The second special feature of Chapter 11B is that questions of the NAFTA interpretation must, upon the request of one party, be transferred to the commission. It must render in writing, within 60 days, an interpretation binding to the arbitration tribunal.[54]

There is an essential need for the Arab MENA countries to promulgate a similar multilateral investment treaty to provide a widely liberalized common market between Arab countries. Indeed, a general encouragement to settle dispute by arbitration or other means of alternative dispute resolution, such as a multilateral treaty between MENA countries, shall contain dispute settlement mechanisms for the protection of the flow of investments between Arab countries.

There are huge investments from Gulf states into most Arab countries, particularly Egypt, North Africa and Lebanon which need protection in investor–state arbitration. These considerable investments in various sectors will find a better threshold of protection in light of a new multilateral investment treaty. It would be significant for the increase of FDI into Arab countries to extend the scope of member states included in a multilateral investment treaty to include some countries of the developed world. European countries would benefit from such a multilateral investment treaty if the European country were not involved with all Arab countries in separate BITs but with a multilateral treaty with all Arab countries together as a multilateral mechanism. A unified multilateral treaty between all Arab countries and the main European and US partners in investments in the Middle East would offer a united threshold of protection for American and European investors in the Middle East in investor–state arbitration. It would avoid developed countries that inject FDI into the MENA region facing unforeseen difficulties due to the lack of necessary protection through BITs.

52 The same meaning see Lew, Mistelis and Kröll, 770.
53 Ibid., 771.
54 Ibid., 771.

Chapter 5
Arbitration and Bilateral Investment Treaties (BITs) in the MENA Region

The Rise of BITs in the MENA Region

Bilateral investment treaties (BITs) have increased over the last three decades as they are effective mechanisms in maintaining protection of foreign investments. BITs contain dispute resolution provisions for certain defined categories of investments, providing for arbitration.

The scope and the content of these clauses differ considerably depending on the states involved and their respective bargaining power. In the majority of cases they constitute a unilateral offer by the state involved to all investors from the other state party to settle disputes by arbitration.[1] The scope of protection for foreign investors varies from one BIT to another. All BITs provide for an arbitration clause which is the final step after failing to settle disputes amicably.

The first BIT was signed between the Federal Republic of Germany and Pakistan on 25 November 1959. BITs have their origins in European legislation. European countries entered into BITs with developing countries at this early stage and during the early 1960s. The Organization for Economic Co-operation and Development (OECD) undertook the work on the protection and promotion of investments. In 1967 the OECD presented a Draft Convention on the Protection of Foreign Property; however the Convention failed to gain sufficient support to be opened for signature. During the nineteenth and twentieth centuries the United States had established its bilateral economic relations on the basis of Friendship, Commerce and Navigation Treaties. In the Middle East, several BITs have been entered into by Egypt, Jordan and Kuwait, and seven other countries have so far entered into at least one treaty each.[2]

The 1992 World Bank guidelines on the treatment of Foreign Direct Investment relied in part on a survey of BITs for the formulation of generally acceptable international standards to promote the flow of foreign investment.[3]

The negotiation of BITs aims at investment promotion and protection; the contracting parties agree to study the main clause of a model protection agreement.

The main issues which are of a fundamental concern to BIT negotiators are:

1. Legal guarantees to ensure faire and equitable treatment and protection of foreign investors;
2. The most-favoured-investor clause;
3. Protection in the event of expropriation and nationalization;
4. The transfer of capital and profits; and
5. International arbitration in the event of disputes between investor and host state.[4]

1 For details see Julian Lew, Loukas Mistelis and Stefan Kröll, *Comparative International Commercial Arbitration* (Kluwer Law International 2003) 768; see also www.unctad.org

2 Rudolf Dolzer and Margrete Stevens, *Bilateral Investment Treaties, International Centre for Settlement of Investment Disputes* (Martinus Nijhoff Publishers 1995) 1–4.

3 Dolzer and Stevens, V.

4 Ibid., 6.

Member states of the Organization of the Islamic Conference concluded an Agreement for Promotion, Protection and Guarantee of Investment, which entered into force in 1988, and which includes provisions similar to those contained in many BITs.

The Agreement for Promotion, Protection and Guarantee of Investment among member states of the Organization of Islamic Conference (OIC Agreement) was opened for signature by Resolution no. 7/12-E of the 21st Islamic Conference of Foreign Ministers, held in Baghdad, Iraq on June 1–5, 1981.[5]

In recent decades, there has been a considerable number of arbitration proceedings, which are based on BIT provisions. In one of the well-known cases, a French investor had entered into a concession contract with *Tucumàn*, a province in Argentina. The contract stipulated that disputes relating to the application and interpretation of the contract should be submitted to the exclusive jurisdiction of the administrative courts in *Tucumàn*. The contract did not make any reference to the BIT between Argentina and France. Vivendi, a French investor in Argentina, started ICSID proceedings against the Republic of Argentina and alleged that the administrative actions of the *Tucumàn* authorities constituted a breach by Argentina of the provisions in the relevant BIT. Vivendi argued that its claims against Argentina were covered by the relevant BIT (Article 8) providing for ICSID arbitration. The tribunal held that it had jurisdiction stating there must be a distinction between the claims for breach of the BIT brought by the investor against Argentina and contractual claims against *Tucumàn*.

Vivendi alleged that, pursuant to the BIT, investors are guaranteed fair and equitable treatment. Further, expropriation is prohibited. Consequently, Vivendi argued that its claims were covered by the relevant BIT providing for ICSID arbitration. The concession contract provides a clause for an exclusive jurisdiction of the administrative courts in *Tucumàn*. The claims for breach of the BIT brought by the investor against Argentina were different from the ICSID tribunal's views from other contractual claims against *Tucumàn* for the interpretation and application of the contract.[6]

BITs have given foreign investors the possibility of relying on dispute resolution options that best suit their needs. Further, many investments made by a subsidiary of a global corporation fall, in most cases, under at least one BIT.[7]

In some cases, the contract clause may apply regardless of the fact that claims are presented as treaty claims. The treaty claim is protected by a BIT or a particular treaty as it is an investment claim or dispute, meanwhile contract claims find their source and basis of the contract and contractual undertakings between the contracting parties. This issue is complicated by the issue of 'umbrella clauses' in which the treaty elevates contractual rights to the level of treaty rights. In such cases, purely contractual claims may also be categorized as treaty claims and jurisdiction should be granted as the dispute is an investment dispute.[8]

---

5 Dolzer and Stevens, ICSID Rev. FILJ 407 (1986).

6 *ICSID, Compania de Augas del Aconquija, SA & Compagnine Générale des Eaux (now Vivendi) v. Argentine Republic, ARB/97/3, 21 November 2000, 40ILM 426 (2001); for more details see Lew, Mistelis and Kröll, 768–9.*

7 Lew, Mistelis and Kröll, 769.

8 Nigel Blackaby and Constantine Partasides, with Alan Redfern and Martin Hunter, *Redfern and Hunter on International Commercial Arbitration* (Oxford University Press 2009), 482–3.

Significance of BITs in the MENA Region

The significance of BITs acquired a new dimension when developing states first entered into BITs between themselves, starting an era of new cooperation. Newly developed industrializing countries of South East Asia and the oil-exporting Arab countries have concluded BITs to facilitate investments of capital and technology in other developing states. It worth stating that, more recently, BITs have been concluded between capital-importing countries, in particular in Central and Eastern Europe and in East Asia. Treaties concluded between developing countries have in substance remained very similar to those concluded by capital exporting counties.[9]

The emergence of newly independent Arab developing countries from the early 1950s onwards brought about economies for which existing treaty arrangements were unsuited.[10]

The objectives of BITs in the Arab world are very broad as many Arab developing countries have come to rely on private foreign capital, technology and management skills, from capital-exporting countries.[11] The development process, in Arab counties, has increased in the early 1960s and consequently, private foreign investment has thus increasingly come to play an integral role in the development process. BITs have served to establish the rules for the promotion and protection of private foreign investments in developing countries. The objectives of BITs are to create incentives for new investment and to maintain economic cooperation. Further, recent BITs explicitly state that their applicability is not restricted to new investments made after entry into force of the treaty but also extends to certain or all existing investments. The US has maintained that the protection of existing investments is fundamental and it views this approach as a way to reaffirm US understanding of traditional international law on foreign investment.[12] Expropriation clauses in BITs play a significant role in the decision of any foreign investor to inject private foreign investment in the Middle East region.[13] The existence of a BIT, its legislative framework and the substantive protection provided to foreign investors, is a signal to the international legal and business communities that Arab countries welcome foreign investments, facilitating and protecting certain foreign ventures. BITs are one of the significant elements which shape a particular country's investment climate, as they determine the Arab state legal framework for private foreign investments.[14] The legal patterns for foreign investments promotion and protection are drawn up in BITs as these treaties are the most effective mechanisms for investment promotion and protection. BITs in Arab host states are fundamental to the increase of IFDI in the Middle East for various economic sectors. Where an Arab contracting state to an investment treaty has agreed to a procedure for the judicial settlement of disputes between an investor and the host state, a claim advanced by the investor in accordance with such procedure is its own claim and the national contracting state of the investor has no legal interest in this respect.[15] BITs in Arab hosting countries reflect the degree of stability and predictability of the existing legislative and regulatory regimes for investments as they are always important and decisive. The global market is a highly competitive global market for Foreign Direct Investment (FDI).[16]

---

9 Dolzer and Stevens, 9–10.

10 For similar meaning, see Dolzer and Stevens, 11.

11 Shihata, 'Promotion of Foreign Direct Investments A General Account, with Particular Reference to the Role of the World Bank Group', *ICSID Review*, FILJ, 6, 486–8 (1991).

12 Dolzer and Stevens, 12.

13 *For* Arab countries' BITs, see US–Egypt BIT; UK–UAE BIT; and China–Kuwait BIT.

14 For the same meaning generally see Dolzer and Stevens.

15 Zachary Douglas, *The International Law of Investment Claims* (Cambridge University Press 2009) 1.

16 Ibid., 1.

It is worth mentioning that BITs operate to reduce the level of sovereign risk inherent in every FDI project by establishing a regime of international minimum standards for the exercise of public power by the host contracting state in relation to investments made in its territory by the nationals of another contracting state.

An Arab state can compete for the increase of FDI by subjecting the conduct of its public institutions to minimum standards of protection granted to foreign investors. The investment treaty obligations which are imposed upon the Arab contracting state impose certain undertakings upon the Arab contracting state as a hosting state.

These certain undertakings constitute a legal framework of a minimum standard of protection such as the prohibition of uncompensated expropriation, fair and equitable treatment, national treatment, full protection and security, and most-favoured-nation treatment.

The investment treaty obligations are generally enforceable against the host state by the investor's recourse to international arbitration. These obligations upon Arab host states are sufficient in assessing predictability for an investor and calculating the investment risks in a feasibility study.

Developed countries which have an increasing outward FDI consider the existence of a BIT as a pre-condition for granting investment insurance to the prospective investors. Germany and France, as they have numerous BITs, make the existence of a BIT a condition for protection under their national investment insurance schemes.[17]

It is appropriate to refer to the fact that sovereign risk will vary from one Arab country to another, regardless of the existence of investment treaties. An investment treaty is fundamental in a developing country to assist it to compete successfully for the increase of foreign direct investment. In North African states, in particular Egypt, and some Arab countries such as Syria, Lebanon, Jordan and Iraq, the cheaper labour and material costs and higher profit margins, etc. are among the factors which foreign investors consider when calculating risks before injecting private foreign investment into the country. It is of fundamental importance to address current developments in international investment law and policy in the Middle East countries. Climate change law, land acquisition, state-controlled entities, third-party funding and the current regime of dispute settlement are fundamental elements which need to be addressed in Arab legal culture.

In addition, quantitative methods of research in international investment law must be addressed and analysed in Arab countries. The legal regime and regulatory framework for international investment law in the Middle East need to be scrutinized in the studies of academics and practitioners.

BITs for the reciprocal encouragement of investments, particularly between capital importing developing states and exporting developed states, numbered 2,573 at the end of 2006.[18]

The most utilized dispute resolution mechanism, which is available under investment treaties, is investor–state arbitration. Investor–state disputes exist through recourse to international arbitration by foreign investors.

The judicial forums specified for the resolution of investor–state disputes generally include one or more of the following at the option of the claimant investor:

- municipal courts of the host state;
- arbitration pursuant to the ICSID Arbitration Rules or the ICSID Additional Facility Rules;
- Ad hoc arbitration pursuant to the UNCITRAL Arbitration Rules;

17 Dolzer and Stevens, 12–13.

18 UNCTAD, World Investment Report 2007 (2007) XVII, www.unctad.org/end/docs/wir 2007p1-fn.pdf; see also Douglas, 2.

– Arbitration pursuant to the Rules of Arbitration of the International Chamber of Commerce;
– Arbitration pursuant to the Rules of Arbitration of the Stockholm Chamber of Commerce;
– Arbitration pursuant to the Rules of the Cour Commune de Justice et d'Arbitrage (CCJA);
– A settlement procedure previously agreed to between the investor and host State.[19]

The Benefits of BITs in the MENA region

Investor's Perspective

The foreign investor takes a decision to inject private foreign investments in an Arab country according to the threshold of protection which is provided by BITs. The minimum standards take the form of investment treaty obligations such as the prohibition of uncompensated expropriation, fair and equitable treatment, national treatment, full protection and most-favoured-nation treatment.

Host State's Perspective

The host state's target is to create a better climate for the encouragement of private foreign investment. The encouragement of private foreign investment is through the promotion and protection of foreign investment.

The high threshold of protection to foreign investors, which is provided through BITs, reflects the degree of success of the host state in enhancing the climate for private foreign investments. Among many legislative mechanisms of protection through BITs, the foreign investor's recourse to arbitration against the Arab hosting state is still the main mechanism for protection provided by BITs.[20] Despite the fact that ICSID enforceable monetary awards for compensation against some Arab states are considered excessive awards in the view of some Arab governments, the latter still endeavour to encourage the increase of FDI through signing and ratifying BITs with developed nations.

The indirect targets behind signing and ratifying BITs are to reduce unemployment rates, import new technologies which are friendly to the environment, increase the yield of foreign currency in Arab states through injecting FDI, and create trained labour through transfer of experience from developed countries. This trained labour can be exported to the surrounding countries. These targets can be achieved through new projects in the Middle East which directly aim at the construction of new infrastructure projects, the building of new public utilities for the public (end users), exploration, and exploitation of natural resources through concession agreements etc.

These new projects are the direct results of the increase of private foreign investments in the region. The total value of projects in the Middle East countries is estimated to be USD 2.288 billion. Some other projects are not disclosed.[21]

---

19 Douglas, 3–5.

20 *Waguih Elie George Siag and Clorinda Vecchi v. Egypt*, ICSID Case No. ARB/05/15, 1 June 2009; *SPP v. Egypt*, ICC Case No. 3493, session 16/2/1983. For details on the *Pyramids* case see Sigvard Jarvin, Yves Derains and J.J. Arnaldez, *Collection of ICC Arbitral Awards*, Vol 1, 1974–1985 (ICC publishing 1990) 124–38; Dr Mohamed A.M. Ismail, *International Construction Contracts Arbitration* (Beirut: El Halabi Publishing Co) 107–8; *SPP v. Egypt* ICSID Case No ARB/84/3, https://icsid.worldbank.org; award was issued on 20/5/1992. See also *Hussein Nuaman Soufraki v. The United Arab Emirates*, ICSID Case No. ARB/02/7, Award of 7 July 2004, https://icsid.worldbank.org.

21 www-zawya-com, last accessed 29 Sept 2011.

The Investor's Protection through BITs: 'The Protection Granted to Foreign Investors in MENA Countries through BITs'

Investors' Substantive Rights: Nationality

BITs include substantive provisions which provide protection to foreign investors and private foreign investments. In addition, BITs provide the foreign investor with direct recourse to international arbitration. The substantive provisions include minimum standards of protection which constitute a threshold of substantive rights to foreign investors to be exercised and to provide protection against the host state. These minimum standards are investment treaty obligations, such as the prohibition of uncompensated expropriation, fair and equitable treatment, national treatment, full protection and security, and most-favoured-nation treatment. The investor's recourse to international arbitration is the most fundamental mechanism of protection.

As all BITs contain similar definitions of the term 'investment' listed in non-exhaustive way to ensure a good amount of flexibility in the treaty's application, similarly, all BITs define the person that makes an investment and that, as a result, is accorded the protection provided by the treaty. Some BITs refer to investors as comprising both 'natural persons' and 'legal entities', other BITs refer to 'nationals', drawing a distinction between 'individuals' and 'companies' (legal entities). Each particular BIT has its own objectives; consequently contracting states are free to choose the nationality requirements that in their view better suit a particular BIT. These views provide contracting states with the flexibility not to be bound by other treaties they have concluded or by their own domestic legislations. The BIT is a '*lex specialis*' within the state's legal system. If any question arises relating to the interpretation of such a term as 'investors', reference may be made to the rules of treaty interpretation (Article 31) of the Vienna Convention on the Law of Treaties which provides 'a treaty shall be interpreted in good faith in accordance with the ordinary meaning to be given to the terms of the treaty in their context and in the light of its object and purpose'.[22]

For 'individuals' defined in some BITs, in addition to the common requirement of the nationality of the contracting state pursuant to its applicable rules, these persons are domiciled in the territory of their nationality. Other BITs require that, whatever their nationality, individuals have a permanent residence in the contracting state's territory. In addition to being nationals of a contracting state, they are authorized to act in their capacity as investors in compliance with their national law. Some BITs consider that a national person who is a dual citizen shall be deemed to be exclusively a citizen of the state of his/her dominant and effective citizenship.[23]

One of the most famous ICSID cases which related to individuals in the Middle East and dealt with the nationality requirement under a BIT is *Hussein Nuaman Soufraki v. The United Arab Emirates*. A concession agreement dated 21 October 2000 was granted to Mr Soufraki in his personal capacity by the Dubai Department of Ports and Customs to develop, manage and operate a port in Dubai. The concession agreement describes Mr Soufraki as a Canadian national. Mr Soufraki initiated ICSID arbitration against the UAE, relying on a BIT between Italy and the United Arab Emirates, claiming breach by respondent of certain provisions of the BIT. In his request for arbitration, Mr Soufraki describes himself as an Italian national. The respondent objected to the tribunal's jurisdiction on the grounds that the claimant was not an Italian investor since he was not

22 Piero Bernardini, *Nationality Requirements Under BITs and Related Case Law, Investment Treaty Law, Current Issues II*, ed. Federico Ortino, Lahra Liberti, Audley Sheppard and Hugo Warner (The British Institute of International and Comparative Law 2007) 18.

23 Ibid., 18–19.

a 'natural person holding the nationality of that state [Italy] in accordance with its law', as required by Article 1(3). The respondent contended that Mr Soufraki had lost his Italian nationality pursuant to Italian law when he had acquired Canadian nationality and had taken up residence in Canada in 1991. As the claimant himself had recognized, he had not applied to reacquire Italian citizenship as allowed by Italian law no. 91 of 1992. This law allows the reacquisition of nationality by taking up residence in Italy for no less than a year but, according to the respondent, the evidence submitted did not demonstrate that the claimant had established his residence in Italy during the required one-year period. Further, the respondent contended that the certificate of Italian nationality issued by the Italian Consulate General in Istanbul on 5 May 2003 could not be relied upon since it had been issued without the Italian authorities knowing that Mr Soufraki had lost his Italian nationality in 1991 by reason of his naturalization as a Canadian. Mr Soufraki pointed out that pursuant to the documents he provided from the Italian Consulate General in Istanbul and other documentation and relying on the BIT he was an Italian citizen. The four certificates of nationality issued by the Italian authorities pursuant to the Italian law were conclusive proof that he had reacquired Italian nationality. On 7 July 2004 the tribunal found that Mr Soufraki had failed to discharge his burden of proof regarding the fact that he had his residence in Italy for more than one year as required by the Italian law no. 91 of 1992.[24]

> It is accepted in international law that nationality is within the domestic jurisdiction of the state, which settles by its own legislation, the rules relating to the acquisition of its nationality. Article 1(3) of the BIT reflects this rule. But it is no less accepted that when, in international arbitral or judicial proceedings, the nationality of a person is challenged the international tribunal is competent to pass upon that challenge and it will in the end decide for itself whether, on the facts and law before it, the person whose nationality is at issue was or was not a national of the state in question.[25]

Accordingly, the tribunal declined jurisdiction.

It is appropriate to refer to the case where a person changes his nationality after making an investment which was protected under a particular investment treaty on the basis of his former nationality. For instance, in the *Soufraki* case, the tribunal declined jurisdiction under the Italy–United Arab Emirates BIT on the basis that the claimant had lost his Italian nationality after acquiring Canadian nationality. He was therefore no longer a protected 'investor' under the BIT.[26]

It is worth mentioning that there is a private foreign juristic entity which differs from natural persons. All BITs extend the benefit of their protection to legal entities such as companies. Some BITs add the requirement that entities also have their seat and/or actually carry out business in the relevant state.[27] Pursuant to many BITs it is required that the entity be established pursuant to the laws of one of the contracting parties.[28]

The Agreement between the Government of the United Kingdom of Great Britain and Northern Ireland and the Government of the United Arab Emirates for the Promotion and Protection of Investments stipulates in the Definitions of Article 1 that:

24 ICSID Case No. ARB/02/7, Award of 7 July 2004; and see Bernardini, 19–20.

25 ICSID Case No. ARB/02/7, Award of 7 July 2004; and see Bernardini, 19–20.

26 https://icsid.worldbank.org

27 Blackaby and Partasides with Redfern and Hunter (2009).

28 www.kluwerarbitration.com; for example, UAE–Italy BIT; Egypt–US BIT; Kuwait–US BIT; Qatar–US BIT; Bahrain–US BIT.

For the purpose of this Agreement:

...

(c) 'nationals' means:

(i) in respect of the United Kingdom: physical persons deriving their status as United Kingdom nationals from the law in force in the United Kingdom.

(ii) in respect of the United Arab Emirates: natural and physical persons deriving their status as United Arab Emirates nationals from the law in force in the United Arab Emirates.

(d) 'companies' means:

(i) in respect of the United Kingdom: corporations, firms and associations incorporated or constituted under the law in force in any part of the United Kingdom or in any territory to which this Agreement is extended in accordance with the provisions of Article 12.

(ii) in respect of the United Arab Emirates: any entity established in accordance with and recognized as a juridical person by the law of the State, such as public and private companies, corporations, business associations, authorities, partnerships, foundations, firms, institutions, establishments, agencies, development funds, enterprises, co-operatives, and organizations or other similar entities irrespective of whether their liabilities are limited or otherwise.

(e) 'investors' means: any national or company of one of the Contracting Parties or the Government of one of the Contracting Parties, or the Government of any of the Emirates of the United Arab Emirates.

...

Thus, a locally incorporated entity may claim against its State of incorporation if controlled by a national or company of the other contracting State. This enables minority shareholders in the local entity (many of whom may be local investors) to obtain indirect relief through treaty arbitration.[29]

It is suggested that tribunals have to review the legislative concept behind the relevant BIT and the language of the treaty provisions. Consequently, it is clear how to reach the real interpretations and if the scope of protection extends to cover a particular corporate entity or not.

In *Waguih Elie George Siag and Clorinda Vecchi v Egypt*, ICSID Case No. ARB/05/15, 1 June 2009,[30] the ICSID tribunal made the following findings of facts:

Mr Siag was born in Egypt on 12 March 1962 to Egyptian parents. He was, therefore, an Egyptian national from birth. On 19 December 1989 Mr Siag submitted an application for

29 Blackaby and Partasides with Redfern and Hunter (2009), 473.

30 *Waguih Elie George Siag and Clorinda Vecchi v. Egypt*, ICSID Case No. ARB/05/15, 1 June 2009; visit kluwerarbitration.com; http://italaw.com/documents/WaguihElieGeorgeSiag-AwardandDissentingOpinion_001.pdf, last accessed, 31 January 2013.

permission to acquire Lebanese nationality under Article 10 of the Nationality Law. On 5 March 1990 the Egyptian Minister of Interior issued his Decree No. 1353 of 1990 acknowledging Mr Siag's prior acquisition of Lebanese nationality and granting him permission to maintain his Egyptian nationality. Mr Siag obtained a Lebanese passport on 14 June 1990.

By the decree of the Italian Minister of Interior, Mr Siag acquired Italian nationality on 3 May 1993 pursuant to Article 5 of the Italian nationality law No. 91 of 1992.[31]

Pursuant to the third paragraph of Article 10 of the Nationality Law, Mr Siag sought permission to maintain his Egyptian nationality.

Mrs Clorinda Vecchi is the mother of Mr Siag. She was born in 1937 of parents who were Italian citizens and she acquired Italian citizenship at birth. It was clear that she had lost her Italian nationality. Mrs Vecchi reacquired her Italian citizenship on 14 September 1993 by making a declaration under Article 17 of the Italian Nationality Law No. 91 of 1992 which accords former Italian citizens the right to reacquire Italian nationality. Mrs Vecchi's Italian nationality was not in dispute.[32]

Egypt claimed that Mr Siag had never relinquished his Egyptian nationality and that the claimants did not possess genuine links to Italy.

The ICSID Tribunal found that:

> The Claimants allege that through a series of acts and omissions commencing in 1995, Egypt expropriated their investment, consisting of the Property owned by Claimants and the Project, and thus destroyed the value of Claimants' investments.

In this leading case, the Claimants seek a declaration that Egypt violated numerous provisions of the Italy–Egypt BIT, as well as international law and Egyptian law. They also claim compensation for all damages suffered, costs, and an award of compound interest.

Egypt also contended that the expropriation had been lawful. It contended that the claimants' claim to damages was vastly exaggerated and said if liability was established, which was strongly resisted, the damages should be nominal only.[33]

Article 9 of the BIT is devoted to dispute resolution and follows the usual pattern of BITs. Thus Article 9(1) provides for the right of investors to have recourse to arbitration pursuant to the ICSID Convention. It reads as follows:

> (1) All kinds of disputes or differences, including disputes over the amount of compensation for expropriation, nationalizations or similar measures, between one Contracting State and an investor of the other Contracting State concerning an investment of that investor in the territory and maritime zones of the former Contracting State shall, if possible, be settled amicably.

If such disputes or differences cannot be settled within six months from the date of request for settlement, the investor concerned may submit the dispute to the competent court of the contracting state for decision or initiate an ICSID arbitration or, if such is not applicable, proceed to arbitration under the 1976 UNCITRAL Arbitration Rules.

---

31 www.kluwerarbitration.com; http://italaw.com/documents/WaguihElieGeorgeSiag-AwardandDissentingOpinion_001.pdf, last accessed 31 January 2013.

32 *Waguih Elie George Siag and Clorinda Vecchi v. Egypt*, ICSID Case No. ARB/05/15, 1 June 2009.

33 www.kluwerarbitration.com; http://italaw.com/documents/WaguihElieGeorgeSiag-AwardandDissentingOpinion_001.pdf, last accessed, 31 January 2013.

The Italy–Egypt BIT provides a number of guarantees and protections to investors including: (1) fair and equitable treatment of investments; (2) a prohibition against unreasonable or discriminatory measures; (3) most-favoured-nation treatment of investments; (4) most-favoured-nation treatment of activity in connection with investments; (5) full protection; (6) a prohibition against measures that limit the right of ownership, possession, control, or enjoyment of investments; and (7) a prohibition against direct or indirect nationalization or expropriation, or measures having an equivalent effect, except for a public purpose in the national interest and against payment of adequate and fair compensation calculated at market value.

The ICSID tribunal pointed out that Italy ratified the ICSID Convention on 29 March 1971. Egypt did so on 3 May 1972.

Articles 25(1) and 25(2)(a) of the ICSID Convention provide as follows:

> (1) The jurisdiction of the Centre shall extend to any legal dispute arising directly out of an investment, between a Contracting State (or any constituent subdivision or agency of a Contracting State designated to the Centre by that State) and a national of another Contracting State, which the parties to the dispute consent in writing to submit to the Centre. When the parties have given their consent, no party may withdraw its consent unilaterally.
>
> (2) 'National of another Contracting State' means:
>
> > (a) any natural person who had the nationality of a Contracting State other than the State party to the dispute on the date on which the parties consented to submit such dispute to conciliation or arbitration as well as on the date on which the request was registered pursuant to paragraph (3) of Article 28 or paragraph (3) of Article 36, but does not include any person who on either date also had the nationality of the Contracting State party to the dispute.

The tribunal referred to the relevant provisions of the Egyptian Nationality Law No. 26 of 1975, 'the Nationality Law':

> Article 1
>
> Egyptian citizens fall under the following categories:
>
> …
>
> Second
>
> Those who were Egyptian citizens as of 22 February 1958 under the provisions of Law No. 391 of 1956 concerned with Egyptian Nationality.
>
> Article 10
>
> An Egyptian may not gain a foreign nationality except after being permitted by virtue of a decree from the Minister of Interior; otherwise such person shall still be considered an Egyptian in every respect and under all circumstances, unless the Cabinet decides to withdraw his nationality under the provision of Article 16 of this Law.

> In the event an Egyptian is permitted to gain a foreign nationality, then this shall lead to the withdrawal of the Egyptian nationality.
>
> However, permission to acquire a foreign nationality may allow the person for whom such permission is given, his wife and minor children to retain the Egyptian nationality, provided he notifies his wish to take advantage of such benefit within a period not exceeding one year from the date of gaining the foreign nationality, and in such case they may retain the Egyptian nationality despite having gained a foreign nationality.
>
> Article 20
>
> Declarations, notifications, documents and applications stipulated under this Law shall be addressed to the Minister of Interior or whomever he delegates in this regard, and issued on the forms determined by virtue of a decree from the Minister of Interior.

Defences to Liability (Italian Nationality) – Egypt's defence against the claimants' case was based on:

> First, that Egypt need not recognise Claimants' Italian nationalities because Claimants did not possess genuine links to Italy; … and fourthly, that Claimants, as foreign nationals, were not permitted to own land in Taba.

The Tribunal dismissed 'each of Egypt's defences to liability. The Tribunal finds that Claimants have genuine links to Italy and Egypt must accordingly recognise Claimants' Italian nationality; … Illegal expropriation was carried out by Egypt.'[34]

Egypt was liable for failing to ensure the fair and equitable treatment of the claimants' investment, in breach of Article 2(2) of the BIT; and for allowing the claimants' investment to be subjected to unreasonable measures, in breach of Article 2(2) of the BIT.

Protected Investors 'Investments'

An applicable treaty between the state where the investment was made and the home state of the investor must be identified to enable a foreign investor to be protected by investment treaty in the Middle East. In practice, the only accurate means of verifying the existence of a BIT, and/or whether it is in force, is by examining the constitutional framework of the host state and if the treaty has been ratified by the host state parliament or merely been signed. Treaties signed in the MENA region may not necessarily be in force. A treaty enters into force in accordance with the procedure provided for in the treaty itself or in the host state constitution. Most BITs contain provisions with regard to their effective date and duration.

BITs after ratification by Arab parliaments are valid legislations. Arab constitutions and civil codes stipulate that legislations must not have retroactivity. It is not applicable to the past

34 www.kluwerarbitration.com; http://italaw.com/documents/WaguihElieGeorgeSiag-AwardandDissenting Opinion_001.pdf, last accessed 31 January 2013.

investments but only applies to future investments, after such legislation (BIT) has been validated. However, recent BITs have taken the view that prior investments are also afforded protection.[35]

For further protection of foreign investments, BITs also include provisions regarding the legal status of investments after the termination or expiry of the particular BIT. Generally, such provisions provide protection to foreign investments for a certain period of time, i.e. between 10 and 15 years after the expiry of a BIT.[36]

Protected Investors

At first, an applicable BIT must be identified to determine if the investor enjoys protection pursuant to such BIT or not. In some cases, it is fundamental to link the eligibility requirement for investors to the definition of 'investment'. Investments currently have a broad meaning in BITs which provide non-exhaustive lists for investments as examples and guides to the definition of 'investments' in practice, particularly when a dispute arises before an ICSID tribunal. Although treaties may vary substantially in this respect, the following provision of the US–Egypt BIT provides:[37]

> 'Investment' means every kind of asset owned or controlled and includes but is not limited to:
>
> (i) tangible and intangible property, including rights, such as mortgages, liens and pledges;
>
> (ii) a company or shares, stock, or other interests in a company or interests in the assets thereof;
>
> (iii) a claim to money or a claim to performance having economic value, and associated with an investment;
>
> (iv) valid intellectual and industrial rights property, including, but not limited to rights with respect to copyrights and related patents, trade marks and trade names, industrial designs, trade secrets and know-how, and goodwill.
>
> (v) licenses and permits issued pursuant to law, including those issued for manufacture and sale of products.
>
> (vi) any right conferred by law or contract, but not limited rights to within the confines of law to search for or utilize natural resources, and rights to manufacture, use and sell products;

35 In international jurisprudence, see: 'The Argentina–US BIT, for example, provides that it shall apply to investments existing at the time of entry into force as well as to investments made or acquired thereafter. However, in *Tecnicas Medioambientales Tecmed SA v. The United Mexican States*, the tribunal made a distinction between application of a BIT to investments made prior to the BIT coming into effect and its application to alleged breaches which occurred prior to such date. It held that while the concerned investment was eligible for protection under the BIT, the BIT could not have retrospective application to actions by the host State prior to the effective date of the BIT'. Blackaby and Partasides with Redfern and Hunter (2009) 470; www.kluwerarbitration.com, last accessed 1 February 2012; http://italaw.com/documents/WaguihElieGeorgeSiag-AwardandDissentingOpinion_001.pdf, last accessed 31 January 2013.

36 Blackaby and Partasides with Redfern and Hunter (2009) 471.

37 Article (1) of the Treaty between the United States of America and the Arab Republic of Egypt concerning the Reciprocal Encouragement and Protection of Investments.

(vii) returns which are reinvested.

Article 2 of the US–Egypt BIT, provides that:

ENCOURAGEMENT AND PROMOTION OF INVESTMENTS

1. Each Party undertakes to provide an maintain a favorable environment for investments in this territory by nationals and companies of the other Party and shall, in applying its laws, regulations, administrative practices and procedures, permit such investments to be established and acquired on terms and conditions that accord treatment no less than that accorded in like situations to investments of nationals or companies of any third country, whichever is more favourable.

Private investors covered by the protection of BITs can be divided into natural persons and juristic legal entities. Most BIT provisions establish the nationality of a natural person by reference to the domestic laws of the respective contracting states._

The Notion of 'Investment' Protected by an Investment Treaty

The definition of protected investments has a broad meaning as it has purposeful interpretations in practice. The investor must establish that he or she has made a protected investment. The ICSID Convention does not contain a definition of 'investment'. This is a great advantage in practice as it provides treaty drafters with a degree of flexibility. Many of the earlier treaties used a general definition such as 'the term "investment" shall comprise all categories of assets including all categories of rights and interests'. Subsequent BITs tend to provide a more elaborate definition by adding a non-exhaustive list of examples. These definitions commence with a broad statement, often referring to 'investments comprise every kind of asset' or 'every kind of investment in the territory'.[38]

These broad definitions exist not only in the Middle East but also worldwide.[39]

In some treaties, there may be a stricter condition requiring that the investment should be specifically approved or 'classified' by the host state.[40]

In the case of *Desert Line Projects LLC v. Republic of Yemen*, the tribunal prevented the state from relying on formal requirements where the investment has otherwise been clearly approved by the state. The tribunal upheld its jurisdiction despite the claimant's failure to produce an 'investment certificate', which is a requirement under the BIT. The tribunal confirmed that the investment had been endorsed at the highest level of the state.[41]

38 Blackaby and Partasides with Redfern and Hunter (2009).

39 For example, UK–Russia treaty, Article 1(a) see: Blackaby and Partasides with Redfern and Hunter (2009) 475; Lew, Mistelis and Kröll.

40 In *Phillipe Gruslin v. Malaysia*, the tribunal declined jurisdiction on the ground that the concerned investment was not made in a project approved by Malaysia which was a precondition to accessing the protection of the agreement.

41 Award ICSID, Case No. ARB/05/17/II c 319, (2008), Paras 116–118; see: Blackaby and Partasides with Redfern and Hunter (2009).

The definition of 'investment' now covers direct and indirect investments and modern contractual and other transactions having economic value. This has been confirmed by numerous decisions of arbitral tribunals in BIT arbitrations.[42]

Further, a shareholding in a local company in the host country is sufficient to constitute investment for the purposes of treaty protection.[43]

As Redfern and Hunter stated, despite the broad interpretation of 'investments', the notion of investments has some limitations. The ICSID Secretary-General refused to register a case because the dispute related to a mere commercial sale and could not be qualified as an investment dispute.[44]

In one of the Middle East disputes, *Joy Mining v. Egypt*, the tribunal found that bank guarantees did not constitute an investment where they were merely contingent liabilities supporting a sales contract[45] which is a common commercial transaction.

In conclusion, the new trend is that the definition of 'investment' should cover direct and indirect investments and any other transactions which have economic value. Indeed, this should offer greater threshold of protection to foreign investors.

Expropriation

The Property and the Project

The *Siag* ICSID case was a clear and recent example of expropriation of foreign investors' property in the MENA region. Siag Touristic is a company established pursuant to Egyptian laws.

On 18 July 1992, Siag Touristic and its shareholders formed Siag Taba, a limited partnership under Egyptian law. Siag Touristic owns 75 per cent of Siag Taba and each of the individual shareholders owns 5 per cent. Siag Touristic transferred 150,000 m^2 of the 650,000 m^2 property to Siag Taba as part of its share purchase.[46]

The project, which the claimants planned to implement on the property, was to consist of a resort with a capacity for 1,560 persons and certain related items of infrastructure, which were to be built in three phases following the grant of the necessary governmental approvals.

42 For example, in *Fedax NV v. The Republic of Venezuela*, Decision on Objections to Jurisdiction, ICSID Case No. ARB/96/3,IIC 101(1997); 5 ICSID Report 186; Blackaby and Partasides with Redfern and Hunter (2009).

43 *AMT v. Zair*, https://icsid.worldbank.org

44 In the case concerning one of the developing countries, *Mihaly International Corporation v. Republic of Sri Lanka*, the arbitral tribunal held that expenses incurred in bidding for a public contract were not an investment under the applicable BIT. The tribunal considered the fact that the respondent State had expressly disclaimed any rights and obligations between the parties of material significance, ICSID Case No. ARB/00/2 IIC 170 (2002); (2002) ICSID Review-Foreign Investment Law Journal, 147. See: Blackby and Partasides with Redfern and Hunter (2009) 477. See also www.kluwerarbitration.com, last accessed 1 February 2012; http://italaw.com/documents/WaguihElieGeorgeSiag-AwardandDissentingOpinion_001.pdf, last accessed 31 January 2013.

45 *Joy Mining Machinery Limited v. Arab Republic of Egypt*, Award on Jurisdiction, ICSID Case No. ARB/03/IIC 147 (2004), Paras 44–7, The BIT defined 'Investments' as every kind of assets meanwhile the tribunal reached this conclusion; see Blackaby and Partasides with Redfern and Hunter (2009) 478.

46 In March and April of 1995, Mr Siag increased his ownership interest in Siag Touristic to 88.15 per cent and Mrs Vecchi decreased her ownership interest to 10.5 per cent. Mona Siag and the Mr Siag's three children hold the remaining 1.35 per cent interest in Siag Touristic.

During the period 1990–1994, Siag Touristic commenced basic construction work on the property, including building a wall along the perimeter of the property and installing a CalTex service station.

On 23 August 1994, Siag Touristic entered into an agreement ('the Lumir Agreement'), with an Israeli Company, Lumir Holdings Ltd, to secure financing for a portion of the first phase of the project.

On 28 March 1995, Mr Siag wrote to the Chairman of the Touristic Development Agency (TDA), a division of the Egyptian Ministry of Tourism, to inform him about the financing which Siag had secured through the Lumir Agreement. Mr Siag's letter specifically stated that the Siag family 'owns the project with all its stock and has not and will not relinquish any shares to any person whether Egyptian or foreign'.[47]

The First Threat of Seizure by Egypt

The ICSID Tribunal found that:

> On 29 May 1995, the Chairman of the TDA, with the explicit approval of the Minister of Tourism, sent a notice to Mr Siag purporting to cancel the sale contract and ordering the return of the Property to the Government of Egypt.[48]

The reason behind the notice was that Mr Siag had a business relation with the Israeli company Lumir.

Mr Siag sent a letter to the Minister of Tourism ('the Minister') on 7 June 1995, confirming that he did not object to terminating the Lumir Agreement, in order not to lose the project.

The tribunal elaborated that: 'One week later, the Minister instructed the Chairman of the TDA to defer its seizure of the Property for one month, indicating that Mr Siag had 'submitted a written acknowledgment to cancel the contract with Lumir company'. The Lumir Agreement was terminated on 26 June 1995 and Mr Siag informed the Minister on 28 June 1995.[49]

Again, there was expropriation of the property by Ministerial Decree from the Egyptian government.

The mere fact was that between May 1995 and May 1996, 8 apartment buildings with 288 individual apartments were constructed on the property, with a capacity of 520 persons.

> On 23 May 1996, the Egyptian Minister of Tourism issued Ministerial Resolution Number 83 for the Year 1996, cancelling the Contract and redeeming 'all the land, subject of this contract with all the structures thereon …'[50]

47 www.kluwerarbitration.com; http://italaw.com/documents/WaguihElieGeorgeSiag-AwardandDissentingOpinion_001.pdf, last accessed 31 January 2013.

48 www.kluwerarbitration.com; http://italaw.com/documents/WaguihElieGeorgeSiag-AwardandDissentingOpinion_001.pdf, last accessed 31 January 2013.

49 www.kluwerarbitration.com; http://italaw.com/documents/WaguihElieGeorgeSiag-AwardandDissentingOpinion_001.pdf, last accessed 31 January 2013.

50 www.kluwerarbitration.com; http://italaw.com/documents/WaguihElieGeorgeSiag-AwardandDissentingOpinion_001.pdf, last accessed 31 January 2013.

The resolution relied on a view that Siag failed to honour its contractual commitments stipulated on time. Siag's attorney requested the protection of the police and the district attorney in safeguarding Siag's rights.

The First Court Decision

The tribunal referred to the Cairo Appeal Administrative Court at the Egyptian Conseil d'Etat on 21 July 1996 and found as follows:

> [The] Resolution is illegal for being issued before the expiration of the deadline set for the completion of the first phase of the project according to the contract concluded between the Ministry and the plaintiff company … In addition the decree included taking the land together with all constructions thereupon, which are valued at millions of Egyptian pounds … Consequently, this decision involved confiscation of the plaintiff company's money, … and this is in violation of the provisions of Article 36 of the Constitution, which stipulates 'Public confiscation of money is prohibited, and the private confiscation is permissible only by virtue of a judicial ruling'.

There was a second seizure of the property by Egypt.

The tribunal pointed out that: 'Siag returned to the Property on 19 August 1996 and took possession of the site. This situation lasted for 36 hours only. On 21 August 1996, Government security forces and the TDA forcibly seized the Property for the second time.'[51]

The Second Court Decision

On 5 February 1997, the Supreme Administrative Court of the Egyptian Conseil d'Etat unanimously dismissed the government's appeal and affirmed the injunction issued by the Appeal Administrative Court.

The ICSID Tribunal pointed to the second court decision and stated that: 'Despite these two decisions, no steps were taken by Egypt to return the Property or the Project to Mr Siag.'[52]

The tribunal added that there was a decision by the Supreme Administrative Court on the merits.

On 7 August 2001, the Supreme Administrative Court held that Resolution no. 83 was illegal and cancelled it. The Supreme Administrative Court also found that the contract was valid, binding and effective and should not have been repudiated by the government.

The dispositive section of the judgment provided as follows:

The decision was

> To accept the appeal in form; and, on the merits, to cancel the lower court's ruling and to cancel the challenged resolution of the Minister of Tourism number 83 for the year 1996, with the resulting effects, including considering the contract entered into with the appellant on January 4, 1989 as valid and effective. The administrative entity is committed to pay the expenses relating to both court judgments.

---

51 www.kluwerarbitration.com; http://italaw.com/documents/WaguihElieGeorgeSiag-AwardandDissentingOpinion_001.pdf, last accessed 31 January 2013.

52 www.kluwerarbitration.com; http://italaw.com/documents/WaguihElieGeorgeSiag-AwardandDissentingOpinion_001.pdf, last accessed 31 January 2013.

> The concerned Ministers and heads of departments shall assist in implementing [this ruling] by force if requested to.

Again, there was a new resolution for the expropriation of Siag property by the Egyptian Minister of Tourism cancelling the agreement with Siag.

On 28 March 2002, the Egyptian Conseil d'Etat rejected Egypt's contentions and held that the decree had been illegally issued.

Egypt unsuccessfully appealed to the Supreme Administrative Court of the Egyptian Conseil d'Etat. The Supreme Administrative Court rejected the Appeal of the Egyptian government.

There was seizure of the property by the President and Prime Minister of Egypt and the transfer of the property to Al-Sharq Gas Company. On 15 July 2002 the President of Egypt issued a decree to expropriate the property.

The tribunal pointed out that:

> This Presidential decree n° 205 of 2002 purported to allocate the Property 'to public benefit' and provided that the Property could only be used as instructed by the Prime Minister. … However, on 24 February 2003, before the case could be heard, the Prime Minister issued another governmental decree to expropriate the Property. Prime Ministerial Resolution n° 315 classified the project of constructing a land natural gas line Areesh/Taba and the beginning of a maritime natural gas line Taba/Aqaba as 'a public benefit work.' As such, it assigned to Al-Sharq Gas Company the piece of land 'concerning which the presidential resolution number 205 for the year 2002 was issued.'[53]

The tribunal added that:

> On 27 April 2003, following Siag's challenges to both Presidential Decree n° 205 and the Prime Minister's Resolution n° 315, the Administrative Court held that by virtue of its sale to Siag, the Property had 'moved out of the scope of State property' and had become the personal property of Siag. … Again, Egypt took no steps to comply with the Court's judgment and Al-Sharq Gas Company retained possession of the Property and proceeded to construct a pipeline and associated facilities.[54]

The Egyptian Prime Minister issued another decree to expropriate the property (Resolution no. 799). The Prime Ministerial Resolution no. 799 was scrutinized by the ICSID tribunal.

Expropriation of Siag's Property

The ICSID tribunal scrutinized the following issues related to liability and found that the claimants' investments were directly expropriated by Egypt. Customary international law stipulates that expropriation is only lawful if certain conditions are met. They are also included to varying degrees in most treaties, including the BIT governing this arbitration. Article 5(1) of the Italy–Egypt BIT states as follows:

53 http://italaw.com/documents/WaguihElieGeorgeSiag-AwardandDissentingOpinion_001.pdf, last accessed 31 January 2013; www.kluwerarbitration.com

54 http://italaw.com/documents/WaguihElieGeorgeSiag-AwardandDissentingOpinion_001.pdf, last accessed 31 January 2013; www.kluwerarbitration.com

NATIONALIZATION OR EXPROPRIATION

(ii) Investments of either Contracting State or any of its natural or juridical persons shall not be directly or indirectly nationalized, expropriated, or subjected to measures having effect equivalent to nationalization or expropriation, in the territory and maritime zones of either Contracting State, except for a public purpose in the national interest of that State, for adequate and fair compensation, according to legal procedures and on condition that such measures are taken on a non-discriminatory basis and in accordance with due process of law.

The tribunal concluded that an expropriation is illegal unless certain conditions are met pursuant to article 5(1)(ii) of the BIT. The tribunal had to scrutinize if Siag's property was expropriated for public purposes or not. The tribunal concluded that the claimants' land was not expropriated 'for a public purpose', pursuant to the stipulations of Article 5 of the BIT.

The tribunal investigated whether Mr Siag had adequate and fair compensation or not. The tribunal held that the claimants had elected to pursue their treaty claim as they were entitled to do under the BIT. Expropriation must be according to the legal procedures and certain stipulations. The tribunal found that the Egyptian government had not followed the legislative stipulations in expropriating the claimant's investments.

The tribunal accepted the claimants' submission that due process may be denied both procedurally and substantively in terms of the substantive abuse despite the fact that there was a delay in the project. The tribunal didn't accept that those delays provided a valid reason to cancel the contract and expropriate the claimants' investments.

In respect of procedural abuse, the claimants based their submissions on the fact that Resolution No. 83 was passed without prior notice to the claimants. The tribunal found that the failure by Egypt to provide such notice constituted a denial of due process pursuant to Article 5 of the BIT.

In conclusion, the tribunal found the evidence overwhelming that Egypt had failed to meet the five cumulative conditions required for lawful expropriation set down by Article 5(1)(ii) of the BIT. Egypt's expropriation of the claimants' investment was held to have been in contravention of Article 5(1)(ii). The tribunal further accepted the claimants' submission that, as the tribunal had found that a breach of Article 5(1)(ii) had taken place, it need not examine the auxiliary claim that Egypt also breached the terms of Article 5(1)(i) of the BIT.

Failure to Provide Full Protection

Article 4(1) of the BIT provides that 'Investments by nationals or companies of either Contracting Party shall enjoy full protection in the territory of the other Contracting Party'.

In conclusion, the tribunal found that Egypt had contravened Article 4(1) of the Italy–Egypt BIT.

Fair and Equitable Treatment, and International Minimum Standards

In the ICSID case *Jan de Nul N.V. and Dredging International N.V. v. Arab Republic of Egypt*, ICSID Case No. ARB/04/13, 6 November 2008, the ICSID tribunal dismissed the claimants' claims in all respects, holding that the acts of the Suez Canal Authority are not attributable to Egypt and that Egypt did not violate either the 1997 or the 2002 BIT between the Belgo–Luxembourg Economic Union and Egypt.

The ICSID Tribunal held that:

> On the merits, the Tribunal dismissed all of Claimants' claims. The Tribunal applied the 1977 BIT with respect to conduct which took place prior to the entry into force of the 2002 BIT, but noted that in substance, the protections of the two treaties were identical. … In applying Article 5, the Tribunal adopted the functional test deployed in by the ICSID tribunal in *Maffezini v. Spain* , namely 'whether specific acts or omissions are essentially commercial rather than governmental in nature.' The Tribunal concluded that the SCA acted like any other contractor in all its dealings with Claimants. However, the Tribunal noted that acts and omissions of various other actors, including the Egyptian courts, were clearly attributable to Egypt and proceeded to review the conduct of those actors for conformity with Egypt's treaty obligations.

The tribunal decided that:

> Egypt had not breached its obligation to afford fair and equitable treatment via a denial of justice, whether procedural or substantive.

The tribunal pointed out that:

> The Tribunal dealt briefly with alleged violations of the continuous protection and security standard and the duty to promote investments. In relation to the continuous protection and security standard, the Tribunal did not consider the precise scope of the standard but held that it had not been breached because Claimants had not established any discriminatory measure, nor that the management and enjoyment of their investment was consequently hindered. The Tribunal left open the question of whether the 1977 or 2002 BIT created a positive duty to promote investments, holding that Claimants had not established that Egypt breached the relevant articles of either BIT in any way, even by an omission.[55]

In the *Siag* ICSID case the tribunal stated that:

> The fair and equitable treatment (FET) standard is a broad requirement, the application of which depends on the particular facts of each case. It is however widely recognised that the principle of good faith underlies fair and equitable treatment.[56]

In the *Siag* case, the claimants submitted that Egypt had violated each of the generally recognized 'strands' of the fair and equitable treatment doctrine and the Tribunal upheld this contention.[57]

55 https://icsid.worldbank.org; http://italaw.com/documents/WaguihElieGeorgeSiag-AwardandDissentingOpinion_001.pdf, last accessed 31 January 2013.

56 Siag ICSID case; http://italaw.com/documents/WaguihElieGeorgeSiag-AwardandDissentingOpinion_001.pdf, last accessed 31 January 2013.

57 Siag ICSID case; http://italaw.com/documents/WaguihElieGeorgeSiag-AwardandDissentingOpinion_001.pdf, last accessed 31 January 2013.

Lack of Due Process/Denial of Justice

The lack of due process/denial of justice, has special meaning in the *Siag* ICSID case. While maintaining that Egypt had also breached the FET standard in several other ways, it was the contended lack of due process and ensuing denial of justice that was relied on most strongly by the claimants.

In this case, it is clear that the application of the FET standard was most forcefully pursued by claimants as having been breached.

> Claimants, in their post-hearing submissions, submit that Egypt's failure to respect the numerous rulings of its courts in favour of Claimants constituted an 'extraordinary violation of the rule of law' and 'a twelve-year denial of justice,' which provided further evidence that the FET standard of the BIT had not been met.[58]

It is appropriate to refer to the fact that Egypt had made an offer of compensation to Siag Touristic which was, in the view of the ICSID tribunal, clear evidence that Egypt respected the court judgement that recognized that Siag Touristic had certain rights in the project.

The tribunal held that Egypt's actions failed to afford the claimants due process of law and there was denial of justice to the claimants. There was a contravention of Article 2(2) of the BIT. Consequently, Egypt failed to ensure the fair and equitable treatment of the claimants' investments.

Unreasonable or Discriminatory Measures

Article 2(2) of the Italy–Egypt BIT provides that:

> Each Contracting State shall ensure that the management, maintenance, use, enjoyment or disposal of investments in its territory and maritime zones of investors of the other Contracting State shall not be in any way subjected to, or impaired by, unreasonable or discriminatory measures.

The tribunal held that Egypt had breached Article 2(2) of the Italy–Egypt BIT by subjecting or impairing the claimants' investment to unreasonable measures.[59]

Most-Favoured-Nation Treatment

In the *Siag* ICSID case, and pursuant to Article 3 of the BIT, the tribunal held that it was clear that obligations had been breached by Egypt:

---

58 Siag ICSID case; http://italaw.com/documents/WaguihElieGeorgeSiag-AwardandDissentingOpinion_001.pdf, last accessed 31 January 2013.

59 http://italaw.com/documents/WaguihElieGeorgeSiag-AwardandDissentingOpinion_001.pdf, last accessed 31 January 2013; www.kluwerarbitration.com

> Given the Tribunal's rulings in Claimants' favour on both expropriation and fair and equitable treatment, the Tribunal considers that nothing would be added to Claimants' claim by the invocation of the most favoured nation doctrine and the 'umbrella clause' of the Egypt–Greece BIT.[60]

Amicable Settlement before ICSID Arbitration: 'Legal Nature of the Time Bar Provided for Amicable Settlement' – Is it Procedural or Jurisdictional?

The ICSID tribunal in *Biwater Gauff v. Tanzania* held that the six-month waiting period under the BIT was 'procedural' in nature, the purpose of which was to facilitate opportunities for amicable settlement, not to deprive investors of starting arbitration proceedings.[61] The tribunal pointed out that:

> Non-compliance with the six month period, therefore, does not preclude this Arbitral Tribunal from proceeding. If it did so, the provision would have curious effects, including: – preventing the prosecution of a claim, and forcing the claimant to do nothing until six months have elapsed, even where further negotiations are obviously futile, or settlement obviously impossible for any reason; – forcing the claimant to recommence an arbitration started too soon, even if the six month period has elapsed by the time the Arbitral Tribunal considers the matter.

Conversely, this approach was not adopted in the ICSID case of *Enron v. Argentina*. The tribunal held that:

> The Tribunal wishes to note in this matter, however, that the conclusion reached is not because the six-month negotiation period could be a procedural and not a jurisdictional requirement as has been argued by the Claimants and affirmed by other tribunals. Such requirement is in the view of the Tribunal very much a jurisdictional one. A failure to comply with that requirement would result in a determination of lack of jurisdiction.[62]

Further, a failure to fulfil such preconditions might result in registration being rejected by the ICSID Secretariat.

It is suggested that the amicable settlement time bar is of an organizational or procedural nature. If either party has not fulfilled this requirement, this will not deprive him from starting arbitration as an international investment dispute. This view offers a greater threshold of protection to foreign investors.

60 http://italaw.com/documents/WaguihElieGeorgeSiag-AwardandDissentingOpinion_001.pdf, last accessed 31 January 2013; www.kluwerarbitration.com

61 Blackaby and Partasides with Redfern and Hunter (2009) 479.

62 Blackaby and Partasides with Redfern and Hunter (2009) 479.

Chapter 6
ICSID Arbitration Practice in the MENA Region

Washington Convention on the Settlement of Investment Disputes between States and Nationals of Other States

ICSID Convention

The International Centre for Settlement of Investment Disputes (ICSID) was established by the 1965 Washington Convention on the Settlement of Investment Disputes between States and Nationals of other States. The Convention was prepared under the auspices of the World Bank and it aims to provide a special forum for the settlement of investment disputes, in order to encourage the increase of foreign investment worldwide. In the Middle East, the 1965 Convention is a safeguard for increasing Foreign Direct Investments (FDI) by private foreign entities from the developed world to the MENA states. In 1978, ICSID created the 'Additional Facility' to cover cases which fall outside the ambit of the ICSID Convention, particularly where one of the parties is not from a contracting state. To date, hundreds of Bilateral Investment Treaties (BITs) in the Middle East have provided for arbitration under ICSID.[1] The 1965 ICSID Convention, which came into force in October 1966, was executed in Washington, DC. The Washington Convention is also known as the ICSID Convention. Today, more than 144 States have both signed and ratified the ICSID Convention (Contracting States).

The International Bank for Reconstruction and Development, the World Bank, sponsored the Convention. As explained by Professor Sir Elihu Lauterpacht,[2] Aron Broches, then General Counsel of the World Bank, conceived the idea for the Convention in the wake of earlier efforts by the Organization for Economic Cooperation and Development (OECD) to create a framework for the protection of international investments. In March 1965, the Executive Directors approved the text of the ICSID Convention. The mandatory minimum 20 states ratified the Convention and it entered into force on the 14 October 1966. Developed and developing countries have signed as contracting states over the years, resulting in the considerably high membership.[3]

The Washington Convention of 1965 established a considerable reform which was made possible by the creation of the ICSID mechanism. This Convention was aimed at creating a new arbitral forum for the resolution of disputes between investors and states through the inclusion of arbitration clauses in state contracts. Nevertheless, the *travaux préparatoires* of the Washington Convention also made it clear that the consent of the state to arbitration could be established through

1 https://icsid.worldbank.org, last accessed 30 March 2012.

2 In his foreword to the second edition of Christoph Schreuer's detailed commentary on the ICSID Convention, see C. Schreuer et al. *The ICSID Convention: A Commentary* (2nd edn, Cambridge University Press 2009) ix–x; on the same topic see Lew, Mistelis and Kröll, *Comparative International Commercial Arbitration* (Kluwer Law International 2003).

3 Report of the Executive Directors on the Convention on the Settlement of Investment Disputes and Nationals of Other States 1965, ICSID Reports 1 (1993) 23–33; Lucy Reed, Jan Paulsson and Nigel Blackaby, *Guide to ICSID Arbitration* (Kluwer Law International 2010) 1–4.

the provisions of an investment law.[4] Many states in the Middle East had begun programmes of Bilateral Investment Treaties (BITs) to encourage Inward Foreign Direct Investments (IFDI). These programmes set out considerable protection in favour of foreign investments. Once the Washington Convention was in place, Middle Eastern countries, particularly in recent decades, began to incorporate a clause in BITs establishing the consent of the state to arbitrate, which covered investors through investor–state arbitration.

Whether or not a contract or agreement has been concluded with the host state, the investor may usually commence arbitration directly against the host state of the investment. Further, foreign investors could have access to litigation before courts of the host states before commencing arbitration. It is worth mentioning that the first case brought by an investor under the investment protection of a BIT was not decided until 1990. However, in 1998 ICSID registered eight cases with 19 cases pending and in 2008, 31 new cases with 128 pending.[5]

> The dramatic growth of BITs since the mid-1980s has led to the adoption of similar provisions in the 'investment chapters' or collateral agreements to multilateral economic cooperation treaties and free trade agreements. Among these are the 1987 ASEAN Agreement for the Promotion and Protection of Investments, Chapter 11 of the 1994 NAFTA, Part 3 and Article 26 of the 1994 Energy Charter Treaty (the ECT). Many foreign investments are therefore protected by investment treaties.[6]

Goals of the ICSID Convention

ICSID jurisprudence has a considerable and increasing role in investor–state arbitration in the Middle East and worldwide. The codification of BITs, international agreements and the continued interest of arbitration by practitioners in the ICSID dispute resolution process have increased in recent decades. It is fundamental to ensure that the main purpose of the ICSID Convention is to protect and promote the flow of private foreign investments worldwide. Further, it is fundamental from the Convention's perspective to promote world developments.[7]

The preamble of the Convention emphasizes this economic goal and the objectives of establishing an effective legal framework for neutral resolutions of investor–state disputes which is attractive to both investors and states:

> The Contracting States:
>
> Considering the need for international cooperation for economic development, and the role of private international investment therein;
>
> Bearing in mind the possibility that from time to time disputes may arise in connection with such investment between Contracting States and nationals of other Contracting States;

4 Nigel Blackaby and Constantine Partasides, with Alan Redfern and Martin Hunter, *Redfern and Hunter on International Commercial Arbitration* (Oxford University Press 2009) 465–7.

5 Ibid., 466–8; https://icsid.worldbank.org, last accessed 30 March 2012.

6 Ibid., 468–9; https://icsid.worldbank.org, last accessed 30 March 2012.

7 Lew, Mistelis and Kröll.

> Recognizing that while such disputes would usually be subject to national legal processes, international methods of settlement may be appropriate in certain cases;
>
> Attaching particular importance to the availability of facilities for international conciliation or arbitration to which Contracting States and nationals of other Contracting States may submit such disputes if they so desire;
>
> Desiring to establish such facilities under the auspices of the International Bank for Reconstruction and Development;
>
> Recognizing that mutual consent by the parties to submit such disputes to conciliation or to arbitration through such facilities constitutes a binding agreement which requires in particular that due consideration be given to any recommendation of conciliators, and that any arbitral award be complied with; and
>
> Declaring that no Contracting State shall, by the mere fact of its ratification, acceptance or approval of this Convention and without its consent, be deemed to be under any obligation to submit any particular dispute to conciliation or arbitration,
>
> Have agreed as follows: …[8]

The Convention contains 10 chapters and 75 articles. It sets out the legal regime for detailed legal procedures. As explained by Ibrahim Shihata, who served as the Secretary-General of ICSID from 1983 to 2000, the goal of the Convention in creating ICSID was:

> to provide a forum for conflict resolution in a framework which carefully balances the interests and requirements of all the parties involved, and attempts in particular to 'depoliticize' the settlement of investment disputes.[9]

The Report of the Executive Directors on the Convention highlights the aim of promoting global economic development through private international investments. The target of partnership and inter-dependence between industrialized and developing countries, protected by a regime of truly independent dispute resolution, is underlined in the report.[10] The main target of the ICSID mechanism is to promote the flow of private international investment, particularly to developing countries, by offering a neutral dispute resolution forum both to investors who are wary of nationalistic decisions by local courts and to host states that are wary of self-interested actions by foreign investors.[11] When a Middle East state is party to an ICSID dispute, the private investor is normally from a developed nation.

---

8 visit https://icsid.worldbank.org; Reed, Paulsson and Blackaby; Blackaby and Partasides with Redfern and Hunter (2009); Lew, Mistelis and Kröll.

9 I. Shihata, 'Towards a Greater Depoliticization of Investment Disputes: The Roles of ICSID and MIGA', *ICSID Review*-FILJ 1 (1986) 22, 4; Reed, Paulsson and Blackaby, 4–6; Lew, Mistelis and Kröll; Blackaby and Partasides with Redfern and Hunter (2009).

10 Reed, Paulsson and Blackaby, 3.

11 Ibid., 4.

ICSID: The Institution

ICSID is located at the World Bank headquarters in Washington, DC. The centre itself does not conduct arbitration proceedings but administers their initiation and functioning. ICSID comprises an Administrative Council and a Secretariat. The former is the governing body. It is chaired ex officio by the President of the World Bank. It consists of one representative from each contracting state.

Article 17 of the ICSID Convention stipulates that the World Bank funds the administrative budget of ICSID.

> If the expenditure of the Centre cannot be met out of charges for the use of its facilities, or out of other receipts, the excess shall be borne by Contracting States which are members of the Bank, in proportion to their respective subscriptions to the capital stock of the Bank, and by Contracting States which are not members of the Bank in accordance with rules adopted by the Administrative Council.

Generally, the World Bank provides the centre with facilities such as hearing rooms, conference facilities and other administrative services.[12]

The secretariat's personnel include a multi-lingual counsel. The ICSID secretariat is located in Washington, DC. Article 9 of the ICSID Convention stipulates that:

> The Secretariat shall consist of a Secretary-General, one or more Deputy Secretaries-General and staff.

The secretariat is generally available for consultations with parties who may require clarification as to matters of procedure. The Secretary-General appoints one of them as the Secretary for each tribunal and the secretariat generally assists the arbitrators.[13]

The ICSID has many publications. The centre publishes, among other things, the *ICSID Review*, a foreign investment law journal, being a highly regarded journal containing articles, case reports and excerpts of the legal reasoning of unpublished decisions, along with other book reviews relating to international investment law and international business transactions. The majority of ICSID's publications are available on the ICSID website.[14]

The question which arises now is: Has ICSID achieved its goals? A possible answer is as follows: statistics which are emphasized by highly regarded analysts show that

> On average, 27 cases have been registered annually with ICSID in recent years, with a peak of 37 cases in 2007. This increase is due in large part to the proliferation of BITs and other international agreements with investment protection provisions, which contain dispute resolution provisions offering ICSID arbitration in the event of disputes. At the end of 2008, the total number of BITs worldwide reached a record 2,676, with the total number of other international agreements with investment provisions having reached 273. Similarly, global foreign direct investment flow reached an historic record of US$1.9 trillion in 2007, before falling an estimated 15 percent in 2008 in the

12 Reed, Paulsson and Blackaby, 4–6; Lew, Mistelis and Kröll; Blackaby and Partasides with Redfern and Hunter (2009).

13 Reed, Paulsson and Blackaby, 9.

14 https://icsid.worldbank.org, last accessed 27 September 2012.

face of the global financial crisis. The fact that many, if not most, BITs and international investment agreements include the option of an ICSID dispute resolution perhaps confirms the connection between increased foreign investment and the availability of a neutral dispute resolution process, as envisioned by the drafters of the ICSID Convention some 40 years ago. The first investment treaty case, *Asian Agricultural Products Ltd. (AAPL) v. Sri Lanka*, was registered in 1987 (23 non-investment treaty cases had been registered at ICSID prior to *AAPL*). The flow of investment treaty cases has increased remarkably since then. As of January 2010, ICSID had registered 305 cases: 271 ICSID Convention arbitration cases, six ICSID Convention conciliation cases and 28 ICSID Additional Facility arbitration cases. These cases involve State parties from South America (30 percent), Eastern Europe and Central Asia (22 percent), Sub-Saharan Africa (16 percent), the Middle East and North Africa (10 percent), South and East Asia and the Pacific (8 percent), Central America and the Caribbean (7 percent), North America (6 percent) and Western Europe (1 percent). The considerable majority of the ICSID Convention arbitration cases and ICSID Additional Facility arbitration cases (73 percent of all registered ICSID cases) are investment treaty cases, initiated under a BIT or other international investment agreement. When compared to the broader universe of known investment treaty cases, ICSID continues to be the leading international arbitral institution for investment treaty arbitration: the 225 registered ICSID investment treaty cases represent 63 percent of the 357 known investment treaty disputes as of January 2010.[15]

As of January 2010, ICSID investment treaty tribunals had rendered more than 200 publicly available decisions, awards and orders, including: (a) 76 awards on merits; (b) 60 decisions on jurisdiction; (c) 26 decisions or orders on provisional measures; (d) ten decisions on annulment; (e) 13 decisions on whether or not to keep enforcement of an award and (f) numerous other decisions and orders on a range of other procedural issues, including arbitrator and counsel challenges, the participation of non-disputing parties, ancillary claims and confidentiality issues. As to the outcomes of these decisions, it is telling that statistical studies by empiricist scholars on decisions and awards rendered by ICSID and other investment treaty tribunals indicate fairly even successes for investors and States.[16]

Professor Lauterpacht pointed out in his foreword to the second edition of Professor Schreuer's commentary, the achievements of the ICSID Convention stating that non-state entities, corporations or individuals could sue the state directly; in which state immunity was much restricted; under which international law principles could be applied directly to the relationship between the investor and host state; and under which circumstances the arbitral award would be directly enforceable within the territories of the state parties.[17]

Contractual v. Non Contractual ICSID Arbitration

Statistics show that as of January 2010, only 22 percent of the arbitrations registered with ICSID were brought under an arbitration clause in an investor-state contract. ICSID also accepts arbitrations that arise from State consent to ICSID arbitration contained in: The host State's national investment laws; a BIT between the host State and the investor's home State; or a multilateral

15 Reed, Paulsson and Blackaby, 7; see also Lew, Mistelis, Kröll, 8; www.unctad.org; and www.kluwerarbitration.com

16 Reed, Paulsson and Blackaby, 8; see also www.unctad.org; https://icsid.worldbank.org, last accessed 1 February 2012; Lew, Mistelis and Kröll.

17 Schreuer; Reed, Paulsson and Blackaby, 7.

investment treaty (*MIT*) or free trade agreement between countries which include the host State and the investor's home State.[18]

Today, about '73 percent of the arbitrations registered with ICSID were brought under a BIT or other international investment agreement and 5 percent under an investment law of the host State'.[19] Most arbitrations arising from disputes in the Middle East were initiated according to BITs.[20]

The Additional Facility

The 1978 the Additional Facility was created by the World Bank to extend the availability of ICSID arbitration to certain types of proceedings between states and foreign nationals which fall outside the scope of the ICSID Convention. The Additional Facility is part of the ICSID and not a separate institution. The same ICSID secretariat serves both. Arbitrations conducted under the Additional Facility include proceedings where either the state party or the home state of the foreign investor is not a member of ICSID. Pursuant to Article 4(3) of the Rules Governing the Additional Facility for the Administration of Proceedings by the Secretariat of the International Centre for Settlement of Investment Disputes (*Additional Facility Rules*) (Annex 4), the Secretary-General of ICSID may approve agreements to use the Additional Facility to resolve disputes even if they do not arise directly out of an investment, but only if he or she is satisfied that 'the underlying transaction has features which distinguish it from an ordinary commercial transaction'.[21]

Article 4 of the Additional Facility Rules stipulates that the access to Additional Facility arbitration is subject to the Secretary-General's specific consent. In practice, it is suggested that parties to an agreement must submit the relevant draft agreement to the Secretary-General for approval before the agreement is signed. The fundamental criterion is that the dispute must 'arise directly out of an investment' and have 'features which distinguish it from an ordinary commercial transaction' (Article 4(3) of the Additional Facility Rules).[22]

Annex 4 stipulates that arbitrations administered under the Additional Facility are subject to: The Additional Facility Rules, the Administrative and Financial Rules (Additional Facility) and the Arbitration (Additional Facility) Rules (*Additional Facility Arbitration Rules*).

> The provisions of the ICSID Convention do not apply to Additional Facility proceedings. It is of fundamental importance in practice to distinguish between the ICSID Convention's special self-contained provisions on recognition and enforcement of awards which are not applicable to Additional Facility arbitrations, which have a seat of arbitration whose courts will exercise supervisory jurisdiction.[23] Additional Facility awards thus may be equated with ordinary international commercial arbitration awards such as those rendered under the ICC, LCIA, ICDR (American Arbitration Association) and UNCITRAL arbitration rules. This explains why Article 19 of the Additional Facility Arbitration Rules provides that arbitral proceedings under the Additional

18 Reed, Paulsson and Blackaby; https://icsdi.worldbank.org, last accessed 1 February 2012.
19 Reed, Paulsson and Blackaby; https://icsid.worldbank.org
20 Reed, Paulsson and Blackaby, 13–14; Lew, Mistelis and Kröll.
21 Reed, Paulson and Blackaby, 17–18.
22 Ibid., 19–20.
23 Ibid., 18–19.

> Facility may be held only in countries which are parties to the New York Convention, otherwise the awards would be unduly vulnerable at the enforcement stage.[24]

Generally, the Additional Facility is being used increasingly in disputes between states and nationals of other states which fall outside the scope of the ICSID Convention under the NAFTA, the ECT and various BITs. Today, approximately 28 arbitration cases have been registered by ICSID under the Additional Facility Rules, 21 of which were registered during the last 10 years up until January 2010.[25]

Alternative Dispute Resolution in the ICSID

Alternative Dispute Resolution (ADR) mechanisms are rarely used in the ICSID framework. This may be the case particularly where an investor and the host state want to maintain good business relations in an infrastructure or public utilities or natural resources project. These projects, in the MENA countries, are huge and long term.

Conciliation as a means of resolving investment disputes is institutionalized in Chapter III, 'Conciliation', Articles 28 to 35, of the ICSID Convention. The final resolution is not binding. Either a contracting state or a national of a contracting state may initiate conciliation by filing a request with the Secretary-General. Consent to conciliation by both parties is necessary. One or three persons comprise the Conciliation Commission, which must be an odd number (Article 29(2/A)). The Secretary-General makes the necessary appointments. Pursuant to Article 32 the conciliation commission is the judge of its own competence.

The ICSID conciliation process is not fundamentally different from other types of third party assisted settlements.[26] The mechanism was mentioned in the Convention's Articles 28 to 35:

> Section 1, Request for Conciliation, Article 28:
>
> (1) Any Contracting State or any national of a Contracting State wishing to institute conciliation proceedings shall address a request to that effect in writing to the Secretary-General who shall send a copy of the request to the other party.
>
> (2) The request shall contain information concerning the issues in dispute, the identity of the parties and their consent to conciliation in accordance with the rules of procedure for the institution of conciliation and arbitration proceedings.
>
> (3) The Secretary-General shall register the request unless he finds, on the basis of the information contained in the request that the dispute is manifestly outside the jurisdiction of the Centre. He shall forthwith notify the parties of registration or refusal to register.
>
> Section 2, Constitution of the Conciliation Commission, Article 29:

24 Ibid., 18–19.
25 www.kluwerarbitration.com; Reed, Paulsson and Blackaby, 19.
26 Reed, Paulsson and Blackaby, 21.

(1) The Conciliation Commission (hereinafter called 'the Commission') shall be constituted as soon as possible after registration of request pursuant to Article 28.

(2) (A) The Commission shall consist of a sole conciliator or any uneven number of conciliators appointed as the parties shall agree.

(B) Where the parties do not agree upon the number of conciliators and the method of their appointment, the Commission shall consist of three conciliators, one conciliator appointed by each party and the third, who shall be the president of the Commission, appointed by agreement of the parties.

Article 30:

If the Commission shall not have been constituted within 90 days after notice of registration of the request has been dispatched by the Secretary-General in accordance with paragraph (3) of Article 28, or such other period as the parties may agree, the Chairman shall, at the request of either party and after consulting with both parties as far as possible, appoint the conciliator or conciliators not yet appointed.

Article 31:

(1) Conciliators may be appointed from outside the Panel of Conciliators, except in the case of appointments by the Chairman pursuant to Article 30.

(2) Conciliators appointed from outside the Panel of Conciliators shall possess the qualities stated in paragraph (1) of Article 14.

Section 3, Conciliation Proceedings, Article 32:

(1) The Commission shall be the judge of its own competence.

(2) Any objection by a party to the dispute that the dispute is not within the jurisdiction of the Centre, or for other reasons is not within the competence of the Commission, shall be considered by the Commission which shall determine whether to deal with it as a preliminary question or to join it to the merits of the dispute.

Article 33:

Any conciliation proceeding shall be conducted in accordance with the provisions of this Section and, except as the parties otherwise agree, in accordance with the Conciliation Rules in effect on the date on which the parties consented to conciliation. If any question of procedure arises which is not covered by this Section or the Conciliation Rules or any rules agreed by the parties, the Commission shall decide the question.

Article 34:

(1) It shall be the duty of the Commission to clarify the issues in dispute between the parties and to endeavour to bring about agreement between them upon mutually acceptable terms. To that end,

> the Commission may at any stage of the proceedings and from time to time recommend terms of settlement to the parties. The parties shall cooperate in good faith with the Commission in order to enable the Commission to carry out its functions, and shall give their most serious consideration to its recommendations.
>
> (2) If the parties reach agreement, the Commission shall draw up a report noting the issues in dispute and recording that the parties have reached agreement. If, at any stage of the proceedings, it appears to the Commission that there is no likelihood of agreement between the parties, it shall close the proceedings and shall draw up a report noting the submission of the dispute and recording the failure of the parties to reach agreement. If one party fails to appear or participate in the proceedings, the Commission shall close the proceedings and shall draw up a report noting that party's failure to appear or participate.
>
> Article 35:
>
> Except as the parties to the dispute shall otherwise agree, neither party to a conciliation proceeding shall be entitled in any other proceeding, whether before arbitrators or in a court of law or otherwise, to invoke or rely on any views expressed or statements or admissions or offers of settlement made by the other party in the conciliation proceedings, or the report or any recommendations made by the Commission.

In practice, it is advisable for the MENA states to use amicable settlement mechanisms as provided in Articles 28 to 35 of the ICSID Convention. Most disputes arise out of or in connection with foreign investments in Arab Middle East states mainly in infrastructure, public utilities and natural resources projects. A project for the construction of an airport (e.g. *Mali Corp v. Egypt*) or in the natural resources sector (e.g. *Joy Mining v. Egypt*) or in any other type of transactions where foreign investments are injected, relates in the majority of cases to the concept of *Le Contrat Administratif* which has unique characteristics in Arab Civil Codes legal systems. It has its excessive clauses (*Les Clauses Exorbitantes*) which are based on the traditional principle of *Le Principe du Déroulement des Utilités Publiques avec Régularité et Continuité*. This principle was emphasized in the French and Egyptian Conseil d'Etat jurisprudence decades ago. This fundamental principle in French and Arab state contracts stipulates the regularity and continuity of the running of public utility. Thus, it is of fundamental importance to Arab Middle East countries to preserve foreign investments in state projects through avoiding arbitration disputes and trying to settle amicably through conciliation. The latter mechanism maintains continuity and regularity of states' projects which in most cases relates to the services which states offer to the public (end-users). PPPs, BOT and BOOT types of transactions are clear illustrations of this view. Further, ADR mechanisms create a better climate for foreign investments and expand protection for foreign investors. Consequently, there will be a significant increase in the IFDI to Arab MENA states in various sectors because a safe investment environment is maintained. In addition to climate enhancement for foreign investments and expanding protection to investors, attitudes towards adopting ADR mechanisms is a fundamental factor in preserving investments in Arab states' projects, whether in infrastructure, public utility projects, natural resources or any other type of transaction. The attitude of Arab states towards adopting ADR will avoid unpredictability resulting from arbitration and this attitude is consistent with the public utilities regularity principle in *Le Contrat Administratif* theory.

The 'Fork in the Road' Provision

Access to National Courts before ICSID

A third issue of consent to arbitration under investment treaties is whether it is rendered ineffectual by the pursuit of remedies before a local court through the operation of a so-called 'fork in the road'. BITs usually provide that investors may choose to submit a dispute either to the local courts of the host state or to arbitration and, once made, the choice is final. Thus, if the investor has already submitted the dispute to the local courts it may no longer consent to arbitration. This is the so-called 'fork in the road' provision.[27]

It is appropriate to refer to the fact that as contractual claims are different from treaty claims, even if there had been or there currently was recourse to local courts for breach of contract, this would not have prevented submission of the treaty claims to arbitration.

International Instruments as Part of the Arab Countries' Legislations

Arab constitutions stipulate that an international treaty, whether bilateral or multilateral, is not in force until it is ratified by Arab countries' parliaments.[28]

Ratification is a process by the Arab parliament to vote on the international treaty and if the parliament agrees with the majority of members of parliament on the treaty, the international treaty is ratified. In some cases, there must be an administrative decree for promulgation, to be issued by the head of the state, whether president or king. Publication in the official gazette is a fundamental process as the treaty is not valid legislation in any Arab state unless a certain period of time has passed after publication. Generally, a treaty is valid legislation after 30 days of publication, unless otherwise stipulated in the treaty itself.[29] Consequently, if these procedures are fulfilled, the BIT or any other international treaty is valid legislation in Arab states and is binding to Arab states and their public juristic entities. Thus, the BIT is valid legislation in Arab countries.[30]

If a BIT contains an arbitration mechanism to provide foreign investor protection, and the BIT has been ratified, it is incumbent on the contracting state to proceed in arbitration. A host state cannot deny jurisdiction on the grounds of not fulfilling certain procedural steps such as the concerned minister's consent pursuant to the Arab arbitration acts.

---

27 Blackaby and Partasides with Redfern and Hunter, 2009.

28 For example see: Egyptian Constitution 1971, Article 151, and Constitutional Declaration by the Military Council, March 2011; Syrian Constitution, Article 71; UAE Constitution, Article 125; Qatar Constitution, Article 68; Bahrain Constitution, Article 37; Omani Constitution, Article 76.; Kuwaiti Constitution, Article 70; Jordanian Constitution, Article 33; Algerian Constitution, Article 132, which influenced by the French Constitution of 1958 and considered an international treaty, after ratification by the Parliament, supersedes legislation; Moroccan Constitution, Article 31; Iraqi Constitution, Article 59; Lebanese Constitution, Article 52.

29 The 1971 Egyptian Constitution, Article 188; the Egyptian Constitutional Declaration by the Military Council, March 2011; Syrian Constitution, Algerian Constitution, Iraqi Constitution; Kuwaiti Constitution; UAE Constitution.

30 It is worth mentioning that, pursuant to French constitution, an international treaty after ratification by the French parliament supersedes normal legislation (Article 55 of the French Constitution of the Fifth Republic, October 1958).

There are some procedural difficulties prior to starting arbitration. Article 1 of the Egyptian Arbitration Act 1994 as amended by Law No. 9 of 1997 stipulates that any disputing party cannot start an arbitration process without the consent of the concerned minister (executive power's consent). The concerned minister cannot delegate this power to any public juristic entity as he is, while exercising his powers as a minister, delegated to by the nation. Monetary awards in arbitration disputes are related to the nation's wealth pursuant to Arab constitutions. The latter concepts are applicable mainly to state contracts. The Egyptian judiciary considers an arbitration clause without the concerned minister's consent to be null and void.[31]

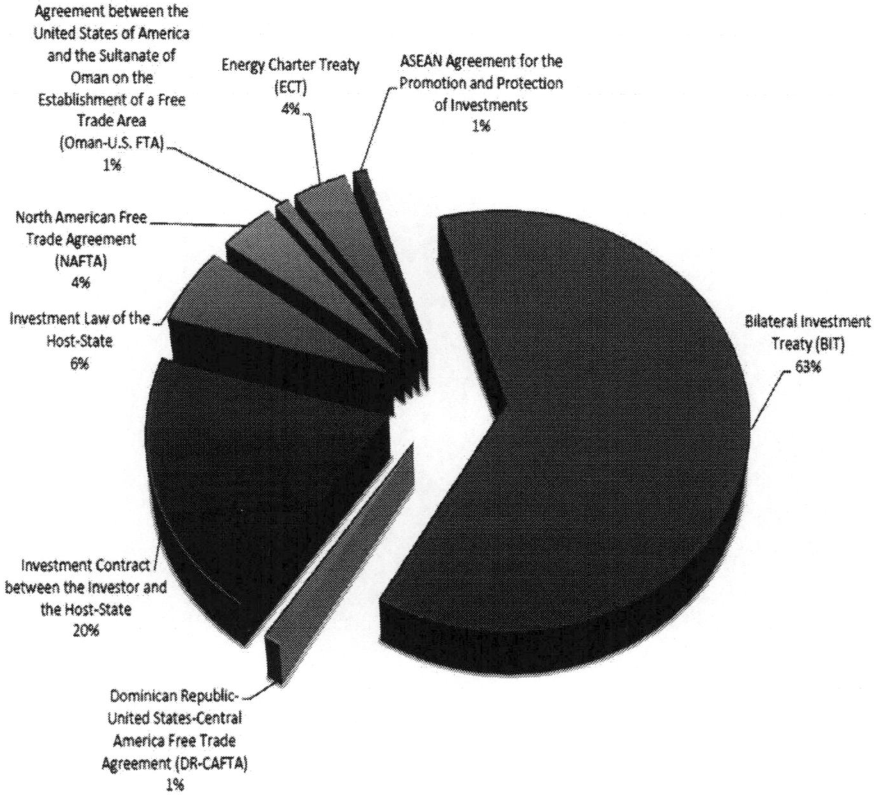

Figure 6.1 Basis of consent invoked to establish ICSID jurisdiction in registered ICSID cases

31 Appeal Administrative Court, *Minister of Civil Aviation v. Mali Corp Co. Ltd*, case No. 18628 of judicial year 59; see Article 1 of the Egyptian Arbitration Act 1994 as amended by Law No. 9 of 1997. See also the Supreme Administrative Court of the Egyptian Conseil d'Etat, case No. 6268 of judicial year 46, session 31/5/2005.

Chapter 7

Conclusions

1) The MENA region has a unique legal culture which characterizes the region's constitutional, legislative, arbitral and judicial pattern. In the past, this legal culture has not accepted arbitration as a dispute settlement mechanism. As a result of the cultural globalization and the integration between the Anglo-American legal culture and Civil Law legal systems, Arab countries in the MENA region have begun to accept arbitration in recent decades.

2) With the emergence of international investment law from the dynamics of state–investor arbitration, ICSID case law has played a fundamental role in codifying the principles of international investment law. ICSID tribunals have applied a subjective test regarding nationality of foreign investors and how a foreign investor can benefit from protection granted to him through BITs. Having scrutinized BIT substantive clauses, it is clear that in each case the court adopted a different approach to achieve a certain conclusion: was the foreign investor protected by BIT or not? The main target of ICSID tribunals is to offer the foreign investor a considerable threshold of protection under investment treaty law.

3) ICSID tribunals have applied clearly the expropriation substantive provisions in BITs to achieve a fair contractual relationship through maintaining a suitable threshold of protection.

4) It is suggested that in all Arab legal systems it is not acceptable to consider an arbitration clause as null and void when there is no clear legislative provision expressly stipulating the nullity of the arbitration clause/agreement. This principle exists in Arab civil codes. The national court cannot consider a contractual provision as null and void without a clear legislative provision. As explained in this book, Arab administrative courts in some Arab countries consider the arbitration clause/agreement null and void if there is no consent from the competent minister. Further, the legislative stipulation for the concerned minister to grant a consent to start arbitration by the private (or domestic) foreign entity, in administrative contracts, is addressed to the public juristic entity to grant permission and not to the private entity to obtain the permission, which in the latter scenario is sometimes impossible if the administration (*L'administration*) is *mala fide*.[1]

5) Arbitration agreement in light of the Washington Convention or a BIT ratified by the host state has no significance. If an Arab state has ratified the ICSID Convention, or a BIT, there is no need for an arbitration agreement as the latter is a stipulation in international commercial arbitration. If the Arab host state has signed and ratified the 1965 ICSID convention, or a BIT, it cannot deny the ICSID tribunal's jurisdiction. There are no grounds for the host state to allege that there is no consent from the public juristic entity of the host state to start arbitration. After ratification of the international treaty (Washington Convention or a BIT), this is valid legislation in the Arab states. Thus, the host state cannot deny the ICSID tribunal's jurisdiction.

6) The inflow of foreign direct investment (FDI) is a result of investment legislation, incentives, policies and international investment law principles which are currently codified by the MENA countries as a result of the emergence of international investment law. Further, constitutional framework plays a significant role in this legislative context.

1 See the *ad hoc* arbitration case enrolled under number 464/2006 at CRCICA, hearing of 2 July 2006.

7) It is expected that, after the Arab revolutions in the MENA region, a new atmosphere of democracy, transparency and anti-corruption will increase the inflow of FDI to the region.
8) The constitutional and legislative stipulations imply that the threshold of protection granted to the foreign investor in Arab countries is greater than the protection granted to the domestic investor. Consequently, the foreign investor may rely on the Washington Convention or a BIT to start arbitration proceedings against a host state, whereas the domestic investor cannot start arbitration, against the state or a public juristic entity, without an arbitration clause/agreement as the domestic investor is not covered by the Washington Convention or a BIT.
9) It is suggested that the amicable settlement time bar in ICSID disputes is of an organizational or procedural nature. If either party has not fulfilled this requirement, this will not deprive him from starting arbitration as an international investment dispute. This view offers a greater threshold of protection to foreign investors.

Annex I
Arab Arbitration Acts

1. Egyptian Arbitration Act, No. 27 of 1994[1] for Promulgating the Law for Arbitration in Civil and Commercial Matters, as Last Amended by Laws No. 9/1997 and No. 8/2000

Article 1

The provisions of the annexed Law shall apply to any arbitration pending at the time of its entry into force or which commences thereafter, even if it is based on an arbitral agreement concluded before the entry into force of this Law.

Article 2

The Minister of Justice shall issue Decrees required for the execution of this Law, and shall establish lists of arbitrators from which selections may be made pursuant to the provisions of Article 17 thereof.

Article 3

Articles 501 to 513 of Law No. 13/1968 promulgating the Code of Civil and Commercial Procedures are hereby repealed. Any provisions contrary to the provisions of this Law are repealed.

Article 4

This Law shall be published in the Official Gazette and shall enter into force one month from the day following the date of its publication.

Issued by the President of the Arab Republic of Egypt on the 18th of April 1994.

Law Concerning Arbitration in Civil and Commercial Matters

Part I – General Provisions

Article 1

Without prejudice to the provisions of international conventions in force in the Arab Republic of Egypt, the provisions of the present Law shall apply to all arbitration between public law or private law persons, whatever the nature of the legal relationship around which the dispute revolves,

1 Entered into force on 22 May 1994; Official Gazette No. 16 bis, 21 April 1994.

when such arbitrations are conducted in Egypt or when the parties to an international commercial arbitration conducted abroad agree to subject it to the provisions of this Law.

In regard to administrative contract disputes, the arbitration agreement shall have the approval of the concerned minister or the official assuming his powers with respect to public juridical persons. No delegation of powers shall be authorized therefore.

Article 2

An arbitration is commercial within the scope of this Law if the dispute arose over a legal relationship of an economic nature, whether contractual or non-contractual. This comprises, in particular, the supply of commodities or services, commercial agencies, construction and engineering or technical Know-how contracts, the granting of industrial, touristic and other licenses, technology transfer, investment and development contracts, banking, insurance and transport operations, exploration and extraction of natural wealth, energy supply, the laying of gas or oil pipelines, the building of roads and tunnels, the reclamation of agricultural land, the protection of the environment and the establishment of nuclear reactors.

Article 3

Arbitration is international within the scope of this Law if the matter thereof relates to international trade as in the following cases:

1. If the respective head offices of the parties to the arbitration are situated in two different countries at the time the arbitral agreement is concluded. If either of the two parties has several business centres, the one most closely linked to the subject matter of the arbitral agreement shall count. Should either of the two parties not have business centre, and then his usual place of abode shall count.
2. If the parties to the arbitration agree to resort to a permanent arbitral organization or to arbitration centre having its headquarters in Egypt or abroad.
3. If the subject matter of the dispute falling within the scope of the arbitral agreement is linked to more than one state.
4. If the respective head offices of the parties to arbitration are located in the same state at the time the arbitral agreement is concluded, and one of the following places is located outside such state:

   a) The place designated as the seat of arbitration in the arbitral agreement, or whose manner of designation is referred to therein.
   b) The place in which an essential part of the obligations arising from the commercial relationship between the parties are to be performed.
   c) The place closely linked to the subject matter of the dispute.

Article 4

1. The word 'arbitration' as used in this Law denotes the arbitration agreed upon by the parties to a dispute of their own free will, whether the body to which the arbitral mission is entrusted by virtue of an arbitral agreement is an institution or permanent arbitration centre or not.

2. The term 'Arbitral Tribunal' denotes the panel composed of one or more arbitrators for the purpose of settlement of the dispute referred to arbitration. As to the word 'court', it means the court belonging to the judicial system of the state.
3. 'The two parties to arbitration' when used in this Law shall denote the parties to the arbitration, whatever their number may be.

Article 5

In those cases where this Law permits the parties to arbitration to select the procedures which must be followed in a given matter, this also includes their right to allow a third party to make such selection. In this regard, third parties are deemed to be any arbitral institution of centre in Egypt or abroad.

Article 6

If the parties to arbitration agree to subject the legal relationship between them to the provisions of a model contract, an international convention or another document, then the provisions of such document, including those related to arbitration, must be enforced.

Article 7

1. If no special agreement exists between the parties to arbitration, any letter or notice shall be delivered to the addressee personally or at his place of work, or at his usual place of abode or at his mailing address, known to both parties or designated in the arbitral agreement or in the document organizing the relationship subject of arbitration.
2. If, after conducting the necessary investigations, any of these addresses cannot be traced, delivery shall be deemed to have been effected if the notice is in the form of a registered letter addressed to the addressee's last known place of work, usual place of adobe or known mailing address.
3. The provisions of this article do not apply to judicial writs before the courts.

Article 8

If one of the parties to a dispute pursues arbitral proceedings while knowing that a condition in the arbitral agreement or one of the mandatory provisions of the present law has been violated and does not raise an objection to such violation by the agreed deadline or within a reasonable period in the absence of agreements, this shall be deemed a waiver by him of his right to object.

Article 9

1. Jurisdiction to review the arbitral matters referred by this law to the Egyptian judiciary lies with the court having original jurisdiction over the dispute.
2. However, in the case of international commercial arbitration, whether conducted in Egypt or abroad, jurisdiction lies with the Cairo Court of Appeal unless the parties agree on the competence of another court of appeal in Egypt.
3. The court vested with jurisdiction in accordance with the preceding paragraph shall continue to exercise exclusive jurisdiction until the completion of all arbitral procedures.

Part II – Arbitral Agreement

Article 10

1. The arbitral agreement is an agreement by which the parties agree to resort to arbitration as a means of resolving all or some of the disputes which arose or which may arise between them in connection with a specific legal relationship, contractual or non contractual.
2. The arbitral agreement may precede the occurrence of the dispute, whether such agreement exists independently or as a clause on a given contract in connection with all or some of the disputes which may arise between the parties. In such case, the subject matter of the dispute must be determined in the statement of claims referred to in paragraph (1) of Article (30) hereof. The arbitral agreement may also be concluded after the occurrence of a dispute, even when such dispute is the subject of a court case, in such case, the agreement must, determine the matters included in the arbitration, otherwise it shall be null and void.
3. Any Reference: in the contract to a document containing an arbitral clause is deemed to be an arbitral agreement, if the reference expressly provides that such clause is an integral part of the contract.

Article 11

Arbitral agreements may only be concluded by natural or juridical persons having capacity to dispose of their rights. Arbitration is not permitted in matters where conciliation is not allowed.

Article 12

The arbitral agreement must, be concluded in writing, otherwise it shall be null and void. It shall be in writing if included in a document signed by both parties or in letters, cables or other means of written communication exchanged between them.

Article 13

1. A court seized with a dispute in respect of which an arbitral agreement exists must rule the case non admissible if the respondent invokes a plea of non admissibility before raising any request or defence in the case.
2. Bringing the action referred to in the preceding paragraph shall not preclude commencing arbitral proceedings, pursuing same or issuing an arbitral award.

Article 14

The court referred to in Article (9) may, on the basis of an application from one of the parties to the arbitration, order that provisional or conservatory measures be taken, whether before the commencement of arbitral proceedings or during the procedure.

Part III – The Arbitral Tribunal

Article 15

1. The arbitral tribunal is composed, by agreement between the parties, of one arbitrator or more. In default of agreement on the number of arbitrators, the tribunal shall be composed of three arbitrators.
2. If there is more than one arbitrator, the tribunal must, on pain of nullity, be composed of an odd number.

Article 16

1. The arbitrator must not be a minor, subject to interdiction or deprived of his civil rights by reason of a judgement against him for a felony or misdemeanour contrary to morality or by reason of declaration of bankruptcy, unless he has been rehabilitated.
2. The arbitrator need not be a specific sex or nationality, unless otherwise provided by agreement between the parties or by provision of law.
3. The arbitrator's acceptance of the mission entrusted to him shall be in writing. When accepting, he must disclose any circumstances which may cast doubts on his independence or neutrality.

Article 17

1. The parties to arbitration may agree on the selection of arbitrators and on the manner and time of their selection. In default of such agreement, the following steps shall be followed:

   a) If the Arbitral Tribunal is composed of a sole arbitrator, the court referred to in Article (9) hereof shall select him on the basis of a request by one of the parties.
   b) If the Arbitral Tribunal is composed of three arbitrators, each of the parties shall select one arbitrator and the two arbitrators shall then select a third. If either party fails to appoint his arbitrator within thirty days from being requested to do so by the other party, or if the two arbitrators fail to select a third arbitrator within the thirty days following the appointment of the more recently appointed one among them, the court referred to in Article (9) hereof shall under take to make such selection on the basis of a request by one of the parties. The arbitrator selected by the two arbitrators appointed as aforesaid or by the court shall preside over the Arbitral Tribunal.

These provisions shall apply to cases where the Arbitral Tribunal is composed of more than three arbitrators.
2. If one of the parties violates the agreed procedures for the selection of arbitrators, or if the two appointed arbitrators fail to agree on a matter entailing their agreement, or if a third party defaults on the performance of a matter entrusted to him in this regard, then the court referred to in Article (9) hereof shall, on the basis of a request by one of the parties, carry out the required procedure or matter unless the agreement provides for another method of completing the said procedure or matter.
3. In selecting the arbitrators, the court shall observe the conditions required by the present Law and those agreed upon by the parties and shall issue its decision in this regard expeditiously without

prejudice to the provisions of Article (18) and (19) hereof. Its decision shall not be amenable to any form of challenge.

Article 18

1. An arbitrator may not be reused unless circumstances arise to cast serious doubts on his neutrality or independence.
2. Neither party may recuse the arbitrator he appointed or in whose appointment he participated except for reasons he discovers after making such appointment.

Article 19

1. The recusance application shall be submitted in writing to the arbitral tribunal, indicating therein the reasons for the recusance, within fifteen days from the dated of the recusance applicant's awareness of the constitution of such tribunal, or of the conditions justifying the recusance. If the arbitrator, whose reply is required, does not step aside within fifteen days from the date of the submission of the application, it shall be referred, without charges, to the court referred to under Article (9) of this law, for decision to be taken in connection therewith by means of an uncontestable ruling.
2. The recusance application shall not be accepted from part of whoever has previously submitted a recusance application related to the recusance of the same arbitrator in relation to the same arbitration.
3. The submission of the recusance application shall not result in the suspension of the arbitration procedures. If recusance of the arbitrator is accepted and sentenced, the arbitration procedures which have been undertaken, including the arbitrator's ruling, shall be consequently considered as null and void.

Article 20

If an arbitrator who is unable to perform his mission or who fails to perform it or interrupts performance in a manner which leads to unjustifiable delay in the arbitral proceedings does not withdraw or is not removed by agreement between the parties, then the court referred to in Article (9) hereof may terminate his mission on the basis of the request of their party.

Article 21

If an arbitrator's mission is terminated by a decision for his recusal, discharge or abstention or for any other reason, a substitute shall be appointed in his place in accordance with the procedures followed for the selection of the arbitrator whose mission has been terminated.

Article 22

1. The arbitral tribunal is empowered to rule on motions related to its non- competence, including motions based on the absence of an arbitral clause, its expiry or nullity, or its failure to include the subject or the dispute.
2. These motions must be invoked by no later than the date of submission of the respondent's memorandum referred to in paragraph 2 of Article (30) hereof. The appointment or participation

in the appointment of an arbitrator by one of the parties to the arbitration shall not disentitle him invoking any of these motions. As to the motion that the arbitral clause does not include matters raised by the other party in the course of the review of the dispute, it must be invoked immediately or the right to invoked it shall lapse. In all cases, the arbitral tribunal may accept motions invoked after the prescribed time limit if it deems the delay to have been for an acceptable reason.
3. The arbitral tribunal may rule on the motions referred to in paragraph (1) of this article before ruling on the merits or join them to the merits in order to adjudicate both together. If it rules to dismiss a motion, such motion may not be invoked except through the institution of a case for the annulment of the arbitral award adjudicating the dispute pursuant to Article (53) of this law.

Article 23

The arbitral clauses is deemed to be an agreement that is independent of the other conditions of the contract. The nullity, repudiation or termination of the contract shall not affect the arbitral clause therein, provided such clause is valid per se.

Article 24

1. The parties to arbitration may agree that the arbitral tribunal shall be entitled pursuant to a request by one of them, to order either party to take whatever provisional or conservatory measures it deems the nature of the dispute requires, as well as to demand the presentation of an adequate guarantee to cover the expenses of the measures it orders.
2. If the party to whom the order is issued defaults on executing it, the arbitral tribunal may, at the request of the other, allow the letter to take the procedures necessary for execution, without prejudice to that party's right to apply to the president of the court referred to in Article (9) of this law for an enforcement order.

Part IV – The Arbitral Proceeding

Article 25

The parties to the arbitration have the right to agree on the procedures to be followed by the arbitral tribunal, including the right to subject such procedures to the provisions in force in any arbitral organization or centre in Egypt or aboard. In the absence of such agreement, the arbitral tribunal may, without prejudice to the provisions of the present law, adopt the arbitration procedures it deems suitable.

Article 26

The parties to arbitration shall be on an equal footing, and each shall be accorded an equal and full opportunity to present his case.

Article 27

The arbitral proceeding shall commence from the date the respondent receives the notice for arbitration from the applicant, unless the parties agree on another date.

Article 28

The parties to arbitration may agree on a place of arbitration in Egypt or abroad. In the absence of such agreement, the arbitral tribunal shall determine where the arbitration shall be held, with due consideration to the circumstance of the dispute and the convenience of the place to the parties, this shall be without prejudice to the power of the power of the arbitral tribunal to convene in any place it deems suitable for conducting any of the arbitral procedures, such as hearing the parties to the dispute or the testimony of witnesses or experts, reviewing documents, inspecting goods or funds, holding deliberations between its members or otherwise.

Article 29

1. Arbitration shall be conducted in Arabic, unless another language or languages is agreed upon by the parties or decided by the arbitral tribunal. The agreement or decision as aforesaid shall apply to the language of written statements and memos, of oral pleadings as well as of all decisions taken, all communications transmitted and all awards issued by the tribunal, unless the agreement between the parties or the decision of the tribunal provides otherwise.
2. The arbitral tribunal may require that all or some of the written documents submitted in the case be accompanied by a translation into the language or languages used in the arbitration. In case of a plurality of such languages, translations may be limited to some of them.

Article 30

1. The claimant shall, by the date agreed between the parties or prescribed by the arbitral tribunal, send to the respondent and to each of the arbitrators a written statement of his claims containing his name and address, the respondent's name and address, an explanation of the facts of the case, a specification of the issues of dispute, his claims and all other matters required to be cited in such statement by the agreement between the parties.
2. The respondent shall, by the date agreed between the parties or prescribed by the arbitral tribunal, send to the applicant and to each of the arbitrators a written statement of defence in reply to the statement of claim. He may include in such statement any incidental claims related to the subject matter or the dispute or invoke a right arising therefrom in the aim of raising a claim for set- off. This right is available to the respondent even at a subsequent stage of the proceedings, if the arbitral tribunal deems that there are circumstances justifying such delay.
3. Either party may annex to his statement of claim or his statement of defence, as the case may be, copies of the documents on which he predicates his claims, and may refer to all or some of the documents and evidence that he intends to present. This shall be without prejudice to the right of the arbitral tribunal, at any stage of the proceedings, to request submission of the originals of the documents or instruments on which either of the parties relies.

Article 31

Copies of the memos, documents and papers submitted to the arbitral tribunal by either party shall be sent to the other. Similarly, copies of experts' reports, documents and other means of evidence submitted to the tribunal shall be sent to each of the parties.

Article 32

Either party may modify his claims or defences or expand thereon during the arbitral proceeding unless the arbitral tribunal decides not to accept such modification or expansion to avoid delaying adjudication of the dispute.

Article 33

1. The arbitral tribunal shall hold pleading hearings to enable each party to explain the subject matter of his claim and to present his arguments and evidence. However, it may limit proceedings to the submission of written memos and documents unless the parties otherwise agree.
2. The parties to arbitration must be notified of the dates of the hearings and meetings that the arbitral tribunal decides to convene sufficiently in advance of the scheduled date as determined by the tribunal according to circumstances.
3. A summary of the facts of each hearing convened by the arbitral tribunal shall be transcribed in minutes, a copy of which shall be transcribed in minutes, a copy of which shall be delivered to each of the parties unless they decide otherwise.
4. Witnesses and experts are without administering of oath.

Article 34

1. If the claimant fails to submit the written statement of claim pursuant to paragraph (1) of Article (30), without an acceptable excuse, the arbitral tribunal shall be held to order the termination of the arbitral proceeding, unless the parties agree otherwise.
2. If the respondent fails to submit a statement of defence pursuant to paragraph (2) of Article (30), the arbitral tribunal shall continue the arbitral proceeding. Such continuation shall not in itself be considered an acknowledgement by the respondent of the claimant's claim, unless the parties agree otherwise.

Article 35

If either party fails to attend one of the hearings or fails to present any of the documents requested from him, the Arbitral Tribunal may continue with the arbitral proceeding and issue an award on the dispute based on the elements of proof present before it.

Article 36

1. The Arbitral Tribunal may appoint one expert or more to present a written or oral report in connection with certain matters it designates. Such report shall be evidenced in the minutes of the hearing. The Tribunal shall furnish each of the parties with a copy of its decision designating the mission entrusted to the expert.
2. The parties shall submit to the expert with any information he may request in connection with the dispute and examine any documents, goods or other assets related thereto. The Tribunal shall adjudicate any dispute arising between the expert and one of the parties in this connection.
3. The Arbitral Tribunal shall send a copy of the expert's report to each party promptly upon its deposition, while allowing each of them to express his opinion thereon. The parties are entitled to review and examine the documents on which the expert based his report.

4. The tribunal may, following submission of the expert's report, decide, either *sua sponte* or on the basis of a request by either party, to convene a hearing to hear the expert's testimony, while allowing the parties to listen to the expert and to discuss with him the contents of his report. Each of the parties shall be entitled to present his own expert or experts at such session to express an opinion on the matters addressed in the report compiled by the expert appointed by the Arbitral Tribunal unless the parties otherwise agree.

Article 37

The President of the Court referred to in Article (9) of this Law, upon request from the Arbitral Tribunal, shall be competent to:

1. Pass judgement against defaulting or intransigent witnesses imposing the penalties prescribed in Article 78 and 80 of the Law of Evidence in Civil and Commercial matters.
2. Order a judicial delegation *commission rogatoire*.

Article 38

The adversial proceeding before the Arbitral Tribunal shall be interrupted in accordance with the conditions prescribed for interruption in the Code of Civil and Commercial Procedures, and interruption as aforesaid shall give rise to the effects prescribed in the said Code.

Part V – The Arbitral Award and the Termination of Proceedings

Article 39

1. The Arbitral Tribunal shall apply the rules agreed by the parties to the subject matter of the dispute. If they agree to apply the law of a specific state, then the substantive rules of that law, not those governing conflict of laws, shall be followed, unless the parties otherwise agree.
2. If the parties fail to agree on the legal rules to be applied to the subject matter of the dispute, the Arbitral Tribunal shall apply the substantive rules of the law it deems most closely connected to the dispute.
3. The Arbitral Tribunal must, when adjudicating the merits of the dispute, take into account the conditions of the contract, subject of the dispute and the usages of commerce in similar transactions.
4. The Arbitral Tribunal may, if it has been expressly empowered to act as an '*amiable compositeur*' by agreement between the parties to arbitration, adjudicate the merits of the dispute according to the rules of justice and equity without being bound by the provisions of law.

Article 40

The award of an Arbitral Tribunal composed of more than one arbitrator shall be issued by a majority of opinions after deliberations conducted in the manner prescribed by the Arbitral Tribunal, unless the parties otherwise agree.

Article 41

If the parties agree, during the arbitral proceeding, on a settlement ending the dispute, they may request that the conditions of the settlement be evidenced before the Arbitral Tribunal, which must in such case issue a decision containing the conditions of the settlement and terminating proceedings. Such decision shall have the force of an arbitral award as far as execution is concerned.

Article 42

The Arbitral Tribunal may issue interlocutory awards or awards that address part of the claim before issuing its final arbitral award ending the entire dispute.

Article 43

1. The arbitral award shall be issued in writing and signed by the arbitrators. If the Arbitral Tribunal is composed of more than one arbitrator, the signatures of the majority of the arbitrators shall be sufficient, provided the reasons why a minority desisted are mentioned in the award.
2. The arbitral award must be motivated, unless the parties to arbitration agree otherwise or the law applicable to the arbitral proceeding does not require the award to cite reasons.
3. The arbitral award must include the names and addresses of the parties, the names, addresses, nationalities and capacities of the arbitrators, a copy of the arbitral agreement, a summary of the parties' claims, statements and documents, the text of the ruling, the date and place it was issued and the reasons therefore when the citing of such reasons is mandatory.

Article 44

1. The arbitral tribunal shall deliver to each of the parties a copy of the arbitral Award signed by the arbitrators who approved it within thirty days from the date of its issuance.
2. The arbitral award may not be published in whole or in part except with a the approval of the parties to arbitration.

Article 45

1. The Arbitral Tribunal shall issue the award finally ending the entire dispute within the time frame agreed by the parties, in the absence of such agreement, the award must be rendered within twelve months from the date of commencement of the arbitral proceedings. In all cases, the Arbitral Tribunal may extend the deadline provided the period of extension shall not exceed six months, unless the parties agree to a longer period.
2. If the arbitral award is not rendered within the period referred to in the preceding paragraph, either of the two parties to arbitration may request the president of the court referred to in Article (9) of this law, to issue an order setting a new deadline or terminating the arbitral proceeding. In such case either party may raise his claims to the court of original jurisdiction.

Article 46

If, in the course of the arbitral proceedings, a matter lying outside the mandate of the Arbitral Tribunal arises. Or if a document submitted to it is challenged for forgery, or if criminal proceedings are instituted for forgery or for any other criminal act, the Arbitral Tribunal may continue to review the merits of the dispute if it deems a decision on such matter, on forgery of the document or on the other criminal act to be unnecessary for the determination of the merits of the dispute. Otherwise, it shall suspend proceedings until a final judgement is issued in this respect.

Such suspension shall entail suspension of the time limit prescribe for rendering the arbitral award.

Article 47

The party in whose favour the arbitral award has been rendered must deposit the original award or a copy thereof in the language in which it was issued, or an Arabic translation thereof authenticated by the competent authority if it was issued in a foreign language, with the clerk of the court referred to in Article (9) of this law.

The court clerk shall evidence such deposit in a *procès verbal* and each of the parties to arbitration may obtain a copy of the said *procès verbal*.

Article 48

1. The arbitral proceedings shall terminate with the issuance or the award ending the dispute in its entirely or with the issuance of an order ending the arbitral proceedings pursuant to paragraph (2) of Article (45), in the following cases:

a) If the parties agree to end the arbitration
b) If the applicant abandons the dispute subject of arbitration, unless the arbitral tribunal decides, on the basis of an objection raised by the respondent, that the latter has a significant interest in the continuance of the arbitral proceeding until the dispute is adjudicated
c) If for any other reason the Arbitral Tribunal deems it useless or impossible to continue the arbitral proceedings

2. Without prejudice to the provisions of Articles (49), (50) and (51) of the present Law, the mission of the Arbitral Tribunal ends with the termination of the arbitral proceedings.

Article 49

1. Either party to arbitration may, within thirty days from receiving the arbitral award, request the arbitral award to interpret any ambiguity appearing in the award. The party requesting interpretation must notify the other party of the request before presenting it to the arbitral tribunal.
2. The interpretation shall be issued in writing within the thirty days following the date the request for interpretation is submitted to the arbitral tribunal. The tribunal may extend the deadline by another thirty days if it deems such extension is necessary.
3. The award rendered to interpret is deemed to be a complementary part of the arbitral award and is subject to its provisions.

Article 50

1. The arbitral tribunal shall correct any material errors in its award, whether involving words or figures, by means of a decision it issues either *sua sponte* or upon request by one of the parties.

The arbitral tribunal shall make the correction without pleadings within thirty days following the issuance of the award or the deposition of the request for correction, as the case may be. The tribunal may extend this deadline by an additional thirty days if it deems this to be necessary.
2. The correction shall be issued in writing by the arbitral tribunal and notified to the parties within thirty days from the date it was issued. if the decision may be invoked by means of an action for nullity, which shall be subject to the provisions of Articles (53) and (54) of thus Law.

Article 51

1. Either of the parties to arbitration may, even after the expiry of the time limit for arbitration, request the arbitral tribunal within thirty days from receiving the arbitral award, to issue an additional award on a claim submitted by such party in the course of the proceedings and overlooked by the arbitral award. Such request must be notified to the other party before it is presented to the tribunal.
2. The arbitral tribunal shall render its award within sixty days from the submission of the request, and may extend such period for a further thirty days if it deems this to be necessary.

Part VI – Challenging the Arbitral Award

Article 52

1. Arbitral awards issued in accordance with the provisions of this law may not be challenged by any of the means of challenge prescribed in the code of civil and commercial procedures.
2. An action for the nullity of the arbitration award may be instituted in accordance with the provisions of the two subsequent articles.

Article 53

1. An action to procure the nullity of the arbitral award is admissible only in the following cases:

a) If no arbitral agreement exists, or if it is void, voidable or expired
b) If at the time of entering into the arbitral agreement one of the parties thereto was minor or incapacitated pursuant to the law governing his capacity
c) If one of the parties to the arbitration was unable to present his defence because he was not properly notified of the appointment of an arbitrator or of the arbitral proceedings, or for any other reason beyond his control
d) If the arbitral award fails to apply the law agreed to by the parties to the subject matter of the dispute
e) If the Arbitral Tribunal was constituted or the arbitrators were appointed in a manner contrary to law or to the agreement between the parties
f) If the arbitral award rules on matters not included in the arbitral agreement or exceeds the limits of such agreement. Nevertheless, if the parts of the award relating to matters which are amenable to arbitration can be separated from the parts relating to matters which are not, then nullity shall apply only to the latter parts
g) If nullity occurs in the arbitral award, or if the arbitral proceedings are tainted by nullity affecting the award.

2. The court seized with the action for nullity shall rule *sua sponte* for the annulment of the arbitral award if its contents violate public policy in the Arab Republic of Egypt.

Article 54

1. Actions to procure the nullity of the arbitral award must be brought within the ninety days following the date the arbitral award is notified to the party against whom it was rendered. An action for nullity is admissible even if the party invoking nullity waived his right to do so before the arbitral award was issued.
2. Jurisdiction over actions for the nullity of arbitral awards rendered in international commercial arbitrations lie with the court referred to in Article (9) of this law. In other than international commercial arbitrations, jurisdiction lies with the court of second instance to which the decisions of the court of original jurisdiction over the dispute are raised.

Part VII – Recognition and Enforcement of Arbitral Awards

Article 55

Arbitral awards rendered in accordance with the provisions of this law have the authority of *res judicata* and shall be forcibly executed without prejudice to the provisions of the present Law.

Article 56

Jurisdiction to issue an order of enforcement of arbitral awards lies with the president of the court referred to in article (9) hereof or with any of the judges of such court that the president may delegate. The application for executing the arbitral award shall be accompanied by:

1. The original award or a signed copy thereof.
2. A copy of the arbitral agreement.
3. An Arabic translation if the award, authenticated by the competent authority, if the award was not issued in Arabic.
4. A copy of the *procès verbal* evidencing the deposition of the award pursuant to Article (47) hereof.

Article 57

The institution of an action for nullity shall not stay execution of the arbitral award. Nevertheless, the court may order a stay of execution if the plaintiff requests same in his request and such request is based on valid reasons. The court shall rule on the request for a stay of execution within sixty days from the date of the first hearing scheduled to hear it. If it orders a stay of execution, it may order the presentation of a surety or money guarantee. Should the court order a stay of execution, it must rule on the motion for nullity within six months from the date such order was issued.

Article 58

1. The application for the enforcement of an arbitral award shall not be accepted before the date prescribed for raising an action for its nullity has lapsed.
2. Enforcement of the arbitral award pursuant to this law may not be ordered except after verifying that:

> a) It is not contrary to a judgement previously issued by the Egyptian courts on the subject matter of the dispute
> b) It does not contradict public policy in the Arab Republic of Egypt
> c) It was properly notified to the party against whom it was rendered

3. Orders issued for the enforcement of arbitral awards may not be petitioned against. However, orders refusing execution may be petitioned against before the competent court pursuant to the provisions of Article (9) hereof within thirty days from the date of its issuance.

2. Kuwaiti Arbitration Law

Code of Civil and Commercial Procedure, Law No. 38 of 1980

Chapter 12: Arbitration

Article 173

Agreement to arbitrate may be made in respect of a specified dispute. Likewise, agreement to arbitrate may be made in respect of all disputes which arise from the implementation of a specific contract. Written proof of arbitration shall be required. Arbitration is not permitted in matters which permit compromise. Likewise, only he who has capacity to dispose of a right which is the subject matter of a dispute may agree on arbitration.

The subject matter of the dispute must be specified in the agreement for arbitration or during the proceedings, otherwise arbitration shall be null and void, even though the arbitrator is authorized to compromise.

The courts shall not be competent to consider disputes which are governed by an arbitration agreement, however, objection to the competence of the court may be waived expressly or implicitly.

Arbitration shall not cover urgent matters otherwise explicitly agreed.

Article 174

An arbitrator may not be a minor, or be under a court interdiction order, or without civil rights by reason of criminal punishment, or be an undischarged bankrupt.

If there are several arbitrators they must be in all cases an uneven number; also, the appointment of the arbitrator must be stated in the agreement for arbitration or in a separate agreement.

Article 175

If a dispute arises and the adversaries have not agreed on the arbitrators or one or more of the agreed arbitrators refuses to carry out this task or resigns or is dismissed or declared ineligible, or there is an impediment preventing any of them from carrying on the work and there is no agreement in this respect among the adversaries, the court originally competent to consider the dispute shall appoint the arbitrators required upon application by any of the adversaries by following the procedures normally taken in the filing of a lawsuit.

The number of arbitrators whom the court may appoint must be equal to or complete the number agreed by the adversaries. No appeal by any means whatever shall be allowed against a court order issued in this respect.

Article 176

Arbitrators may not be authorized to compromise, nor may they make an award in their capacity as compromise arbitrators unless their names were stated when they were appointed in the arbitration agreement.

Article 177

The Ministry of Justice may set up one or more arbitral tribunals to hold sittings at the seat of the general court or in any other place designated by the board president. The tribunals shall have as president a senior judge chosen by the general assembly of the competent court. The members of the tribunal shall be two businessmen or other professionals. They shall be selected from a roll prepared for this purpose in accordance with the rules and procedures issued in this regard by order of the Minister of justice. A member of staff of the court shall carry out the duties of secretary for the tribunal. The tribunal shall consider without fee the dispute referred to it in writing by the parties concerned. The tribunal shall apply the rules laid down in this chapter. However, it may issue the award and orders referred to in Para. A, B and C of Art. 180.

Article 178

Without prejudice to any provision in the preceding article or in any other law the arbitrator must signify his acceptance of appointment as arbitrator and written proof of such acceptance shall be required.

If the arbitrator resigns his duties without a reason after accepting arbitration he may be liable for payment of compensation.

An arbitrator may not be dismissed, except by agreement of all the adversaries.

The arbitrator may not be relieved of his duties, except for reasons which occur or appear after his appointment. The request to relieve him must be for the same reasons for which a judge may be relieved or may be considered unfit to give judgment. The application to relieve an arbitrator will be submitted to a court which is originally competent to hear the dispute within five days of the date the adversary has been notified of the appointment of the arbitrator, or from the date of the occurrence of the reason for his relief, or of his knowledge of it if it was subsequent to the date of his notification of the appointment of the arbitrator.

In all cases application to relieve an arbitrator shall not be accepted if the arbitrator's award has been issued, or if the hearing of the case has been closed.

The party applying for removal of the arbitrator may appeal against the judgment in this respect regardless of the value of the dispute which is submitted to the arbitrator.

Article 179

The arbitrator, within at the latest thirty days from the date of his acceptance of the arbitration, shall notify the adversaries of the date of the first sitting for the hearing of the dispute and its place, without the need to observe the rules laid down in this law for service of notification. He shall fix a date for them to submit their documents, memoranda and arguments. An award may be made in accordance with a submission by one party if the other party has failed to appear on the date fixed.

If there are several arbitrators they must collectively take part in the investigative proceedings and each one will sign the minutes of it, unless they have unanimously agreed to delegate one of them to carry out certain proceedings and have established his delegation in the minutes of that sitting, or if the agreement for arbitration permits such delegation to any one of them.

Article 180

The dispute before the arbitrator shall be interrupted for any reason laid down in this law for interruption of disputes, and the results of interruption laid down by law shall come into effect.

If during the arbitration a preliminary matter outside the jurisdiction of the arbitration arises, or if there is an allegation of forgery in any document, or if there are any criminal proceedings as a result of forgery or any other criminal event, the arbitrator shall suspend his work until final judgment has been issued in its respect. Also, the arbitrator shall suspend his work in order to refer to the president of the court which is originally competent to hear the dispute to carry out the following:

A. To order the punishment laid down in the law against a witness who fails to attend or fails to give answer.
B. To order third parties to produce a document in their possession which is necessary for the award.
C. To order a judicial act of delegation.

Article 181

If there is no stipulation by adversaries in their arbitration agreement on a date for the award, the arbitrator shall make the award within six months of the date of notification of the parties to the dispute of the arbitration sitting, otherwise any of the parties to the dispute may refer the dispute to the court or continue with the litigation before that court if the case was already filed with it.

If the dates of the notification of the parties differ, effect shall be given to the later date of notification.

The adversaries may agree expressly or implicitly to extend the date whether it was fixed by agreement or law, and may also authorize the arbitrators to extend it to a certain date.

The date shall also be suspended whenever a dispute before an arbitrator has been suspended or interrupted. The date shall resume from the date the arbitrator learns of removal of the cause of suspension or interruption and if the remainder of the date is less than two months it shall be extended to two months.

Article 182

The arbitrator shall issue his award without being bound by the procedure laid down by law, except those laid down in this chapter. Nevertheless, the adversaries may agree on certain procedures which the arbitrator shall follow.

The award of the arbitrator shall be issued in accordance with the basic rules of law, unless he has been authorized to compromise, in which case he shall not be bound by these rules except those relating to public policy.

The rules relating to expedited execution of judgment shall apply to the awards of arbitrators. The award of the arbitrator must be issued in Kuwait, otherwise it shall be subject to the basic rules governing awards issued by arbitrators in a foreign country.

Article 183

The arbitrators' award shall be issued by majority, shall be in writing, shall include in particular a copy of the adversaries, the reasons for the award and its pronouncement, date and place of issue of the award and signatures of the arbitrators.

If one or more of the arbitrators refuse to sign the award the award shall mention the fact. It shall be valid if it is signed by the majority of arbitrators.

The award shall be written in Arabic, unless the adversaries otherwise agree, in which case there must be attached to it an official translation when the award is filed.

The award shall be deemed to be issued on the date it is signed by the arbitrators after writing it.

Article 184

The original of the award even though it may have been issued for the purpose of carrying out measures of investigation—together with the original of the arbitration agreement shall be filed with the clerical section of the court originally competent to consider the dispute, within the ten days following the issue of the award which ends the dispute.

The clerk shall draw up a *procès verbal* of such filing.

Article 185

The arbitrator's award shall not be capable of execution except by order issued by the president of the court after it is filed with its clerical section upon request of any of the interested parties. The order for execution shall be issued after review of the award and the arbitration agreement after ascertaining the absence of impediments for execution and the lapse of the time for appeal, if the award was appealable and was not under expedited execution. The order for execution shall be placed at the end of the original of the award document.

Article 186

The award of the arbitrator may not be appealed except where the adversaries have agreed otherwise, before its issue, in which case the appeal shall be before the general court sitting in an appeal capacity. Appeal shall be subject to the rules laid down for appeal against court judgments and the date for the appeal shall begin from the day the original of the award was filed with the clerical section of the court in accordance with Art. 184.

In any case, the award shall not be subject to appeal if the arbitrator was authorized to compromise, or was an arbitrator in appeal, or if the value of the case did not exceed KD. 500, or if the award was issued by the tribunal constituted under Art. 177.

Any interested party may ask for annulment of a final award issued by the arbitrator in any of the following cases, even though there was agreement to the contrary before its issue.

A. If it has been issued without an arbitration agreement or under an invalid one or if the agreement has lapsed by exceeding the period fixed for it or if the arbitrator has gone beyond the terms of the arbitration agreement.
B. If there should exist any of the reasons which give rise to a request for review of the award.
C. If there is a basic invalidity in the award or a basic invalidity in the proceedings which affected the award.

Article 187

A lawsuit for annulment shall be instituted with the court which is originally competent to hear the dispute in the usual manner for the institution of lawsuits, but it must take place within thirty days from notification of the award. This period shall begin in accordance with the provision of Art. 149 in cases where there are reasons which will give rise to a review of judgment.

The complaint sheet shall include the reasons for the request of annulment, without which it will be invalid. The complainant must deposit upon filing of the complaint sheet KD. 20 as guarantee for expenses, and the clerical section of the court shall not accept said filing if there is no proof of deposit of guarantee. It shall be sufficient to deposit one guarantee in the case of a multiplicity of complainants where they have instituted one complaint sheet even though for different reasons for annulment. The government shall be exempted from depositing a guarantee and likewise, those who are exempted from judicial fees.

The guarantee shall be forfeited by law if the lawsuit is pronounced not accepted by the court, or that it may not be instituted, or that it has lapsed, or that it is annulled, or that it is dismissed.

If the court ordered the annulment of the arbitration's award it will consider the substance of the dispute and at the same time give judgment on it.

Article 188

The institution of a lawsuit for annulment shall not imply suspension of the execution of the arbitrator's award.

In any case, the court which is considering the lawsuit may order, in accordance with the request of the plaintiff, suspension of the execution of the award, if it is feared great damage will result from execution and where the reasons for annulment appear to be likely to prevail.

The court may, when ordering suspension of the execution, order the provision of a guarantee or order whatever is deemed sufficient to protect the right of the defendant. The order suspending execution of the award shall also be extended to cover the execution measures which have been taken by the award creditor from the date of the suspension of execution.

3. Bahrain Arbitration Act, 1994

Law No. 9 of 1994 Promulgating the Law on International Commercial Arbitration

Article 1

The provisions of the Model Law on International Commercial Arbitration of 1985 which is attached to this Law shall apply to every international commercial arbitration where the parties have not subjected to another law.

Article 2

The provisions of part Seventh of the Law of Civil and Commercial Procedures issued by Decree Law No. 12 of 1971 with respect to arbitration shall not apply to any international commercial arbitration subjected to the provisions of this Law. The other provisions of the Law of Civil and Commercial Procedures shall apply to this arbitration only to the extent it is not contrary with the provisions of this Law.

Article 3

The High Court of Appeal shall have jurisdiction to perform the functions referred to in Article 6 of the Model Law on International Commercial Arbitration of 1985 which is attached to this Law.

Article 4

Ministers, each in his/her respective capacity, shall implement the provisions of this Law which shall come into effect from the date of its publication in the Official Gazette.

Legislative Decree No. (30) for the year 2009 with respect to the Bahrain Chamber for Economic, Financial and Investment Dispute Resolution

Preliminary Chapter

Article 1

In applying the provisions of this law the following words and expressions shall have the meanings assigned to them unless the context requires otherwise:
Chamber: Bahrain Chamber for Dispute Resolution.
Minister: The Minister concerned with Justice Affairs.
Regulation: The regulation of dispute resolution procedures stipulated in Section (1) of Chapter (2) of this law which shall be issued by an order of the Minister after the approval of the Supreme Judicial Council.
Procedural Rules: The procedural rules for the resolution of disputes stipulated in Section (2) of Chapter (2) of this law which shall be issued by resolution of Board of Trustees.
Dispute Resolution Tribunal: One or more natural person(s) designated to settle the disputes. In all disputes conducted under the provisions of Section 1 of Chapter 2 of this law, the Tribunal shall

include one or more Judges deputized by the Supreme Judicial Council upon a request from the Minister. A majority of the Tribunal shall consist of deputized Judges.
Chief Executive: The Chamber Chief Executive designated pursuant to article (6) of this law.
Board of Trustees: The Chamber Board of Trustees.

Chapter 1

Establishment and Organization of the Bahrain Chamber for Dispute Resolution

Article 2

An independent Chamber shall be established for the settlement of economic, financial and investment disputes and shall be called the 'Bahrain Chamber for Dispute Resolution' it shall have legal entity, and be subject to the administrative supervision and oversight of the Minister.

Article 3

The Chamber shall be composed of:

a) The Board of Trustees.
b) The Administrative and Technical apparatus.

Article 4

a) The Board of Trustees shall be composed of not less than seven members including the chair person. Their appointment and duration of their membership shall be determined by a decree.
b) The remuneration of the chairperson and members of the Board of Trustees shall be determined by a decree.

Article 5

a) The Board of Trustees shall be the supreme authority that deals with the Chamber's affairs devising the policies to be implemented and supervising their implementation. The Board of Trustees shall undertake what it deems necessary to conduct its duties and authorities, especially the following:

1. Devising and approving the Chambers financial and administrative bylaws, issuing regulations and resolutions, and undertaking the necessary measures to implement the provisions of this law.
2. Approving the organizational structure of the chamber and issuing a regulation regulating Chamber employees' affairs; including procedures and rules of appointment, promotion, transfer and determination of salaries, indemnities and disciplinary procedures and work ethics and values in the Chamber and all other such matters subject to the provisions of the Civil Service Law.

3. Issuing the procedural rules.
4. Approving the Chamber's annual budget draft, and approve its final audited account.
5. Studying the periodic reports submitted by the Chief Executive about the conduct of work in the Chamber, and responding by taking the measures it deems necessary.
6. Appointing the Chamber Chief Executive.
7. Appointing one or more Chief Registrar(s) for the Chamber upon the Chief Executive's suggestion.
8. Approving the annual report of the Chamber's work and activities.
9. Devising the Chamber's work plan at the beginning of each year.
10. Determining the authorities and duties of the Chief Executive and the Chief Registrar(s) and evaluating their performance.
11. Appointing an External Auditor to audit the Chamber's Accounts and determining the fee of the External Auditor.
12. Communicating with local, regional and international institutions working in the same field for exchanging experiences and visits, concluding cooperation agreements and training in a manner that will enable the Chamber to achieve the objectives it was established for, and to acquire global reputation in the field of its mandate.

b) The Board of Trustees may delegate specific tasks to one or more committees composed of Board members, or to the Chairman, or to any Board members, or to the Chief Executive.

Article 6

a) The Board of Trustees shall convene at least four times a year. The Chairperson of the Board shall call an extraordinary meeting when deemed necessary, or upon a reasoned written request from the Minister, at least two members of the Board of Trustees, the Chief Executive, or the external Auditor of the Chamber. This call for an extraordinary meeting shall be made within thirty days of the date of receiving the written request.
b) The invitation to the meeting shall contain a statement of the purpose thereof and an attached agenda.
c) The Chief Executive shall attend all meetings of the Board of Trustees except in the instances specified in the internal bylaws. The Board may invite to its meetings experts and others concerned to discuss or hear their opinions as nonvoting participants.
d) The Board of Trustees shall appoint a Board Secretary who prepares Board agendas, writes down minutes of meetings, retains all documents and records pertaining to the Board of Trustees, and undertakes any other tasks assigned by the Board within the scope of work of the Chamber.
e) Within a period not exceeding six months from the issuance of the law, The Board of Trustees shall draft its internal bylaws.

The bylaws must include provisions to organize its work and to conduct its meetings through appropriate modern technical methods as well as the mechanisms and means to make resolutions in urgent matters that arise between the meetings of Board of Trustees.

Article 7

The Chief Executive shall be the head of the Administrative and Technical Apparatus of the Chamber, and shall represent the Chamber before the courts and in dealings with others.

Article 8

a) The Chamber shall have an independent budget based on commercial pattern. The Budget revenues shall consist of the following:

1. Fees and revenues levied by the Chamber in lieu of its services.
2. Sums allocated to the Chamber by the Government in the general budget of the State.
3. Any other revenues approved by the Board of Trustees, which are not contrary to the provisions of the law.

b) The surplus of the Chamber's budget shall be forwarded from one year to the next.
c) An annual statement of the Chamber shall be published after its endorsement by the external auditor and the Board of Trustees.

Chapter 2: Chamber Jurisdiction

Section 1: Chamber Jurisdiction by law

Article 9

The Chamber shall have jurisdiction to settle the following disputes originally within the jurisdiction of Bahrain courts or other entities having judicial jurisdiction, for cases in which the value of the claim exceeds Five Hundred Thousand Dinars:

1. Disputes among financial institutions licensed according to the provisions of the Law of Central Bank of Bahrain or between these institutions and other institutions, companies, and individuals.
2. International Commercial Disputes. The dispute shall be deemed international if the location of one of the disputant parties or the place where a substantial part of the obligations of the commercial relationship is to be performed, or the location most closely connected with the dispute is outside the Kingdom.

A dispute shall be deemed commercial if its subject matter, contractual or non-contractual, concerns relationships of a commercial nature including any transaction of supplying goods or services or the exchange thereof, distribution agreements, commercial representation or commercial agency, managing rights before others, hiring to purchase, construction of factories, consultation services, engineering works, issuing licenses, investment and financing, banking transactions, insurance, franchising agreements, joint ventures, any other forms of industrial or commercial cooperation, and transporting commodities or passengers by air, sea or land.

Article 10

Subject to the restraints stipulated in the Legislative Decree No. (3) for the year 1972, with respect to Judicial Fees, if the dispute before the Chamber is to be conducted in accordance with the provisions of this section, no procedures shall be conducted before the Chamber unless the due fees are obtained in advance. Fee categories shall be determined and modified by a resolution from the Minister after the approval of the Cabinet of Ministers, not exceeding 5% (five per-cent) of the value of the claim. A resolution by the minister may postpone the payment of fees or exempt all or part of the fees.

Article 11

a) Parties to the dispute before the Chamber, in accordance with the provisions of this section, may agree upon the applicable law relevant to the subject matter of the dispute provided that the provisions of the agreed law do not contradict the public order in the Kingdom. If the parties did not agree upon the applicable law, the Law of Bahrain shall be the applicable law to the subject matter of the dispute.
b) If the parties have agreed to choose a law other than the Law of Bahrain in accordance with the provisions of Paragraph (a) of this Article, parties are obliged to submit that law to the Dispute Resolution Tribunal in accordance with the regulations and procedures cited in the regulation.

Article 12

a) If the parties did not agree upon a chosen language(s) to be used in the dispute resolution procedures, conducted before the Chamber in accordance with the provisions of this section, the Arabic language shall be the language to be used.
b) The regulation shall stipulate the provisions regulating the translation of documents and papers to the language(s) used in the dispute resolution procedures.

Article 13

The parties to the dispute before the Chamber, in accordance with the provisions of this section, may challenge before the Cassation Court requesting nullification of the award issued by the Dispute Resolution Tribunal in any of the following cases:

1. The Challenging party was not properly served a notice of the appointment of a member of the Dispute Resolution Tribunal or the dispute resolution procedures, or was not enabled to present his defense.
2. The composition of the Dispute Resolution Tribunal or the dispute resolution procedures is contrary to what is stipulated in the regulation.
3. The award of the Dispute Resolution Tribunal contradicts the public order in the Kingdom of Bahrain.
4. If an act of deception or fraud that influenced the Dispute Resolution Tribunal award was committed by a party or his representative.
5. If after the Dispute Resolution Tribunal award, an admission that papers upon which the award was based were forged or were adjudicated forged, or if the award was based upon testimony of a witness which was adjudged false.
6. If after the Dispute Resolution Tribunal award, a party obtained decisive papers of the case, the submission of which was obstructed by his opponent.
7. If the Dispute Resolution Tribunal award ruled in a matter not claimed by the opponents or by more than what had been claimed. However, if it was possible to isolate the orders related to the claims of the opponents from the other orders, then it is not permissible to annul from the dispute resolution tribunal award other than that part which contains the

orders related to the matters which the award had adjudicated in matters not claimed by the opponents or by more than they claimed.

8. If the dispute resolution tribunal award contradicts another award having *res judicata* status provided that all the opponents in the both cases are the same persons and status and the subject matter of the case is the same subject matter in the previous case.

Article 14

The challenge stipulated in Article (13) of this law shall be filed in the ordinary manner for filing the case within thirty days of the date of the award, or its notification as the case may be, such period shall be calculated in regard to the instances stipulated in paragraphs (4) to (6) of Article (13) of this law, from the first day the fraud appeared or the admission of the forger or the judgment evidencing the forgery or the judgment against the committer of the false testimony or the day the withheld paper appeared.

The plaint of challenge must include the challenge reasons, otherwise it shall be void. The challenger must deposit upon filing the plaint a sum equivalent to 2% of the awarded sum or ten thousand Bahrain Dinars whichever is more. The plaint of challenge shall not be accepted unless accompanied by proof of deposit. It is sufficient to provide a single deposit when multiple challengers file their challenge in a single plaint; even if the challenge reasons were different, the court shall confiscate the deposit or a part thereof if the court adjudged denying the challenge or non acceptance or its lapse.

Article 15

Without prejudice to provision of Articles (14) of this law, the award issued by the Dispute Resolution Tribunal in accordance with the provisions of this section, shall be deemed a final judgment issued by the courts of Bahrain, and the regulation shall stipulate the provisions attesting the enforcement of the award.

The Dispute Resolution Tribunal's award issued in accordance with the provisions of this section shall be enforceable unless the Cassation Court suspends its enforcement upon the request of the Challenger in a Challenge plaint.

Article 16

Until the Chamber commences its jurisdictions stipulated in Chapter (2) of this Law, the courts and the entities that have judicial jurisdiction shall continue to adjudicate the cases that fall in the jurisdiction of the Chamber in accordance with the provisions of this law until a final judgment is reached therein.

Article 17

The Cassation Court alone shall have the jurisdiction to determine whether the Chamber or one of the courts has the jurisdiction to settle a dispute if the case concerning the same subject was filed before both of them and neither of them waived its jurisdiction or both of them waived their jurisdictions. The Cassation Court shall have the jurisdiction to settle the dispute concerning execution of two contradictory judgments, one issued by the Chamber and the other issued by one of the courts.

The request shall be filed in a plaint submitted to the court's clerk section and the disputants shall be notified in accordance with the rules related to notification stipulated in the Civil and Commercial Procedures law. The disputants are entitled to submit a memorandum of response thereon within eight days following the date of their notification.

After the opinion of the Technical Bureau of the court in the request, the Bureau shall submit it to the Chief of the Court to determine a session to examine the matter before the court and notify the disputants at least three days before the session. Unless the Cassation Court decides otherwise, the filed request shall not suspend the conduct of the concerned case. If the request is submitted after the judgment in the case the Cassation Court may suspend any or both of the contradictory judgments.

Article 18

The Supreme Judicial Counsel shall oversee the conduct of the work in the Chamber in connection with the disputes under its jurisdiction, as an entity with a judicial jurisdiction in accordance with the provisions of this section and pursuant to the provision stipulated in the regulation.

Section 2: Chamber Jurisdiction by Parties Agreement

Article 19

The Chamber shall be competent in disputes that the parties agree in writing to settle by the Chamber.

Article 20

If the dispute before the Chamber has been conducted in accordance with the provisions of this section, then determination of cost and remuneration shall be in accordance with provisions mentioned in the Procedural Rules.

Article 21

If the parties did not agree upon the applicable law on the subject matter of the dispute and the dispute before the Chamber has been conducted in accordance with the provisions of this section, the Dispute Resolution Tribunal shall determine the law specified by the rules of conflict of laws that the Tribunal deems applicable to the subject matter of the dispute.

Article 22

a) If the parties did not agree upon the language(s) to be used in the disputes resolution procedures and the dispute is conducted before the Chamber in accordance with the provisions of this section, the dispute resolution tribunal shall specify the language(s) to be used in these procedures.
b) The Procedural Rules shall stipulate the provisions regulating translation of documents and papers to the language(s) used in the dispute resolution procedures.

Article 23

a) The award of the Dispute Resolution Tribunal issued in accordance with the provisions of this section shall be enforceable by an order issued by a High Court of Appeal Judge upon a request petition submitted by the enforcement order applicant accompanied with the original Dispute Resolution Tribunal award and a copy of the dispute resolution agreement, and after seeing the award and the agreement, and assuring that it does not contravene with Public Order in the Kingdom.
b) The order of the High Court of Appeal Judge concerning the request of the enforcement of the Dispute Resolution Tribunal award shall be reasoned, the dispute parties may petition thereof, before the High Court of Appeal within thirty days from its issuance or its notification, as the case may be, for any reasons stipulated in paragraph (a) in article (24) of this law.
c) The Judge who issued the order concerning the enforcement request, shall not be included in the composition of the court selected to adjudicate the petition.

Article 24

a) The parties before the Chamber, in accordance with the provisions of this section, may challenge before the Cassation Court the award issued by the Dispute Resolution Tribunal.
They may also submit before the same court a petition against the order issued by the High Court of Appeal concerning the enforcement request, within the period stipulated in article (23) of this law, for any of the following reasons:

1. Nullity of the Agreement to settle the dispute before the Chamber due to incapacity of one of the parties or due to this agreement contravening provisions of the applicable law chosen by the parties.
2. The challenger or the petitioner was not served a notice in a proper manner regarding the appointment of a member of the Dispute Resolution Tribunal or the dispute resolution procedures or was not enabled to present his defense.
3. Composition of the Dispute Resolution Tribunal or the dispute resolution procedures are contrary to what was stipulated in the parties' agreement.
4. The Dispute Resolution Tribunal award dealt with an unintended dispute or one not contained in the submitted agreement or contains orders in matters outside the scope of the agreement. However, if it was possible to isolate the orders related to the submitted matters to the Tribunal from the other orders not submitted thereto, then it is not permissible to set-aside the Dispute Resolution Tribunal award except that part which contains the orders related to the matters which were not to be submitted to the tribunal.
5. The award of the Dispute Resolution Tribunal contradicts the public order in the Kingdom of Bahrain.

b) The challenge or petition stipulated in paragraph (a) of this article shall be filed in the ordinary manner for filing the case, and its plaint must include the reasons upon which it was based, otherwise it shall be void.

The challenger or the petitioner must provide upon filing the plaint the deposit stipulated in the law of Cassation Court. The plaint of challenge or petition shall not be accepted if it was not accompanied by proof of the deposit. It is sufficient to provide a single deposit when multiple

challengers or petitioners file their challenge or petition in a single plaint; even if the reasons were different the court shall confiscate the deposit or a part thereof if the court adjudged denying the challenge or the petition or non acceptance or its lapse.
c) Filing the Challenge or the petition stipulated in this article, shall not suspend the enforcement of the award of the Dispute Resolution Tribunal Unless the Cassation Court decides to suspend the enforcement upon the challenger or the petitioner requests in the challenge or petition plaint.

Article 25

Without prejudice to the procedures stipulated in Articles (23) and (24) of this law concerning enforcement of the Dispute Resolution Tribunal award, parties to the dispute shall not be entitled to challenge on nullity base against the award issued by the Dispute Resolution Tribunal in accordance with Article (24) of this law, if the parties have agreed in writing to choose a foreign law concerning the dispute, and they shall not be entitled to challenge the award before Bahrain's Courts, and that the challenge against the award shall be before the competent authority in another state.

Chapter 3: Regulation of Procedures before the Chamber

Article 26

Rules specified in the Civil and Commercial Procedures Law and the Evidence Law in Civil and Commercial Matters, in so far not contradicting the nature of the Chamber's jurisdiction and the situations before it, shall apply upon the procedures and the dates to be applicable to disputes pending before the Chamber in *accordance* with the provisions of section (1) of Chapter (2) of this law, including the procedures of submission of the case, its management, terms of appointment and choosing members of the Dispute Resolution Tribunal, the rules governing their challenge, and reasons for their refusal and terms of the parties' representation before the Dispute Resolution Tribunal, *instances* of disqualification of those appointed to settle the dispute, the provisions regulating payment of fees and costs and its deposit with the Chamber and other related matters necessary to regulate the procedures, including provisions of appearance, absence, intervention, joinder, construe the awards, correcting typos, arithmetical mistakes and lapse of claims. Details of such shall be contained in a regulation issued by the Minister after the approval of the Supreme Judicial Counsel within a period not exceeding six months from the issuance of the law.

Article 27

a) The Board of Trustees, within a period not exceeding six months from the issuance of the law, shall issue the Procedural Rules that stipulate the means for the resolution of disputes before the Chamber, the applicable rules and procedure before the Chamber, the dates applicable to disputes pending before the Chamber subject to the provisions of section (2) of Chapter (2) of this law, including the procedures of submission of the case, its management, terms of selection and appointment of members of the Dispute Resolution Tribunal, the rules governing their challenge, and reasons for their refusal and terms of the parties' representation before the Dispute Resolution Tribunal, *instances* of disqualification of those appointed to settle the dispute, rules to determine the fees of Dispute Resolution Tribunal, and the provisions regulating payment of fees and costs and deposits with the Chamber and other related matters necessary to regulate the procedures,

including provisions of appearance, absence, construe the awards, correcting typos and arithmetical mistakes and lapse of claims.
b) The Board of Trustees may issue special procedural rules containing rules and procedures to be applicable in certain types of disputes before the Chamber subject to the provisions of Section (2) of Chapter (2) of this law.

Article 28

If the Chamber has jurisdiction over the dispute, the Chamber shall be the authority to appoint whom it deems to resolve the dispute no matter what procedural rules are to be applied to the dispute.

Article 29

Chosen Members of the Dispute Resolution Tribunal shall be neutral and independent. Every member chosen to resolve the dispute, and before his appointment, shall disclose to the appointing authority any circumstances or conflicts that might arise or lead one to have any doubt about his neutrality or independence.

Article 30

On application of the provisions of this Law, and subject to the provisions of the Regulation and the Procedural Rules:

a) It is not permitted for non Bahraini lawyers to represent disputants unless accompanied by a Bahraini Lawyer licensed before the Cassation Court; if the submitted dispute has been conducted in accordance with the provisions of Section (1) of Chapter (2) of this law.
b) Non Bahraini lawyers may represent disputants; if the submitted dispute has been conducted in accordance with the provisions of Section (2) of Chapter (2) of this law.

Article 31

A judge, deputed by the Supreme Judicial Council, shall have jurisdiction in the following:

a) Issuing necessary decision to conduct dispute resolution procedures which required a judicial intervention upon the Dispute Resolution Tribunal request.
b) Deal with interim matters which fall between the submission of the dispute to the Chamber and the composition of the Dispute Resoltion Tribunal or in exceptional situations that might prevent the Dispute Resolution Tribunal for dealing with the interim application. The deputed Judge shall refer the application to the Dispute Resolution Tribunal immediately after its composition without any interruption of the jurisdiction of the Dispute Resolution Tribunal to deal with the interim applications.

The petition against the interim decision shall be submitted to the Judge who issued the decision or to the Dispute Resolution Tribunal after its composition, as the case may be. The issued decision in the petition shall be final and not subject to challenge by any means. The regulation and the procedural rules shall specify the provisions governing the submission of such petition and the decision to be taken thereof.

Article 32

The award of the Dispute Resolution Tribunal shall be issued in writing and signed by the Dispute Resolution Tribunal in accordance with the rules stipulated in the regulation and the procedural rules.

Chapter 4: Licensing of Dispute Resolution Institutions

Article 33

The Minister, after the approval of the Cabinet of Ministers, may license Dispute Resolution Institutions to practice in the Kingdom of Bahrain and to have the Kingdom as a centre, and determine the due fees. The licenses shall govern the performance of their operations.

Article 34

Provisions of Articles (23), (24), (25), (30/b), (35) and (36) of this law, shall apply to all the Institutions mentioned in the previous article.

Chapter 5: General Provisions

Article 35

Provisions of Civil and Commercial Procedures Law and Evidence Law shall not be applicable to any dispute falling within the jurisdiction of the Chamber according to the provision of this Law, only to the extent that they do not contradict with the provisions of this law.

Article 36

a) The Chairperson and the Members of the Board of trustees, or the Chief executive, or the Chief Registrar, or any employee of the Chamber shall not be liable for any act of commission or omission that result in damages for others if such was due to carrying their duties within their limits of their authorities stipulated in this Law or regulations or decisions to implement therefore, unless it was committed with bad intention or it was a result of a gross mistake.
b) Any Dispute Resolution Tribunal member had been appointed in accordance with the provisions of this Law, shall not be liable for any act of commission or omission in the manner of performing his duties, unless the act was committed with bad intention or it was a result of a gross mistake. This provision shall apply to those who work for the Dispute Resolution Tribunal member or deputies authorized by him to perform some of the duties related to tasks assigned to him. This shall not waive the responsibility of the Dispute Resolution Tribunal member if he steps aside without any serious reason or in improper time.

c) The Chamber shall not be liable for any act of commission or omission emanating from the Chairperson and the Members of the Board of trustees, or the Chief executive, or the Chief Registrar, or any employee of the Chamber, or any Dispute Resolution Tribunal member, or any other official acts on its name or on its behalf, unless such act of commission or omission was committed with bad intention or it was a result of a gross mistake.

Article 37

The Provisions of the Law No. (13) for the Year 1975 with respect to the Pension and Retirement Benefits for Civil Servants and its amendments shall apply on the Chamber's employees.

Article 38

The legislative decree No. (9) for the year 1993 with respect to the establishment of Bahrain International Commercial Arbitration Center shall be revoked, as well as any text that contradicts the provisions of this law.

Article 39

The Prime Minister and the Ministers, each within his respective jurisdiction, shall implement the provisions of this Law which shall become effective from the following day of the date of its publication in the Official Gazette; provided that the chamber shall commence its jurisdiction stipulated in Chapter 2 of this law after six months from its effectiveness' date.

The King of the Kingdom of Bahrain
Hamad Bin Isa Al-Khalifa
The Prime Minister
Khalifa Bin Salman Al-Khalifa
The Minster of Justice and Islamic Affairs
Khalid Bin Ali Al-Khalifa
Issued in Riffa Palace
Issued on the 29th of June 2009

4. The UAE Code of Civil Procedure, Federal Law No. (11) of 1992

Chapter Three: Arbitration

Article 203

1. The parties to a contract may generally stipulate in the basic contract or by a supplementary agreement that any dispute arising between them in respect of the performance of a particular contract shall be referred to one or more arbitrators and may also agree to refer certain disputes to arbitration under special conditions.
2. No agreement for arbitration shall be valid unless evidenced in writing.

3. The subject of the dispute shall be specified in the terms of reference or during the hearing of the suit even if the arbitrators were authorized to act as amiable compositors; otherwise the arbitration shall be avoid.
4. Arbitration shall not be permissible in matters, which are not capable of being reconciled. An arbitration agreement may be made only by the parties who are legally entitled to dispose of the disputed right.
5. If the parties to a dispute agree to refer the dispute to arbitration, no suit may be filed before the courts. Notwithstanding the foregoing, if one of the parties files a suit, irrespective of the arbitration provision, and the other party does not object to such filing at the first hearing, the suit may be considered, and in such case, the arbitration provision shall be deemed cancelled.

Article 204

1. If a dispute arises between the parties prior to the execution of an agreement between them to refer the same to arbitration, or if one or more of the nominated arbitrators refuses to act as such, withdraws, is dismissed, has his appointment revoked, or is prevented from acting due to an encumbrance, and no agreement exists between the parties in this respect, the court which has jurisdiction to consider the dispute shall appoint the necessary number of arbitrators at the request of one of the parties filed in the normal procedure for filing a suit. The number of arbitrators appointed by the court shall be equal, or complementary, to the number agreed between the parties to the dispute.
2. The court's decision in respect of the foregoing may not be contested in any way whatsoever.

Article 205

1. Unless their names are specifically mentioned in the arbitration agreement or a subsequent document, arbitrators may not be authorized to act as *amiable compositors*.

Article 206

1. An arbitrator may not be a minor, bankrupt, legally incapacitated or deprived of his civil rights due to a criminal offence unless he has been rehabilitated.
2. If there are more than one arbitrators, the number shall, at all times be odd.

Article 207

1. The acceptance of the appointment of an arbitrator shall be in writing or may be evidenced by recording the same in the minutes of the sessions.
2. If an arbitrator, after having accepted his appointment, withdraws without good reason, he may be held liable for compensation.
3. No arbitrator may be removed except with the approval of all the parties to the dispute. However, if it is established that the arbitrator has willfully neglected to act in accordance with the terms of reference, despite a written notice to him in this respect, the court which had jurisdiction to consider the dispute may, at the request of one of the parties, dismiss the arbitrator and order a replacement in the same manner as he was originally appointed.
4. An arbitrator may not be disqualified except for reasons occurring or appearing after his appointment. A request for disqualification must be based on the same grounds on which a judge

may be dismissed or deemed unfit for passing judgement. The request for disqualification shall be filed with the court which has jurisdiction to consider the dispute within five days from notifying the parties of the appointment of the arbitrator or from the date on which the reason for disqualification arose or from the time it became known if subsequent to the notification of the appointment of the arbitrator. In all events, the request for disqualification shall not be granted if the court has already passed a judgement or if the hearing of pleadings has been concluded.

Article 208

1. Within a maximum period of thirty days from the acceptance of his appointment, the arbitrator shall, without the need to comply with the rules provided under this Law in respect of serving of notices, notify the parties to the dispute of the date of the first hearing scheduled for consideration of the dispute and the venue thereof. The arbitrator shall fix a date for the parties to the dispute to submit their documents, memoranda and pleadings.
2. A decision may be issued on the basis of the documents submitted by only one of the parties to the dispute if the other party fails to submit his documents within the time specified.
3. If there shall be more than one arbitrator, they shall jointly conduct the investigation and each of them shall sign the minutes of sessions.

Article 209

1. The hearing of a dispute before the arbitrator shall terminate if a reason for such termination, as stipulated under this Law, exists. Unless the matter has been reserved for award, such termination shall have the legal effects stipulated under the law.
2. If, during the course of arbitration, a preliminary issue, which is outside the powers of the arbitrator, arises or if a challenge has been filed that a document has been counterfeited, or if criminal proceedings have been taken regarding such counterfeiting or for any other criminal act, the arbitrator shall suspend the proceedings until a final judgement on the same has been passed. In addition, the arbitrator shall suspend the proceedings to refer to the President of the competent court the following:

a) To pass a judgement in accordance with the law to penalize any witness who fails to appear or refuses to give statement.
b) To order a party to submit any documents in its possession which are necessary for the issue of the arbitration award.
c) To decide on evidence by commission.

Article 210

1. If the parties to the dispute did not specify in the arbitration agreement a date for the issue of the award, the arbitrator shall pass his award within six months from the date of the first arbitration session; otherwise any of the parties shall be entitled to refer the dispute to the court or, if a suit has already been filed, to proceed with the same before the court.
2. The parties to the dispute may, expressly or impliedly, agree to extend the date fixed by agreement or under the law and may authorize the arbitrator to extend the same for a specified period. The court may, at the request of the arbitrator or one of the parties, extend the period specified under the above paragraph for such a period, as the court may deem sufficient to decide on the dispute.

3. The period specified as aforesaid shall cease to run whenever the arbitration is discontinued or terminated before the arbitrator and shall recommence from the date on which the arbitrators are notified of the removal of the reason for which the dispute was discontinued or terminated. If the remaining period is less than a month, it shall be extended to one full month.

Article 211

1. The arbitrators shall cause the witnesses to take oath. Whoever makes a false statement before the arbitrators shall be deemed to have committed the crime of perjury.

Article 212

1. The arbitrator shall issue his award without being bound by any procedures other than those stipulated in this Chapter and those pertaining to calling of the parties, hearing of their pleas and enabling them to submit their documents. Notwithstanding the foregoing, the parties to the dispute may agree on certain procedures to be followed by the arbitrator.
2. The arbitrators award shall be in conformity with the provisions of law unless the arbitrator was authorized to reconcile the dispute, in which event he shall not be bound to comply with such rules except in matters which concern public order.
3. The special rules pertaining to immediate enforcement shall apply to arbitration awards.
4. The arbitrators' award shall be issued within the United Arab Emirates; otherwise, the rules applicable to arbitration awards passed in foreign countries shall apply thereto.
5. The arbitrators' award shall be passed by a majority and shall be made in writing and accompanied by the dissenting vote. In particular, the award shall contain a copy of the arbitration agreement, a summary of the statements of the parties, their documents, the grounds and context of the award, the date and place of issue and the signatures of the arbitrators. Should one or more arbitrators refuse to sign the award, such refusal shall be stated in the award; provided, however, that the award shall be valid if signed by a majority of the arbitrators.
6. Unless otherwise agreed between the parties to the dispute, the award shall be in the Arabic language; otherwise, the award shall, at the time of filing, be accompanied by a legalized translation thereof.
7. The award shall be deemed to have been issued from the date of signing the same by the arbitrators.

Article 213

1. When arbitration is conducted through court, the arbitrators shall, within fifteen days following the issue of their award, file with the competent court the award together with the original terms of reference, minutes of sessions and documents. They shall also file with the court a copy of the award to be delivered to each of the parties within five days from the date of filing of the original copy thereof. The court clerk shall prepare a report on the said filing to be submitted to the judge or the head of the department, as the case may be, so as a hearing may be convened within fifteen days for the purpose of approving the award. The parties of the dispute shall be notified of the date fixed for the hearing as aforesaid.
2. Where the arbitration is conducted in connection with an appeal suit, the filing shall be made with the court, which has jurisdiction to consider the appeal.

3. Where arbitration is conducted between the parties to a dispute outside the court, the arbitrators shall provide each party with a copy of their award within five days from the date of the issue of the same. The court shall, at the request of one of the parties filed within the normal course of filing the suit, consider whether the award shall be approved or nullified.

Article 214

1. While considering the request for approving the arbitrators' award, the court may refer the same back to the arbitrators to reconsider any issues which they have omitted or to clarify the award if it was not specific to the extent that the enforcement of the same is not possible. Unless otherwise decided by the court, the arbitrators shall, in both cases, issue their revised award within three months from the date of their notification of the court's decision.
2. The decision of the court may not be contested except upon the passing of the final judgment in respect of the approving or nullifying of the award.

Article 215

1. The arbitrators' award may not be enforced unless the same has been approved by the court with which the award was filed; provided that the court has reviewed the award and the terms of reference and ensured that there is no encumbrance to such enforcement. The said court shall, at the request of one of the parties concerned, correct the material errors in the arbitrators award in accordance with the legally prescribed manners applicable to correction of errors.
2. The national court is concerned with all matters related to arbitral award enforcement.

Article 216

1. The parties to a dispute may, at the time of consideration of the arbitrators award, request the nullification of the same in the following events:

> a) If the award was issued without, or was based on invalid terms of reference or an agreement which has expired by time prescription, or if the arbitrator has exceeded his limits under the terms of reference.
> b) If the award was issued by arbitrators who were not appointed in accordance with the law, or by only a number of the arbitrators who were not authorized to issue the award in the absence of the others, or if it was based on terms of reference in which the dispute was not specified, or if it was issued by a person who is not competent to act as an arbitrator or by an arbitrator who does not satisfy the legal requirements.
> c) If the award of the arbitrators or the arbitration proceedings become void and such voidness affected the award.

2. A request for nullification of the award shall not be rejected on the grounds of a waiver by a party of its right to the same prior to the issue of the award.

Article 217

1. The award of the arbitrators may not be contested by any manner of appeal.

2. The judgement approving the arbitrators' award may be contested in any of the appropriate manners of appeal.
3. Notwithstanding the preceding paragraph, the award shall not be appealable if the arbitrators were authorized to reconcile the dispute or, if the parties have expressly waived their rights to file an appeal or if the disputed amount was not in excess of Dirhams ten thousand.

Article 218

1. The arbitrators shall estimate their fees and arbitration expenses and may decide that such amount, in whole or in part, be borne by the party against whom the award was issued. The court may, at the request of one of the parties, amend the said estimation taking into account the efforts of the arbitrators and the nature of the dispute.

Chapter Four: Execution of Foreign Judgments

Article 235

1. Judgments and orders passed in a foreign country may be ordered for execution and implementation within UAE under the same conditions provided for in the law of foreign state for the execution of judgments and orders passed in the state.
2. Petition for execution order shall be filed before the Court of First Instance under which jurisdiction execution is sought under lawsuit filing standard procedures. Execution may not be ordered unless the following was verified:-

> a) State courts have no jurisdiction over the dispute on which the judgment or the order was passed and that the issuing foreign courts have such jurisdiction in accordance with the International Judicial Jurisdiction Rules decided in its applicable law.
> b) Judgment or order was passed by the competent court according to the law of the country in which it was passed.
> c) Adversaries in the lawsuit on which the foreign judgment was passed were summoned and duly represented.
> d) Judgment or order had obtained the absolute degree in accordance with law of the issuing court.
> e) It does not conflict or contradict with a judgment or order previously passed by another court in the State and does not include any violation of moral code or public order.

Article 236

1. Provisions of the preceding Article shall apply to the arbitration decision passed in foreign countries. Arbitration decisions must be passed on a matter which may be decided on by arbitration according to the law of the country and must be enforceable in the country it was passed in.

Article 237

1. Attested documents and conciliation reports authenticated by Courts in foreign countries may be ordered to be executed in the State under the same conditions provided for the execution of similar orders and reports passed in the UAE as stated in the law of the foreign country.
2. Execution order referred to in the preceding para shall be requested vide a petition filed with the execution judge. Execution order may not be passed unless the conditions for the implementation of such document or report were verified to have been met in accordance with the laws of the country in which it was attested or authenticated and after verifying it to be free from any thing in violation of moral code or public order.

Article 238

1. Rules provided for in the preceding Articles do not prejudice rules and regulations provided for in conventions signed between the UAE and other countries in this respect.

Annex II
Arab BITs with the Developed World

1. Treaty between the United States of America and the Arab Republic of Egypt concerning the Reciprocal Encouragement and Protection of Investments

Whereas, the United States of America and the Arab Republic of Egypt (each hereinafter referred to as a 'Party'), both recognize the importance of providing mutually beneficial support for the major efforts that each has contributed in fostering international peace both within and beyond their respective regions, and

Whereas, each Party recognizes that economic expansion and development are basic elements in the process of strengthening the efforts for and the bonds of international peace and friendship within an atmosphere of stability and security, and

Whereas, each agrees that economic cooperation through the pursuit of policies an practices which foster bilateral trade and investment, will contribute substantially to the long-term benefit and welfare of the peoples of each Party, and

Recognizing that agreement on a general framework for the encouragement and non discriminatory treatment of investments will stimulate the flow of productive capital and technology and thereby provide for a more effective use of capital and technical resources for development needs, further promoting economic stability and durable peace,

Both have resolved to conclude a bilateral Treaty pertaining to the reciprocal encouragement and protection of investments, and

Have agreed as follows:

Article I Definitions

1. For the purposes of this Treaty,

[*The original text contains a paragraph 1, but no paragraph 2*]

(a) 'Company' means any kind of juridical entity, including any corporation, company association, or other juridical entity, that is duly incorporated, constituted, or otherwise duly organized, regardless of whether or not the entity is organized for pecuniary gain, privately or publicly owned, or organized with limited or unlimited liability.

(b) 'company of a Party' means a company duly incorporated, constituted or otherwise duly organized under the applicable laws and regulations of a Party or its subdivisions in which

(i) natural persons who are nationals of such Party, or

(ii) such Party or its subdivision or its agencies or instrumentalities have a substantial interest.

The juridical status of a company of a Party shall be recognized by the other Party and its subdivisions.

(c) 'Investment' means every kind of asset owned or controlled and includes but is not limited to:

(i) tangible and intangible property, including rights, such as mortgages, liens and pledges;
(ii) a company or shares, stock in a company or interests in the assets thereof;
(iii) a claim to money or a claim to performance having economic value, due under an investment agreement.
(iv) valid intellectual and industrial property rights, including, but not limited to rights with respect copyrights and related patents, trade marks and trade names, industrial designs, trade secrets and know-how, and goodwill.
(v) licenses and permits issued pursuant to law, including those issued for manufacture and sale of products.
(vi) any right conferred by law or contract, but not limited rights to within the confines of law to search for or utilize natural resources, and rights to manufacture, use and sell products;
(vii) returns which are reinvested.

(d) 'own or control' includes ownership or control exercised through subsidiaries or affiliates.
(e) 'national' of a Party means a natural person who is a national of a party under its applicable law.
(f) 'return' means an amount derived from an investment, including, but not limited to, profit; dividend; interest; royalty payment; management, technical assistance or other fee; and payment in kind.

Article II Encouragement and Promotion of Investments

1. Each Party undertakes to provide an maintain a favorable environment for investments in this territory by nationals and companies of the other Party and shall, in applying its laws, regulations, administrative practices and procedures, permit such investments to be established and acquired on terms and conditions that accord treatment no less favorable than the treatment it accords to investments of its own nationals and companies of any third country, whichever is more favorable.
2. (a) Each Party shall accord investments in its territory, and associated activities in connection with these investments of nationals or companies of the other Party, treatment no less favorable than that accorded in like situations to investments and associated activities of its own nationals and companies, or nationals and companies of any third country, whichever is most favorable. Associated activities in connection with an investment include, but are not limited to:

(i) the establishment, control and maintenance of branches, agencies, offices, factories or other facilities for the conduct of business;
(ii) the organization of companies under applicable laws and regulations; the acquisition of companies or interests in companies or in the property; and the management, control, maintenance, use, enjoyment and expansion, and the sale, liquidation, dissolution or other disposition, of companies organized or acquired;
(iii) the making, performance and enforcement of contracts related to investment;
(iv) the acquisition (whether by purchase, lease or any other legal means), ownership and disposition (whether by sale, testament or any other legal means) of personal property of all kinds, both tangible and intangible;
(v) the leasing of real property appropriate for the conduct of business;
(vi) acquisition, maintenance and protection of copyrights, patents, trademarks, trade secrets, trade names, licenses and other approvals or products and manufacturing processes,

and other industrial property rights; and

(vii) the borrowing of funds at market terms and conditions from local financial institutions, as well as the purchase and issuance of equity shares in the local financial markets, and, in accordance with national regulations and practices, the purchase of foreign exchange for the operation of the enterprise.

(b) This Treaty shall also apply to investments by nationals or companies of either Party, made prior to the entering into force of this Treaty and accepted in accordance with the respective prevailing legislation of either party.

3.(a) Notwithstanding the preceding provisions of this Article, each Party reserves the right to maintain limited exceptions to the standard of national treatment otherwise required concerning investments or associated activities if exceptions fall within one of the sectors listed in the Annex to this Treaty. Both Parties hereby agree to maintain the number of such exceptions to a minimum. In addition, each Party shall notify the other Party of any specific measures which constitute exceptions to the standard of national treatment provided herein. In no event, however, shall the treatment to be accorded pursuant to any exception be less favorable than that accorded in like situations to investments and associated activities of nationals or companies of any third country. Moreover, no exception, within the sectors contained in the Annex, introduced after the date of entry into force of this Treaty shall apply to investments of nationals or companies of the other Party existing in that sector at the time the exception becomes effective.

(b) Each Party retains the discretion to approve investments according to national plans and priorities on a nondiscriminatory basis consistent with paragraphs (1) and (3)(a) of this Article.

4. The treatment, protection and security of investments shall never be less than that required by international law and national legislation.

5. (a) Subject to the laws relating to the entry and sojourn of aliens, nationals of either Party shall be permitted to enter and to reside in the territory of the other Party for the purpose of establishing, developing, directing, administering or advising on the operations of an investment to which they or the companies that employ them have committed or are in the process of committing a substantial amount of capital or other resources.

(b) Nationals and companies of either Party, and their companies which they own or control in the territory of the other Party, shall be able to engage the managing director of their choice. Further, subject to employment laws of each Party, nationals and companies of either Party shall be permitted to engage, within the territory of the other Party, professional and technical personnel of their choice, for the particular purpose of rendering professional, technical and managerial assistance necessary for the planning and operation of investments.

6. In the context of its national economic policies and objectives, each Party shall seek to avoid the imposition of performance requirements of the investment of nationals and companies of the other Party.

7. Each Party recognizes that in order to maintain a favorable environment for investments in its territory by nationals or companies of the other Party, it should provide effective means of asserting claims and enforcing rights with respect to investment agreements, investments authorizations and properties. Each Party shall grant to nationals or companies of the other Party, on terms and conditions no less favorable than those which it grants in like situations to its own nationals or companies or to nationals or companies of any third country, whichever is the most favorable treatment, the right of access to its courts of justice, administrative tribunals and agencies, and all other bodies exercising adjudicatory authority, and the right to employ persons of their choice, who

otherwise qualify under applicable laws and regulations of the forum for the purpose of asserting claims, and enforcing rights, with respect to their investments.
8. Each Party and its subdivisions shall make public all laws, regulations, administrative practices and procedures, and adjudicatory decisions that pertain to [or] affect investments in its territory of nationals or companies of the other Party.

Article III Compensation for Expropriation

1. No investment or any part of an investment of a national or company of either Party shall be expropriated or nationalized by the other Party or by a subdivision thereof-or subjected to any other measure, direct or indirect, if the effect of such other measure, or a series of such other measures, would be tantamount to expropriation or nationalization (all expropriations, all nationalizations and all such other measures hereinafter referred to as 'expropriation') -unless the expropriation

(a) is done for a public purpose;
(b) is accomplished under due process of law;
(c) is not discriminatory;
(d) is accompanied by prompt and adequate compensation, freely realizable; and
(e) does not violate any specific contractual engagement.

Compensation shall be equivalent to the fair market value of the expropriated investment on the date of expropriation. The calculation of such compensation shall not reflect any reduction in such fair market value due to either prior public notice or announcement of the expropriatory action, or the occurrence of the events that constituted or resulted in the expropriatory action. Such compensation shall include payments for delay as may be considered appropriate under international law, and shall be freely transferable at the prevailing rate of exchange for current transactions on the date of the expropriatory action.
2. If either Party or a subdivision thereof expropriates the investment of any company duly incorporated, constituted or otherwise duly organized in its territory, and if nationals or companies of the other Party, directly or indirectly, own, hold or have other rights with respect to the equity of such company, then the Party within whose territory the expropriation occurs shall ensure that such nationals or companies of the other Party receive compensation in accordance with the provisions of the preceding paragraph.
3. Except as otherwise provided in an agreement between the Parties, or between a Party and a national or company of the other Party, a national or company of either Party that asserts that all or part of its investment in the territory of the other Party has been expropriated shall have a right to prompt review by the appropriate judicial or administrative authorities of such other Party to determine whether any such expropriation has occurred and, if so, whether such expropriation, and any compensation thereof, conforms to the principals of international law.

Article IV Compensation for Damages Due to War and Similar Events

Nationals or companies of either Party whose investments or returns in the territory of either Party suffer

(a) damages due to war or other armed conflict between such other Party and a third country or
(b) damages due to any kind of civil disturbance or insurrection in the territory of such other Party,

shall be accorded treatment no less favorable than that which such other Party accords to its own nationals or companies or to nationals or companies of any third country, whichever is the most favorable treatment, when making restitution, indemnification, compensation or other appropriate settlement with respect to such damages.

Article V Transfers

1. Either Party shall in respect to investments by nationals or companies of the other Party grant to those nationals or companies the free transfer of:

(a) returns;
(b) royalties and other payments deriving from licenses, franchises and other similar grants or rights;
(c) installments in repayment of loans;
(d) amounts spent for the management of the investment in the territory of the other Party or a third country;
(e) additional funds necessary for the maintenance of the investment;
(f) the proceeds of partial or total sale or liquidation of the investment, including a liquidation effected as a result of any event mentioned in Article IV; and
(g) compensation payments pursuant to Article III.

2. To the extent a national or company of either Party has not made another arrangement with the appropriate authorities of the other Party in whose territory the investment of such national or company is situated, currency transfers made pursuant to Paragraph 1 of this Article shall be permitted in the currency of the original investment or in any other freely convertible currency. Such transfers shall be made at the prevailing rate of exchange on the date of transfer with respect to current transactions in the currency to be transferred.
3. Notwithstanding the preceding paragraphs, either Party may maintain laws and regulations: (a) requiring reports of currency transfer; and (b) imposing income taxes by such means as a withholding tax applicable to dividends or other transfers. Furthermore, either Party may protect the rights of creditors, or ensure the satisfaction of judgements in adjudicatory proceedings, through the equitable, nondiscriminatory and good faith application of the law.

Article VI Consultations and Exchange of Information

1. The Parties shall, upon the written request of either of them, promptly hold consultations to discuss the interpretation or application of this Treaty or to resolve any disputes in connection therewith.

2. Further, for the purpose of reviewing the operation of this Treaty in encouraging investments, consultations should be held biennially between the two Parties. Those consultations should aim at exchanging information and views on the progress regarding investments.
3. If one Party requests in writing that the other Party supply information in its possession concerning investments in its territory by nationals or companies of the Party making the request, then the other Party shall, consistent with its applicable laws and regulations and with due regard for business confidentiality, endeavor to establish appropriate procedures and arrangements for the provision of any such information.

Article VII Settlement of Legal Investment Disputes Between One Party and a National or Company of the Other Party

1. For purposes of this Article, a legal investment dispute is defined as a dispute involving (i) the interpretation or application of an investment agreement between a Party and a national or company of the other Party; or (ii) an alleged breach of any right conferred or created by this Treaty with respect to an investment.
2. In the event of a legal investment dispute between a Party and a national or company of the other Party with respect to an investment of such national or company in the territory of such Party, the parties shall initially seek to resolve the dispute by consultation and negotiation. The Parties may, upon the initiative of either of them and as a part of their consultation and negotiation, agree to rely upon non-binding, third-party procedures. If the dispute cannot be resolved through consultation and negotiation, then the dispute shall be submitted for settlement in accordance with the applicable dispute-settlement which a Party and national or company of other Party have previously agreed. With respect to expropriation by either Party, any dispute-settlement procedures specified in an investment agreement between such Party and such national or company shall remain binding and shall be enforceable in accordance with the terms of the investment agreement and relevant provisions of domestic laws of such Party and treaties and other international agreements regarding enforcement of arbitral awards to which such Party has subscribed.
3. (a) In the event that the legal investment dispute is not resolved under procedures specified above, the national or company concerned may choose to submit the dispute to the International Centre for the Settlement of Investment Disputes ('Centre') for settlement by conciliation or binding arbitration, if, within six (6) months of the date upon which it arose: (i) the dispute has not been settled through consultation and negotiation; or (ii) the dispute has not, for any good faith reason, been submitted for resolution in accordance with any applicable dispute-settlement procedures previously agreed to by the Parties to dispute: or (iii) the national or company concerned has not brought before the courts of justice or administrative tribunals or agencies of competent jurisdiction of the Party that is a Party to the dispute.
(b) Each Party hereby consents to the submission of an investment dispute to the Centre for settlement by conciliation or binding arbitration.
(c) Conciliation or binding arbitration of such disputes shall be done in accordance with the provisions of the Convention on the Settlement of Investment Disputes Between States and Nationals of Other States ('Convention') and the Regulations and Rules of the Centre.
4. In any proceeding, judicial, arbitral or otherwise, concerning a legal investment dispute between it and a national or company of the other Party, A Party Shall not assert, as a defense, counterclaim, right of set-off or otherwise, that the national or company concerned has received or Will receive, pursuant to an insurance contract, indemnification or other compensation for all or part of its alleged

damages from any third Party whatsoever, whether public or private, including such other Party and its subdivisions, agencies and instrumentalities. Notwithstanding the foregoing, a national or company of the other Party shall not be entitled to compensation for more than the value of its affected assets, taking into account all sources of compensation within the territory of the Party liable for the compensation.
5. For the purpose of any proceedings initiated before the Centre in accordance with this Article, any company that, immediately prior to the occurrence of the event or events giving rise to the dispute was a company of the other Party, shall be treated as a national or company of such other Party.
6. The provisions of this Article shall not apply to a dispute arising under an official export credit, guarantee, or insurance arrangement, pursuant to which the Parties have agreed to other means of settling disputes.

Article VIII Settlement of Disputes Between the Parties Concerning Interpretation or Application of this Treaty

1. Any dispute between the Parties concerning the interpretation or application of this Treaty should, if possible, be resolved through diplomatic channels.
2. If the dispute cannot be resolved through diplomatic channels, it shall, upon the agreement of the Parties, be submitted to the International Court of Justice.
3. (a) In the absence of such agreement, the dispute shall, upon the written request of either Party, be submitted to an arbitral tribunal for binding decision in accordance with the applicable rules and principles of international law.
(b) The Tribunal shall consist of three arbitrators, one appointed by each Party, and a Chairman appointed by agreement of the other two arbitrators. The Chairman shall not be a national of either Party. Each Party shall appoint an arbitrator within 60 days, and the Chairman shall be appointed within 90 days, after a Party has requested arbitration of a dispute.
(c) If the period set forth in (b) above are not met, and in the absence of some other arrangement between the Parties, either Party may invite the President of the International Court of Justice to make the necessary appointment. If the President is a national of either of the Parties or is unable to act for any reason, either Party may invite the Vice President, or if he is also a national of either Party or otherwise unable to act, the next most senior member of the International Court of Justice, to make the appointment.
(d) In the event that an arbitrator is for any reason unable to perform his duties, a replacement shall be appointed within thirty (30) days of determination thereof, utilizing the same method by which the arbitrator being replaced was appointed. If a replacement is not appointed within the time limit specified above, either Party may invite the President of the International Court of Justice to make the necessary appointment. If the President is a national of either of the Parties or is unable to act for any reason, either Party may invite the Vice President, or if he is also a national of either Party or otherwise unable to act, the next most senior member of the International Court of Justice, to make the appointment.
(e) Unless otherwise agreed to by the Parties to the dispute, all submissions shall be made. and all hearings shall be completed within one hundred and twenty (120) days of the date of the selection of the third arbitrator, and the Tribunal shall render its decision within thirty (30) days of the date of the final submissions or the date of the closing of the hearings, whichever is later, and such decision shall be binding on each Party.

(f) Except as otherwise agreed to by the Parties, arbitration proceedings shall be governed by the Model Rules on Arbitral Procedure adopted by the United Nations International Law Commission in 1958 ('Model Rules') and commended to Member States by the United Nations General Assembly in Resolution 1262 (XIII). To the extent that procedural questions are not resolved by this Article or the Model Rules they shall be resolved by the Tribunal. Notwithstanding any other provision of this Treaty or the Model Rules, the Tribunal shall in all cases act by majority vote.
(g) Each Party shall bear the costs of its own arbitrator and counsel in the arbitral proceeding. Expenses incurred by the Chairman and other costs of the proceedings shall be paid for equally by the Parties. The Tribunal may, however, at its discretion, direct that a higher proportion of the costs be paid by one of the Parties. Such a decision shall be binding.
4. The provisions of this Article shall not apply to a dispute arising under an official export credit, guarantee or insurance arrangement, pursuant to which the Parties have agreed to other means of settling disputes.

Article IX Preservation of Rights

1. This Treaty shall not supersede, prejudice, or otherwise derogate from (a) laws, regulations, administrative practices or procedures, or adjudicatory decisions of either Party, (b) international legal obligations, or (c) obligations assumed by either Party, including those contained in an investment agreement or an investment authorization, whether extant at the time of entry into force of this Treaty or thereafter, that entitle investments or associated activities of nationals or companies of the other Party to treatment more favorable than that accorded by this Treaty in like situations.
2. This Treaty shall not derogate from or terminate any other agreement entered into by the two Parties and in force as between the two Parties on the date on which this Treaty enters into force.

Article X Measures Not Precluded by Treaty

1. This Treaty shall not preclude the application by either Party or any subdivision thereof of any and all measures necessary for the maintenance of public order and morals, the fulfillment of its existing international obligations, the protection of its own security interests, or such measures deemed appropriate by the Parties to fulfill future international obligations.
2. This Treaty shall not preclude either Party from prescribing special formalities in connection with the establishment of investments in its territory of nationals and companies of the other Party, but such formalities shall not impair the substance of any of the rights set forth in this Treaty.

Article XI Taxation

With respect to its tax policies, each Party should strive to accord fairness and equity in the treatment of investments of nationals or companies of the other Party. Nevertheless, all matters relating to the taxation of nationals or companies of a Party, or their investments in the territories of the other Party or a subdivision thereof shall be excluded from this Treaty, except with regard to measures covered by Article III and the specific provisions of Article V.

Article XII Application of Treaty to Political or Administrative Subdivisions of the Parties

This Treaty shall apply to the political and/or administrative subdivisions of each Party.

Article XIII Entry into Force and Duration and Termination

1. This Treaty shall be ratified by each of the Parties, and the instruments of ratification thereof shall be exchanged as soon as possible.
2. This Treaty shall enter into force thirty (30) days after the date of exchange of the instruments of ratification. It shall remain in force for a period of ten (10) years and shall continue in force unless terminated in accordance with Paragraph 3 of this Article.
3. Either Party may, by giving one (1) year's written notice to the other Party, terminate this Treaty at the end of the initial ten (10) year period or at any time thereafter.
4. With respect to investments made or acquired prior to the date of termination of this Treaty and to which this Treaty otherwise applies, the provisions of all of the other Articles of this Treaty shall continue to be effective for a further period of ten (10) years from such date of termination.
5. The attached Annex and Protocol are integral parts of this Treaty.

DONE in duplicate at Washington this Twenty-ninth day of September 1982 in the English and Arabic languages, both texts being equally authentic.

2. Agreement between the Government of the United Kingdom of Great Britain and Northern Ireland and the United Arab Emirates for the Promotion and Protection of Investments

The Government of the United Kingdom of Great Britain and Northern Ireland and the Government of the United Arab Emirates;
Desiring to create favourable conditions for greater investment by investors of one State in the territory of the other State, and for the transfer of technology between the two countries;
Recognising that the encouragement and reciprocal protection under international agreement of such investments will be conducive to the stimulation of individual business initiative and will increase prosperity in both States;
Have agreed as follows:

ARTICLE 1

Definitions

For the purpose of this Agreement:

(a) 'investment' means every kind of asset owned or controlled by investors of either of the Contracting Parties and in particular, though not exclusively, includes:

(i) movable and immovable property and any other property rights such as mortgages, liens, or pledges.

(ii) shares in and stock and debentures of a company and any other form of participation in a company.
(iii) liquid assets, deposits and claims to money or to any performance under contract having a financial value.
(iv) intellectual property rights, goodwill, technical processes and know-how.
(v) business concessions conferred by law or under contract, including concessions to search for, cultivate, extract or exploit natural resources.

A change in the form in which assets are invested does not affect their character as investments and the term 'investment' includes all investments, whether made before or after the date of entry into force of this Agreement;
(b) 'returns' means the amounts yielded by an investment and in particular, though not exclusively, includes profit, interest, capital gains, dividends, royalties and fees.
(c) 'nationals' means:

(i) in respect of the United Kingdom: physical persons deriving their status as United Kingdom nationals from the law in force in the United Kingdom.
(ii) in respect of the United Arab Emirates: natural and physical persons deriving their status as United Arab Emirates nationals from the law in force in the United Arab Emirates.

(d) 'companies' means:

(i) in respect of the United Kingdom: corporations, firms and associations incorporated or constituted under the law in force in any part of the United Kingdom or in any territory to which this Agreement is extended in accordance with the provisions of Article 12.
(ii) in respect of the United Arab Emirates: any entity established in accordance with and recognized as a juridical person by the law of the State, such as public and private companies, corporations, business associations, authorities, partnership foundations, firms, institutions, establishments, agencies, development funds, enterprises, co-operatives, and organizations or other similar entities irrespective of whether their liabilities are limited, or otherwise.

(e) 'investors' means: any national or company of one of the Contracting Parties or the Government of one of the Contracting Parties, or the Government of any of the Emirates of the United Arab Emirates.
(f) 'territory' means:

(i) in respect of the United Kingdom: Great Britain and Northern Ireland, including the territorial sea and any maritime area situated beyond the territorial sea of the United Kingdom which has been or might in the future be designated under the national law of the United Kingdom in accordance with international law as an area within which the United Kingdom may exercise rights with regard to the sea-bed and subsoil and the natural resources and any territory to which this Agreement is extended in accordance with the provisions of Article 12,
(ii) in respect of the United Arab Emirates: all land territory including the territorial sea, economic zone and continental shelf.

(g) 'associated activities' means the organization, control, operation, maintenance and disposal of juridical persons, branches, agencies, offices or other facilities for the conduct of business: the acquisition, use, protection and disposal of property of all kinds, including intellectual and industrial property rights, and the borrowing of funds, the purchase, issue and disposal of equity, shares and the purchase and disposal of foreign exchange for imports, all subject to the laws and regulations of the Contracting Party in whose territory the investment is made.

ARTICLE 2

Promotion and Protection of Investment

(1) Each Contracting Party shall encourage and create favourable conditions for investors of the other Contracting Party to invest in its territory, and, subject to its right to exercise powers conferred by its laws and regulations shall admit such investment and permit associated activities.
(2) Investments of investors of each Contracting Party shall at all times be accorded fair and equitable treatment and shall enjoy full protection and security in the manner consistent with international law in the territory of the other Contracting Party. Neither Contracting Party shall in any way impair by unreasonable, arbitrary or discriminatory measures the management, maintenance, use, enjoyment or disposal of investments in its territory of investors of the other Contracting Party. Each Contracting Party shall observe any obligation it may have entered into with regard to investments of investors of the other Contracting Party.

ARTICLE 3

National Treatment and Most-favoured-Nation Provisions

(1) Neither Contracting Party shall in its territory subject investments, associated activities or returns of investors of the other Contracting Party to treatment less favourable than that which it accords to investments, associated activities or returns of its own investors or to investments, associated activities or returns of investors of any third State.
(2) Neither Contracting Party shall in its territory subject investors of the other Contracting Party, as regards their management, maintenance, use, enjoyment or disposal of their investments, to treatment less favourable than that which it accords to its own investors or to investors of any third State.

ARTICLE 4

Compensation for Losses

(1) Investors of one Contracting Party whose investments in the territory of the there Contracting Party suffer losses owing to war or other armed conflict, revolution, state of national emergency, revolt, insurrection or riot in the territory of the latter Contracting Party shall be accorded by the latter Contracting Party treatment, as grads restitution, indemnification, compensation or other settlement no less favourable an that which the latter Contracting Party accords to its own investors or to vectors of any third State. Resulting payments shall be freely transferable.

(2) Without prejudice to paragraph (1) of this Article, investors of one Contracting Party who in any of the situations referred to in that paragraph suffer losses in the territory of the other Contracting Party resulting from:
(a) requisitioning of their property by its forces or authorities, or
(b) destruction of their property by its forces or authorities, which was not caused in combat action or was not required by the necessity of the situation.
shall be accorded restitution or adequate compensation. Resulting payments shall be freely transferable.

ARTICLE 5

Exceptions

The provisions of this Agreement relative to the grant of treatment not less favourable than that accorded to the investors of either Contracting Party or of any third State shall not be construed so as to oblige one Contracting Party to extend to the investors of the other the benefit of any treatment, preference or privilege resulting from:
(a) any existing or future customs union or similar international agreement to which either of the Contracting Parties is or may become a party, or
(b) any international agreement or arrangement relating wholly or mainly to taxation or any domestic legislation relating wholly or mainly to taxation.

ARTICLE 6

Expropriation

(1) Investments of investors of either Contracting Party shall not be nationalized, expropriated or subjected to measures having the effect of dispossession, direct or indirect, or having effect equivalent to nationalization or expropriation (hereinafter referred to as 'expropriation') in the territory of the other Contracting Party except for a public purpose related to the internal needs of that Party on a non-discriminatory basis, under due process of law, not being contrary to any contractual obligation undertaken by a Contracting Party in favour of an investor, and against prompt, adequate and effective compensation. Such compensation shall amount to the genuine value of the investment expropriated immediately before the expropriation or before the impending expropriation became public knowledge, whichever is the earlier, shall include interest at a normal commercial rate until the date of payment, shall be made without delay, be effectively realizable and be freely transferable. The investor affected shall have a right, under the' law of the Contracting Party making the expropriation, to prompt review, by a judicial or other independent authority of that Party, of the lawfulness pf the expropriation and of the valuation of his or its investment in accordance with the principles set but in this paragraph.
(2) Where a Contracting Party expropriates the assets of a company which, is incorporated or constituted under the law in force in any part of its own territory, and in which investors of the other Contracting Party own shares, it shall ensure that the provisions of paragraph (1) of this Article are applied to the extent necessary to guarantee prompt, adequate and effective compensation in respect of their investment to such investors of the other Contracting Party who are owners of those shares.

ARTICLE 7

Repatriation of Investment and Returns

Each Contracting Party shall in respect of investments guarantee to investors of the other Contracting Party the unrestricted transfer of their investments and returns. Transfers shall be effected without delay in the convertible currency in which the capital was originally invested or in any other convertible currency agreed by the investor and the Contracting Party concerned. Unless otherwise agreed by the investor transfers shall be made at the rate of exchange applicable on the date of transfer pursuant to the exchange regulations in force.

ARTICLE 8

Reference to International Centre for Settlement of Investment Disputes

(1) If any dispute should arise between a Contracting Party and an investor of the other Contracting Party concerning an investment of the latter in the territory of the former, and settlement cannot be reached within three months between the parties to this dispute through negotiation, consultation, pursuit of local remedies or otherwise then, if the investor affected also consents in writing to submit the dispute to the International Centre for the Settlement of Investment Disputes (hereinafter referred to as 'the Centre') for settlement by conciliation or arbitration under the Convention on the Settlement of Investment Disputes between States and Nationals of other States opened for signature at Washington on 18 March 19651 (hereinafter referred to as 'the Convention') either Party may institute proceedings by addressing a request to that effect to the Secretary-General of the Centre as provided in Articles 28 and 36 of the Convention. In the event of disagreement as to whether conciliation or arbitration is the more appropriate procedure, the investor affected shall have the right to choose. The Contracting Party which is a party to the dispute shall not raise as an objection at any stage of the proceedings or enforcement of an award the fact that the investor which is the other party to the dispute has received in pursuance of an insurance contract an indemnity in respect of some or all of his or its losses.
(2) Each Contracting Party hereby consents to submit to the Centre for settlement by conciliation or arbitration under the Convention any legal dispute arising between that Contracting Party and an investor of the other Contracting Party concerning an investment of the latter in the territory of the former.
(3) A company which is incorporated or constituted under the law in force in the territory of one Contracting Party and in which before such a dispute arises the majority of shares are owned by investors of the other Contracting Party shall in accordance with Article 25(2)(b) of the Convention be treated for the purposes of the Convention as a company of the other Contracting Party.
(4) Neither Contracting Party shall pursue through the diplomatic channel any dispute referred to the Centre unless:
(a) the Secretary-General of the Centre, or a conciliation commission or an arbitral tribunal constituted by it, decides that the dispute is not within the jurisdiction of the Centre, or
(b) the other Contracting Party should fail to abide by or to comply with any award rendered by an arbitral tribunal.

ARTICLE 9

Disputes between the Contracting Parties

(1) The Contracting Parties shall consult promptly at the request of either of them to resolve any dispute in connection with this Agreement or to discuss any matter relating to the interpretation or application of this Agreement.
(2) If such a dispute is not resolved the Contracting Parties should endeavour to settle it through the diplomatic channel.
(3) If a dispute between the Contracting Parties cannot thus be settled, it shall upon the request of either Contracting Party be submitted to an arbitral tribunal.
(4) Such an arbitral tribunal shall be constituted for each individual case in the following way, within two months of the receipt of the request for arbitration; each Contracting Party shall appoint one member of the tribunal. Those two members shall then select a national of a third State with which both Contracting Parties have diplomatic relations who on approval by the two Contracting Parties shall be appointed Chairman of the tribunal. The Chairman shall be appointed within two months from the date of appointment of the other two members,
(5) If within the periods specified in paragraph (4) of this Article the necessary appointments have not been made, either Contracting Party may, in the absence of any other agreement, invite the President of the International Court of Justice to make any necessary appointments. If the President is a national of either Contracting party or if he is otherwise prevented from discharging the said function, the Vice-President shall be invited to make the necessary appointments. If the Vice-President is a national of either Contracting Party or if he too is prevented from discharging the said function, the Member of the International Court of Justice next in seniority who is not a national of either Contracting Party shall be invited to make the necessary appointments.
(6) The arbitral tribunal shall reach its decision by a majority of votes. Such decision shall be binding on both Contracting Parties. Each Contracting Party shall bear the cost of its own member of the tribunal and of its representation in the arbitral proceedings; the cost of the Chairman and the remaining costs shall be borne in equal parts by the Contracting Parties. The tribunal may, however, in its decision direct that a higher proportion of costs shall be borne by one of the two Contracting Parties and this award shall be binding on both Contracting Parties. The tribunal shall determine its own procedure.

ARTICLE 10

Subrogation

(1) If one Contracting Party or its designated Agency makes a payment under an indemnity given in respect of an investment, the latter Contracting Party shall recognize the assignment to the former Contracting Party or its designated Agency by law or legal transaction of all the rights and claims of the Party indemnified and that the former Contracting Party or its designated Agency is entitled to exercise such rights and enforce such claims by virtue of subrogation, to the same extent as the party indemnified.
(2) The former Contracting Party or its designated Agency shall be entitled in all circumstances to the same treatment in respect of the rights and claims acquired by it by virtue of the assignment and any payments received in pursuance of those rights and claims as the Party indemnified was

entitled to receive by virtue of this Agreement in respect of the investment concerned and its related returns.

(3) Any payments received in non-convertible currency by the former Contracting, Party or its designated Agency in pursuance of the rights and claims acquired shall be freely available to the former Contracting Party for the purpose of meeting any expenditure incurred in the territory of the latter Contracting Party.

(4) This Article shall, notwithstanding the final sentence of Article l(a) of this Agreement, apply only to investments made after the entry into force of this Agreement, where the investment has received the prior consent of the Contracting Party in whose territory it is made if such consent is required by the Contracting Party.

ARTICLE 11

Application of other Rules

If the provisions of law of either Contracting Party or obligations under international law existing at present or established hereafter between the Contracting Parties in addition to the present Agreement contain rules, whether general or specific, entitling investments by investors of the other Contracting Party to a treatment more favourable than is provided for by the present Agreement, such rules shall to the extent that they are more favourable prevail over the present Agreement.

ARTICLE 12

Territorial Extension

At the time of ratification of this Agreement, or at any time thereafter, the provisions of this Agreement may be extended to such territories for whose international relations the Government of the United Kingdom are responsible as may be agreed between the Contracting Parties in an Exchange of Notes.

ARTICLE 13

Entry into Force

This Agreement shall be ratified and shall enter into force on the exchange of instruments of Ratification1.

ARTICLE 14

Duration and Termination

This Agreement shall remain in force for a period of ten years. Thereafter it shall continue in force until the expiration of twelve months from the date on which either Contracting Party shall have

given written notice of termination to the other. Provide that in respect of investments made whilst the Agreement is in force, its provisions shall continue in effect with respect to such investments for a period of twenty years after the date of termination and without prejudice to the application thereafter of the rule of general international law.
In witness whereof the undersigned, duly authorised thereto by their respective Governments, have signed this Agreement.
Done in duplicate at Dubai this Eighth day of December 1992 corresponding to the Thirteenth of Jamadi Al Thani 1413H in the English and Arabic languages, both text being equally authoritative.

3. Agreement Between the Government of the People's Republic of China and the Government of the State of Kuwait for the Promotion and Protection of Investments[1] 23/11/1985[2]

The government of the People's Republic of China and the Government of the State of Kuwait (hereinafter collectively referred to as the Contracting States and each referred to as a Contracting State); Desiring to create favorable conditions for greater economic co-operation between them and in particular for investments by investors of one Contracting State in the territory and maritime zones of the other Contracting State; Recognizing that the encouragement and reciprocal protection under international agreements of such investments will be conducive to the stimulation of business initiative and will increase prosperity in both Contracting States; Have agreed as follows:

Article 1 Definitions

For the purposes of this Agreement
(1) The term 'investment' shall comprise every kind of assets invested before of after the entry into force of this Agreement by natural or juridical persons of one Contracting State in the territory and maritime zones of the other Contracting State in accordance with the laws and regulations of that State. Without restricting the generality of the foregoing, the term 'investment' shall include:
(a) movable and immovable property as well as any other property rights in rem such as mortgages, lines, pledges, usufruct and similar rights;
(b) shares, stocks and debentures of companies or other rights or interests in such companies; loans and bonds issued by a Contracting State or any of its natural or juridical person and returns retained for the purpose of re-investment;
(c) claims to money or to any performance having economic value associated with an investment;
(d) copyrights, trademarks, patents, and other industrial property rights, know-how, trade names and goodwill;
(e) any right conferred by law or contract and any licences and permits pursuant to law. Any alteration of the form in which assets are invested shall not affect their classification as investments, provided that such alteration is not contrary to the admission, if any, granted in respect of the assets originally invested.
(2) The term 'investor' shall mean any natural or juridical person of a Contracting State who invests in the territory and maritime zones of the other Contracting State.

1 http://unctad.org/sections/dite/iia/docs/bits/china_kuwait.pdf
2 Entered into force on 24 December 1986.

(3) The term 'natural person' shall mean with respect to either Contracting State a natural person holding the nationality of that State in accordance with its laws.
(4) The term 'juridical person' shall mean with respect to either Contracting State, any entity established in its territory and in accordance with, and recognized as a juridical person by the law of the State, such as public institutions, authorities, corporations, foundations, agencies, development funds, enterprises, cooperatives, societies, associations, and similar entities and private companies, firms, partnerships, establishments and organizations irrespective of whether their liabilities are limited or otherwise. If natural or juridical persons of a Contracting State have an interest in a juridical person which was established within the territory of a third State, and this juridical person invests in the other Contracting State, it shall be recognized as a juridical person of the former Contracting State. This Paragraph of this Article can be applied only when the said third State has no right or abandons its right to protect the said juridical person.
(5) The term 'returns' shall mean amounts yielded by an investment and in particular, though not exclusively, includes profits, interest, capital gains, share dividends, royalties or fees.
(6) The term 'host government' shall mean the government of the Contracting State in whose territory and maritime zones the relevant investment is made or is to be made.
(7) Maritime zones mean the marine and submarine zones over which the Contracting States exercise, under international law, sovereignty, sovereign rights or jurisdiction.

Article 2 Promotion and Protection of Investments

(1) Each Contracting State shall encourage and create favorable conditions for investors of the other Contracting State to make investments in its territory and maritime zones and, in exercise of powers conferred by its laws, shall admit such investments.
(2) Each Contracting State shall at all times ensure fair and equitable treatment to the investments and returns of investors of the other Contracting State. Each Contracting State shall ensure, subject to its laws and regulations, that the management, maintenance, use, enjoyment or disposal of investments in its territory and maritime zones of investors of the other Contracting State shall not in any way be subjected to or impaired by any unreasonable or discriminatory measures. Each Contracting State shall observe any obligation it may have entered into in the documents of approval of investments or the approved investment contracts by investors of the other Contracting State.
(3) The Contracting States shall periodically consult between themselves concerning investment opportunities within the territory and maritime zones of each other in various sectors of the economy to determine where investments from one Contracting State into the other may be most beneficial in the interest of both Contracting States, and accord them appropriate facilities, incentives and other forms of encouragement to such an extent and on such terms and conditions as shall, from time to time, be determined by agreement between the Contracting States hereto.

Article 3 Most-favored-nation Provisions

(1) Each Contracting State shall in its territory and maritime zones accord investments and returns of investors of the other Contracting State treatment not less favorable than that which it accords to investments and returns of investors of any third State.

(2) Each Contracting State shall in its territory and maritime zones accord investors of the other Contracting State, as regards management, maintenance, use, enjoyment or disposal of their investments, treatment not less favorable than that which it accords to investors of any third State. PROVIDED that nothing in this Article or in the immediately preceding Article shall be interpreted as imposing a legal obligation on either Contracting State to extend to the investors of the other, the benefit of any treatment, preference or privilege which may be accorded to any investor of other states by virtue of the formation of a customs union, a free trade area or any other agreement or arrangement relating wholly or mainly to taxation or any regional or sub-regional arrangement relating to movement of capital to which such State may be a party.

Article 4 Compensation for Damage or Loss

(1) Investors of one Contracting State whose investments in the territory and maritime zones of the other Contracting State suffer losses owing to war or other armed conflict, a state of national emergency, revolt, insurrection or riot in the territory and maritime zones of the latter Contracting State shall be accorded by the latter Contracting State treatment, as regards relevant compensatory measures adopted, not less favorable than that which the latter Contracting State accords to investors of any third State.

(2) Without prejudice to Paragraph (1) of this Article, investors of one Contracting State who in any of the events referred to in that Paragraph suffer damage or loss in the territory and maritime zones of the other Contracting State resulting from.

(a) requisitioning of their property by its forces or authorities,

(b) destruction of their property by its forces or authorities which was not caused in combat action or was not required by the necessity of the situation, shall be accorded fair, reasonable and non-discriminatory compensation for the damage or loss sustained during the period of requisitioning or as a result of the destruction of the property. Resulting payments shall be in convertible currency and freely transferable.

Article 5 Nationalization, Expropriation or Similar Measures

(1) (i) Investments of any natural or juridical person of either Contracting State shall not be subject to sequestration or confiscation or any similar measures save with the order of a competent court issued in accordance with laws in force.

(ii) Investments of any natural or juridical person of either Contracting State can be nationalized or expropriated or subjected to measures having effect equivalent to nationalization or expropriation in the territory and maritime zones of the other Contracting State only for a public purpose in the national interest of that Contracting State and by giving fair and reasonable compensation and on condition that such measures are taken on a nondiscriminatory basis and in accordance with domestic laws of general application.

(iii) Such compensation shall be computed on the basis of the market value of the investment immediately prior to the point of time when the decision for expropriation was announced or became publicly known. Where the market value cannot be readily ascertained, the compensation shall be determined in accordance with generally recognized principles of valuation and on equitable principles taking into account, inter alia, the capital invested, depreciation, capital already repatriated, replacement value and other relevant factors. The compensation shall include interest

at the current rate of interest applicable to the currency in which the investment was originally undertaken from the date of expropriation until the date of payment. The determination of the amount of compensation, in the absence of agreement being reached between the investor and the host State, shall be referred to arbitration. The amount of compensation finally determined shall be paid to investors in freely convertible currencies and allowed to be repatriated without undue delay.
(iv) Where a Contracting State nationalizes or expropriates the assets of a company, firm or other business association or business concern, which is established or licenced under the law in force in its territory and in which any natural or juridical person of the other Contracting State owns shares, stocks, debentures or other rights or interest, it shall ensure that fair and reasonable compensation is received in freely convertible currencies and allowed to be repatriated. Such compensation shall be determined on the basis of the recognized principles of valuation such as the market value of the assets immediately prior to the point of time when the decision for nationalization or expropriation was announced or became publicly known. The compensation shall include interest at the current rate of interest applicable to the currency in which the investment was originally undertaken from the date of nationalization or expropriation until the date of payment.
(2) The provisions of Paragraph (1) of this Article shall also apply to the current returns from an investment as well as, in the event of liquidation, to the proceeds from the liquidation.

Article 6 Repatriation of Investment and Returns

(1) Each Contracting State shall, in accordance with its laws and regulations, allow without undue delay the transfer in any convertible currency of:
(a) the net profits, dividends, royalties, technical assistance and technical service fees, interest and other returns, accruing from any investment by an investor of the other Contracting State;
(b) the proceeds accruing from the total or partial liquidation of any investment made by an investor of the other Contracting State;
(c) funds in repayment of borrowings which both Contracting States have recognized as investment; and
(d) the earnings of nationals of the other Contracting State and their employees who are allowed to work in connection with an investment in its territory and maritime zones.
(2) Without restricting the generality of Article 5 of this Agreement the Contracting States undertake to accord to transfers referred to in Paragraph (1) of this Article a treatment as favorable as that accorded to transfers originating from investments made by investors of any third State.
(3) For the purpose of this Agreement, exchange rates shall be determined in accordance with the official rates agreed with the International Monetary Fund or, where such rates do not exist, the official exchange rates for Special Drawing Rights or United States Dollars or any other convertible currency agreed between the Contracting States. (4) Such transfers as above shall, however, be subject to the right of the host government to impose reasonable restrictions beyond its existing regulations relating to foreign exchange controls for temporary periods not exceeding six months to meet situations of fundamental economic disequilibrium provided that fifty percent (50%) of such transfers are allowed to be repatriated during such periods.

Article 7 Subrogation

(1) If a Contracting State (or its designated Agency) makes payment to any of its investors under an indemnity or a guarantee it has granted in respect of an investment or any part thereof in the territory and maritime zones of the host State, or has otherwise become subrogated to any of the rights of such investors with respect to such investments, the host State shall recognize:
(a) the right of the other Contracting State (or its designated Agency) arising from the assignment, indemnity or other subrogation, whether under law or pursuant to a legal transaction, and
(b) that the other Contracting State (or its designated Agency) is entitled by virtue of subrogation to enforce such right and to undertake any obligations in relation to such right. Such other Contracting State (or its designated Agency) shall accordingly, if it so desires, be entitled to assert any such right to the same extent as its predecessor in title before a competent Court or Tribunal in the host State or submit the dispute to arbitration according to the procedures of Article 9 of this Agreement.
(2) If such other Contracting State acquires any amount in such manner as above, it shall be accorded in respect thereof treatment not less favorable than that accorded to the funds of any third State deriving from investment activities similar to those in which the party indemnified was engaged.

Article 8 Settlement of Investment Disputes

(1) Disputes or differences between one Contracting State and an investor of the other Contracting State concerning an investment of that investor in the territory and maritime zones of the former Contracting State shall, if possible, be settled amicably.
(2) If such disputes or differences cannot be settled according to the provisions of Paragraph (1) of this Article within a period of six months from the date either party requested amicable settlement and the parties have not agreed to any other dispute settlement procedures, the investor concerned may choose one or both of the following means of resolutions:
(a) file complaint with and seek relief from the competent administrative authority or agency of the Contracting State in whose territory or maritime zones the investment was made;
(b) file suit with the competent court of law of the Contracting State in whose territory or maritime zones the investment was made.
(3) The dispute relating to the amount of compensation and any other dispute agreed upon by both parties may be submitted to an international Arbitral Tribunal. The international Arbitral Tribunal mentioned above shall be especially constituted in the following way: each party to the dispute shall appoint an arbitrator. The two arbitrators shall appoint an arbitrator as Chairman who shall be a national of a third State which shall have diplomatic relations with both Contracting States. The arbitrators shall be appointed within two months and the Chairman within four months from the date when the concerned party notified the other party of its submission of the dispute to arbitration. If the necessary appointments are not made within the period specified in the previous Paragraph, either party may, in the absence of any other agreement, request the Chairman of the International Arbitration Institute of the Stockholm Chamber of Commerce to make the necessary appointments. The Arbitral Tribunal shall determine its own arbitral procedures by referring either to the Convention on the Settlement of Investment Disputes between States and Nationals of other States done at Washington on March 18, 1965 or the Arbitration Rules of the United Nations Commission on International Trade Law (UNCITRAL). The Arbitral Tribunal shall reach its award based upon the provisions of this Agreement, the relevant domestic laws, the agreements

both Contracting States have concluded and the generally recognized principles of international law. The Arbitral Tribunal shall meet in a third State selected by common accord by the parties concerned or, if the choice has not been made within forty five (45) days of the appointment of the final member of the Tribunal, in Stockholm. The Tribunal shall reach its decision by a majority of votes. The award shall be final and binding on both parties. When the Tribunal renders an award, it shall state its legal basis and, upon request of either party, shall interpret it. Each party shall bear the costs of the arbitrator it has appointed and of its own expenses during the arbitration proceedings. The expenses of the Chairman of the Tribunal and other costs shall be borne equally by both parties.

(4) In addition to the foregoing provisions of this Article, disputes between investors of a Contracting State and the investors of the other Contracting State in whose territory or maritime zones the investment was made may be settled by international arbitration in accordance with the arbitration clause between the parties.

(5) Neither Contracting State shall pursue through diplomatic channels any matter referred to arbitration until the proceedings have terminated and a Contracting State has failed to abide by or to comply with the award rendered by the Arbitral Tribunal.

Article 9 Settlement of Disputes between Contracting States

(1) Should any dispute arise concerning the interpretation or application of this Agreement the Governments of the Contracting States shall try to settle the same by negotiation or conciliation.

(2) If the dispute cannot be so settled it shall, upon the request of either Contracting State, be submitted to an Arbitral Tribunal in accordance with the provisions of this Article.

(3) The Arbitral Tribunal shall be constituted in the following way: within two months of the receipt of the request for arbitration, each Contracting State shall appoint one arbitrator. The two arbitrators shall then select a national of a third State who shall act as the Chairman of the Tribunal (hereinafter referred to as the Chairman). The Chairman shall be appointed within two months from the date of appointment of the other two arbitrators.

(4) If within the periods specified in Paragraph (3) of this Article either party shall not have appointed its arbitrator or the two arbitrators shall not have agreed on the Chairman, a request may be made to the President of the International Court of Justice to make the appointment. If he happens to be a national of either Contracting State or if he is otherwise prevented from discharging the said function, the Vice-President shall be invited to make the appointment. If the Vice-President also happens to be a national of either Contracting State or is also otherwise prevented from discharging the said function, the member of the International Court of Justice next in seniority who is not a national of either Contracting State shall be invited to make the appointment.

(5) The Arbitral Tribunal shall reach its decision by a majority of votes. Such decision shall be binding. Each Contracting State shall bear the cost of its own arbitrator and its counsel in the arbitral proceedings; the cost of the Chairman and the remaining costs shall be borne in equal parts by both Contracting States. The Arbitral Tribunal shall determine its own procedure.

Article 10 Relations between Contracting States

The provisions of the present Agreement shall apply irrespective of the existence of diplomatic or consular relations between the Contracting States.

Article 11 Application of Other Rules and Special Commitments

(1) Where a matter is governed simultaneously by this Agreement and by other agreements in which the Contracting States are parties or principles of law commonly recognized by both Contracting States or the domestic laws of the host State, nothing in this Agreement shall prevent investors of either Contracting State who own investments in the territory and maritime zones of the other Contracting State from taking advantage of whichever rules are the more favorable to their cases.
(2) Investments subject to special commitments undertaken by one Contracting State with respect to the investors of the other Contracting State shall be governed, without prejudice to the provisions of this Agreement, by the terms of those commitments insofar as their provisions are more favorable than those provided by this Agreement.

Article 12 Entry into Force

This Agreement shall enter into force on the date on which the two Contracting States have notified each other that the internal requirements necessary for the entry into force of this Agreement have been fulfilled.

Article 13 Duration and Termination

(1) This Agreement shall remain in force for a period of twenty years and shall continue in force thereafter unless, after the expiry of the initial period of nineteen years, either of the Contracting States notifies the other Contracting State of its intention to terminate the Agreement. The notice of termination shall become effective one year after it has been received by the other Contracting State.
(2) In respect of investments made prior to the date when the notice of termination of this Agreement becomes effective, the provisions of this Agreement shall, *mutatis mutandis*, remain in force for a further period of twenty years from that date.
In witness whereof the undersigned duly authorized thereto by their respective Governments, have signed this Agreement. Signed in two originals in Kuwait this 11th day of Rabi 1406H corresponding to 23rd day of November 1985 in the Chinese, Arabic and English languages, all texts being equally authentic. In case of divergency, the English text shall prevail.

Annex III
ICSID Arbitration Rules

Rules of Procedure for Arbitration Proceedings – Arbitration Rules

Table of Contents

28 Cost of Proceeding

IV Written and Oral Procedures

29 Normal Procedures
30 Transmission of the Request
31 The Written Procedure
32 The Oral Procedure
33 Marshalling of Evidence
34 Evidence: General Principles
35 Examination of Witnesses and Experts
36 Witnesses and Experts: Special Rules
37 Visits and Inquiries; Submissions of Non-disputing Parties
38 Closure of the Proceeding

V Particular Procedures

39 Provisional Measures
40 Ancillary Claims
41 Preliminary Objections
42 Default
43 Settlement and Discontinuance
44 Discontinuance at Request of a Party
45 Discontinuance for Failure of Parties to Act

VI The Award

46 Preparation of the Award
47 The Award
48 Rendering of the Award
49 Supplementary Decisions and Rectification

VII Interpretation, Revision and Annulment of the Award

50 The Application
51 Interpretation or Revision: Further Procedures
52 Annulment: Further Procedures
53 Rules of Procedure
54 Stay of Enforcement of the Award
55 Resubmission of Dispute after an Annulment

VIII General Provisions

56 Final Provisions

The Rules of Procedure for Arbitration Proceedings (the Arbitration Rules) of ICSID were adopted by the Administrative Council of the Centre pursuant to Article 6(1)(c) of the ICSID Convention.

The Arbitration Rules are supplemented by the Administrative and Financial Regulations of the Centre, in particular by Regulations 14–16, 2231 and 34(1).
The Arbitration Rules cover the period of time from the dispatch of the notice of registration of a request for arbitration until an award is rendered and all challenges possible to it under the Convention have been exhausted.
The transactions previous to that time are to be regulated in accordance with the Institution Rules.

I Establishment of the Tribunal

Rule 1: General Obligations

(1) Upon notification of the registration of the request for arbitration, the parties shall, with all possible dispatch, proceed to constitute a Tribunal, with due regard to Section 2 of Chapter IV of the Convention.
(2) Unless such information is provided in the request, the parties shall communicate to the Secretary-General as soon as possible any provisions agreed by them regarding the number of arbitrators and the method of their appointment.
(3) The majority of the arbitrators shall be nationals of States other than the State party to the dispute and of the State whose national is a party to the dispute, unless the sole arbitrator or each individual member of the Tribunal is appointed by agreement of the parties.

Where the Tribunal is to consist of three members, a national of either of these States may not be appointed as an arbitrator by a party without the agreement of the other party to the dispute. Where the Tribunal is to consist of five or more members, nationals of either of these States may not be appointed as arbitrators by a party if appointment by the other party of the same number of arbitrators of either of these nationalities would result in a majority of arbitrators of these nationalities.
(4) No person who had previously acted as a conciliator or arbitrator in any proceeding for the settlement of the dispute may be appointed as a member of the Tribunal.

Rule 2: Method of Constituting the Tribunal in the Absence of Previous Agreement

(1) If the parties, at the time of the registration of the request for arbitration, have not agreed upon the number of arbitrators and the method of their appointment, they shall, unless they agree otherwise, follow the following procedure:

> (a) the requesting party shall, within 10 days after the registration of the request, propose to the other party the appointment of a sole arbitrator or of a specified uneven number of arbitrators and specify the method proposed for their appointment;
> (b) within 20 days after receipt of the proposals made by the requesting party, the other party shall:
>
> > (i) accept such proposals; or
> > (ii) make other proposals regarding the number of arbitrators and the method of their appointment;
>
> (c) within 20 days after receipt of the reply containing any such other proposals, the requesting party shall notify the other party whether it accepts or rejects such proposals.

(2) The communications provided for in paragraph (1) shall be made or promptly confirmed in writing and shall either be transmitted through the Secretary-General or directly between the parties with a copy to the Secretary-General. The parties shall promptly notify the Secretary-General of the contents of any agreement reached.
(3) At any time 60 days after the registration of the request, if no agreement on another procedure is reached, either party may inform the Secretary-General that it chooses the formula provided for in Article
37(2)(b) of the Convention. The Secretary-General shall thereupon promptly inform the other party that the Tribunal is to be constituted in accordance with that Article.

Rule 3: Appointment of Arbitrators to a Tribunal Constituted in Accordance with Convention Article 37(2)(b)

(1) If the Tribunal is to be constituted in accordance with Article 37(2)(b) of the Convention:

(a) either party shall in a communication to the other party:

(i) name two persons, identifying one of them, who shall not have the same nationality as nor be a national of either party, as the arbitrator appointed by it, and the other as the arbitrator proposed to be the President of the Tribunal; and
(ii) invite the other party to concur in the appointment of the arbitrator proposed to be the President of the Tribunal and to appoint another arbitrator;

(b) promptly upon receipt of this communication the other party shall, in its reply:

(i) name a person as the arbitrator appointed by it, who shall not have the same nationality as nor be a national of either party; and
(ii) concur in the appointment of the arbitrator proposed to be the President of the Tribunal or name another person as the arbitrator proposed to be President;

(c) promptly upon receipt of the reply containing such a proposal, the initiating party shall notify the other party whether it concurs in the appointment of the arbitrator proposed by that party to be the President of the Tribunal.

(2) The communications provided for in this Rule shall be made or promptly confirmed in writing and shall either be transmitted through the Secretary-General or directly between the parties with a copy to the Secretary-General.

Rule 4: Appointment of Arbitrators by the Chairman of the Administrative Council

(1) If the Tribunal is not constituted within 90 days after the dispatch by the Secretary-General of the notice of registration, or such other period as the parties may agree, either party may, through the Secretary-General, address to the Chairman of the Administrative Council a request in writing to appoint the arbitrator or arbitrators not yet appointed and to designate an arbitrator to be the President of the Tribunal.
(2) The provision of paragraph (1) shall apply *mutatis mutandis* in the event that the parties have agreed that the arbitrators shall elect the President of the Tribunal and they fail to do so.

(3) The Secretary-General shall forthwith send a copy of the request to the other party.
(4) The Chairman shall use his best efforts to comply with that request within 30 days after its receipt. Before he proceeds to make an appointment or designation, with due regard to Articles 38 and 40(1) of the Convention, he shall consult both parties as far as possible.
5) The Secretary-General shall promptly notify the parties of any appointment or resignation made by the Chairman.

Rule 5: Acceptance of Appointments

(1) The party or parties concerned shall notify the Secretary-General of the appointment of each arbitrator and indicate the method of his appointment.
(2) As soon as the Secretary-General has been informed by a party or the Chairman of the Administrative Council of the appointment of an arbitrator, he shall seek an acceptance from the appointee.
(3) If an arbitrator fails to accept his appointment within 15 days, the Secretary-General shall promptly notify the parties, and if appropriate the Chairman, and invite them to proceed to the appointment of another arbitrator in accordance with the method followed for the previous appointment.

Rule 6: Constitution of the Tribunal

(1) The Tribunal shall be deemed to be constituted and the proceeding to have begun on the date the Secretary-General notifies the parties that all the arbitrators have accepted their appointment.
(2) Before or at the first session of the Tribunal, each arbitrator shall sign a declaration in the following form:
'To the best of my knowledge there is no reason why I should not serve on the Arbitral Tribunal constituted by the International Centre for Settlement of Investment Disputes with respect to a dispute between ____________________ and ____________________.
'I shall keep confidential all information coming to my knowledge as a result of my participation in this proceeding, as well as the contents of any award made by the Tribunal.
'I shall judge fairly as between the parties, according to the applicable law, and shall not accept any instruction or compensation with regard to the proceeding from any source except as provided in the Convention on the Settlement of Investment Disputes between States and Nationals of Other States and in the Regulations and Rules made pursuant thereto.
'Attached is a statement of (a) my past and present professional, business and other relationships (if any) with the parties and (b) any other circumstance that might cause my reliability for independent judgment to be questioned by a party. I acknowledge that by signing this declaration, I assume a continuing obligation promptly to notify the Secretary-General of the Centre of any such relationship or circumstance that subsequently arises during this proceeding.'
Any arbitrator failing to sign a declaration by the end of the first session of the Tribunal shall be deemed to have resigned.

Rule 7: Replacement of Arbitrators

At any time before the Tribunal is constituted, each party may replace any arbitrator appointed by it and the parties may by common consent agree to replace any arbitrator. The procedure of such replacement shall be in accordance with Rules 1, 5 and 6.

Rule 8: Incapacity or Resignation of Arbitrators

(1) If an arbitrator becomes incapacitated or unable to perform the duties of his office, the procedure in respect of the disqualification of arbitrators set forth in Rule 9 shall apply.
(2) An arbitrator may resign by submitting his resignation to the other members of the Tribunal and the Secretary-General. If the arbitrator was appointed by one of the parties, the Tribunal shall promptly consider the reasons for his resignation and decide whether it consents thereto. The Tribunal shall promptly notify the Secretary-General of its decision.

Rule 9: Disqualification of Arbitrators

(1) A party proposing the disqualification of an arbitrator pursuant to Article 57 of the Convention shall promptly, and in any event before the proceeding is declared closed, file its proposal with the Secretary- General, stating its reasons therefore.
(2) The Secretary-General shall forthwith:

> (a) transmit the proposal to the members of the Tribunal and, if it relates to a sole arbitrator or to a majority of the members of the Tribunal, to the Chairman of the Administrative Council; and
> (b) notify the other party of the proposal.

(3) The arbitrator to whom the proposal relates may, without delay, furnish explanations to the Tribunal or the Chairman, as the case may be.
(4) Unless the proposal relates to a majority of the members of the Tribunal, the other members shall promptly consider and vote on the proposal in the absence of the arbitrator concerned. If those members are equally divided, they shall, through the Secretary-General, promptly notify the Chairman of the proposal, of any explanation furnished by the arbitrator concerned and of their failure to reach a decision.
(5) Whenever the Chairman has to decide on a proposal to disqualify an arbitrator, he shall use his best efforts to take that decision within 30 days after he has received the proposal.
(6) The proceeding shall be suspended until a decision has been taken on the proposal.

Rule 10: Procedure during a Vacancy on the Tribunal

(1) The Secretary-General shall forthwith notify the parties and, if necessary, the Chairman of the Administrative Council of the disqualification, death, incapacity or resignation of an arbitrator and of the consent, if any, of the Tribunal to a resignation.
(2) Upon the notification by the Secretary-General of a vacancy on the Tribunal, the proceeding shall be or remain suspended until the vacancy has been filled.

Rule 11: Filling Vacancies on the Tribunal

(1) Except as provided in paragraph (2), a vacancy resulting from the disqualification, death, incapacity or resignation of an arbitrator shall be promptly filled by the same method by which his appointment had been made.
(2) In addition to filling vacancies relating to arbitrators appointed by him, the Chairman of the Administrative Council shall appoint a person from the tribunal of Arbitrators:

(a) to fill a vacancy caused by the resignation, without the consentof the Tribunal, of an arbitrator appointed by a party; or
(b) at the request of either party, to fill any other vacancy, if no new appointment is made and accepted within 45 days of the notification of the vacancy by the Secretary-General.

(3) The procedure for filling a vacancy shall be in accordance with Rules 1, 4(4), 4(5), 5 and, *mutatis mutandis,* 6(2).

Rule 12: Resumption of Proceeding after Filling a Vacancy

As soon as a vacancy on the Tribunal has been filled, the proceeding shall continue from the point it had reached at the time the vacancy occurred. The newly appointed arbitrator may, however, require that the oral procedure be recommenced, if this had already been started.

II Working of the Tribunal

Rule 13: Sessions of the Tribunal

(1) The Tribunal shall hold its first session within 60 days after its constitution or such other period as the parties may agree. The dates of that session shall be fixed by the President of the Tribunal after consultation with its members and the Secretary-General. If upon its constitution the Tribunal has no President because the parties have agreed that the President shall be elected by its members, the Secretary-General shall fix the dates of that session. In both cases, the parties shall be consulted as far as possible.
(2) The dates of subsequent sessions shall be determined by the Tribunal, after consultation with the Secretary-General and with the parties as far as possible.
(3) The Tribunal shall meet at the seat of the Centre or at such other place as may have been agreed by the parties in accordance with Article 63 of the Convention. If the parties agree that the proceeding shall be held at a place other than the Centre or an institution with which the Centre has made the necessary arrangements, they shall consult with the Secretary-General and request the approval of the Tribunal.
Failing such approval, the Tribunal shall meet at the seat of the Centre.
(4) The Secretary-General shall notify the members of the Tribunal and the parties of the dates and place of the sessions of the Tribunal in good time.

Rule 14: Sittings of the Tribunal

(1) The President of the Tribunal shall conduct its hearings and preside at its deliberations.
(2) Except as the parties otherwise agree, the presence of a majority of the members of the Tribunal shall be required at its sittings.
(3) The President of the Tribunal shall fix the date and hour of its sittings.

Rule 15: Deliberations of the Tribunal

(1) The deliberations of the Tribunal shall take place in private and remain secret.
(2) Only members of the Tribunal shall take part in its deliberations.

No other person shall be admitted unless the Tribunal decides otherwise.

Rule 16: Decisions of the Tribunal

(1) Decisions of the Tribunal shall be taken by a majority of the votes of all its members. Abstention shall count as a negative vote.
(2) Except as otherwise provided by these Rules or decided by the Tribunal, it may take any decision by correspondence among its members, provided that all of them are consulted. Decisions so taken shall be certified by the President of the Tribunal.

Rule 17: Incapacity of the President

If at any time the President of the Tribunal should be unable to act, his functions shall be performed by one of the other members of the Tribunal, acting in the order in which the Secretary-General had received the notice of their acceptance of their appointment to the Tribunal.

Rule 18: Representation of the Parties

(1) Each party may be represented or assisted by agents, counsel or advocates whose names and authority shall be notified by that party to the Secretary-General, who shall promptly inform the Tribunal and the other party.
(2) For the purposes of these Rules, the expression 'party' includes, where the context so admits, an agent, counsel or advocate authorized to represent that party.

III General Procedural Provisions

Rule 19: Procedural Orders

The Tribunal shall make the orders required for the conduct of the proceeding.

Rule 20: Preliminary Procedural Consultation

(1) As early as possible after the constitution of a Tribunal, its President shall endeavor to ascertain the views of the parties regarding questions of procedure. For this purpose he may request the parties to meet him. He shall, in particular, seek their views on the following matters:

(a) the number of members of the Tribunal required to constitute a quorum at its sittings;
(b) the language or languages to be used in the proceeding;
(c) the number and sequence of the pleadings and the time limits within which they are to be filed;
(d) the number of copies desired by each party of instruments filed by the other;
(e) dispensing with the written or the oral procedure;
(f) the manner in which the cost of the proceeding is to be apportioned; and
(g) the manner in which the record of the hearings shall be kept.

(2) In the conduct of the proceeding the Tribunal shall apply any agreement between the parties on procedural matters, except as otherwise provided in the Convention or the Administrative and Financial Regulations.

Rule 21: Pre-Hearing Conference

(1) At the request of the Secretary-General or at the discretion of the President of the Tribunal, a pre-hearing conference between the Tribunal and the parties may be held to arrange for an exchange of information and the stipulation of uncontested facts in order to expedite the proceeding.
(2) At the request of the parties, a pre-hearing conference between the Tribunal and the parties, duly represented by their authorized representatives, may be held to consider the issues in dispute with a view to reaching an amicable settlement.

Rule 22: Procedural Languages

(1) The parties may agree on the use of one or two languages to be used in the proceeding, provided, that, if they agree on any language that is not an official language of the Centre, the Tribunal, after consultation with the Secretary-General, gives its approval. If the parties do not agree on any such procedural language, each of them may select one of the official languages (i.e., English, French and Spanish) for this purpose.
(2) If two procedural languages are selected by the parties, any instrument may be filed in either language. Either language may be used at the hearings, subject, if the Tribunal so requires, to translation and interpretation. The orders and the award of the Tribunal shall be rendered and the record kept in both procedural languages, both versions being equally authentic.

Rule 23: Copies of Instruments

Except as otherwise provided by the Tribunal after consultation with the parties and the Secretary-General, every request, pleading, application, written observation, supporting documentation, if any, or other instrument shall be filed in the form of a signed original accompanied by the following number of additional copies:

(a) before the number of members of the Tribunal has been determined: five;
(b) after the number of members of the Tribunal has been determined: two more than the number of its members.

Rule 24: Supporting Documentation

Supporting documentation shall ordinarily be filed together with the instrument to which it relates, and in any case within the time limit fixed for the filing of such instrument.

Rule 25: Correction of Errors

An accidental error in any instrument or supporting document may, with the consent of the other party or by leave of the Tribunal, be corrected at any time before the award is rendered.

Rule 26: Time Limits

(1) Where required, time limits shall be fixed by the Tribunal by assigning dates for the completion of the various steps in the proceeding.
The Tribunal may delegate this power to its President.
(2) The Tribunal may extend any time limit that it has fixed. If the Tribunal is not in session, this power shall be exercised by its President.
(3) Any step taken after expiration of the applicable time limit shall be disregarded unless the Tribunal, in special circumstances and after giving the other party an opportunity of stating its views, decides otherwise.

Rule 27: Waiver

A party which knows or should have known that a provision of the Administrative and Financial Regulations, of these Rules, of any other rules or agreement applicable to the proceeding, or of an order of the Tribunal has not been complied with and which fails to state promptly its objections thereto, shall be deemed—subject to Article 45 of the Convention—to have waived its right to object.

Rule 28: Cost of Proceeding

(1) Without prejudice to the final decision on the payment of the cost of the proceeding, the Tribunal may, unless otherwise agreed by the parties, decide:

> (a) at any stage of the proceeding, the portion which each party shall pay, pursuant to Administrative and Financial
> Regulation 14, of the fees and expenses of the Tribunal and the charges for the use of the facilities of the Centre;
> (b) with respect to any part of the proceeding, that the related costs (as determined by the Secretary-General) shall be borne entirely or in a particular share by one of the parties.

(2) Promptly after the closure of the proceeding, each party shall submit to the Tribunal a statement of costs reasonably incurred or borne by it in the proceeding and the Secretary-General shall submit to the Tribunal an account of all amounts paid by each party to the Centre and of all costs incurred by the Centre for the proceeding. The Tribunal may, before the award has been rendered, request the parties and the Secretary-General to provide additional information concerning the cost of the proceeding.

IV Written and Oral Procedures

Rule 29: Normal Procedures

Except if the parties otherwise agree, the proceeding shall comprise two distinct phases: a written procedure followed by an oral one.

Rule 30: Transmission of the Request

As soon as the Tribunal is constituted, the Secretary-General shall transmit to each member a copy of the request by which the proceeding was initiated, of the supporting documentation, of the notice of registration and of any communication received from either party in response thereto.

Rule 31: The Written Procedure

(1) In addition to the request for arbitration, the written procedure shall consist of the following pleadings, filed within time limits set by the Tribunal:

(a) a memorial by the requesting party;
(b) a counter-memorial by the other party; and, if the parties so agree or the Tribunal deems it necessary:
(c) a reply by the requesting party; and
(d) a rejoinder by the other party.

(2) If the request was made jointly, each party shall, within the same time limit determined by the Tribunal, file its memorial and, if the parties so agree or the Tribunal deems it necessary, its reply; however, the parties may instead agree that one of them shall, for the purposes of paragraph (1), be considered as the requesting party.
(3) A memorial shall contain: a statement of the relevant facts; a statement of law; and the submissions. A counter-memorial, reply or rejoinder shall contain an admission or denial of the facts stated in the last previous pleading; any additional facts, if necessary; observations concerning the statement of law in the last previous pleading; a statement of law in answer thereto; and the submissions.

Rule 32: The Oral Procedure

(1) The oral procedure shall consist of the hearing by the Tribunal of the parties, their agents, counsel and advocates, and of witnesses and experts.
(2) Unless either party objects, the Tribunal, after consultation with the Secretary-General, may allow other persons, besides the parties, their agents, counsel and advocates, witnesses and experts during their testimony, and officers of the Tribunal, to attend or observe all or part of the hearings, subject to appropriate logistical arrangements. The Tribunal shall for such cases establish procedures for the protection of proprietary or privileged information.
(3) The members of the Tribunal may, during the hearings, put questions to the parties, their agents, counsel and advocates, and ask them for explanations.

Rule 33: Marshalling of Evidence

Without prejudice to the rules concerning the production of documents, each party shall, within time limits fixed by the Tribunal, communicate to the Secretary-General, for transmission to the Tribunal and the other party, precise information regarding the evidence which it intends to produce and that which it intends to request the Tribunal to call for, together with an indication of the points to which such evidence will be directed.

Rule 34: Evidence: General Principles

(1) The Tribunal shall be the judge of the admissibility of any evidence adduced and of its probative value.
(2) The Tribunal may, if it deems it necessary at any stage of the proceeding:

(a) call upon the parties to produce documents, witnesses and experts; and
(b) visit any place connected with the dispute or conduct inquiries there.

(3) The parties shall cooperate with the Tribunal in the production of the evidence and in the other measures provided for in paragraph (2). The Tribunal shall take formal note of the failure of a party to comply with its obligations under this paragraph and of any reasons given for such failure.
(4) Expenses incurred in producing evidence and in taking other measures in accordance with paragraph (2) shall be deemed to constitute part of the expenses incurred by the parties within the meaning of Article 61(2) of the Convention.

Rule 35: Examination of Witnesses and Experts

(1) Witnesses and experts shall be examined before the Tribunal by the parties under the control of its President. Questions may also be put to them by any member of the Tribunal.
(2) Each witness shall make the following declaration before giving his evidence:
'I solemnly declare upon my honour and conscience that I shall speak the truth, the whole truth and nothing but the truth.'
(3) Each expert shall make the following declaration before making his statement:
'I solemnly declare upon my honour and conscience that my statement will be in accordance with my sincere belief.'

Rule 36: Witnesses and Experts: Special Rules

Notwithstanding Rule 35 the Tribunal may:

(a) admit evidence given by a witness or expert in a written deposition; and
(b) with the consent of both parties, arrange for the examination of a witness or expert otherwise than before the Tribunal itself. The Tribunal shall define the subject of the examination, the time limit, the procedure to be followed and other particulars. The parties may participate in the examination.

Rule 37: Visits and Inquiries; Submissions of Non-disputing Parties

(1) If the Tribunal considers it necessary to visit any place connected with the dispute or to conduct an inquiry there, it shall make an order to this effect. The order shall define the scope of the visit or the subject of the inquiry, the time limit, the procedure to be followed and other particulars. The parties may participate in any visit or inquiry.
(2) After consulting both parties, the Tribunal may allow a person or entity that is not a party to the dispute (in this Rule called the 'nondisputing party') to file a written submission with the Tribunal regarding a matter within the scope of the dispute. In determining whether to allow such a filing, the Tribunal shall consider, among other things, the extent to which:

(a) the non-disputing party submission would assist the Tribunal in the determination of a factual or legal issue related to the proceeding by bringing a perspective, particular knowledge or insight that is different from that of the disputing parties;
(b) the non-disputing party submission would address a matter within the scope of the dispute;
(c) the non-disputing party has a significant interest in the proceeding.

The Tribunal shall ensure that the non-disputing party submission does not disrupt the proceeding or unduly burden or unfairly prejudiceeither party, and that both parties are given an opportunity to presenttheir observations on the non-disputing party submission.

Rule 38: Closure of the Proceeding

(1) When the presentation of the case by the parties is completed, the proceeding shall be declared closed.
(2) Exceptionally, the Tribunal may, before the award has been rendered, reopen the proceeding on the ground that new evidence is forthcoming of such a nature as to constitute a decisive factor, or that there is a vital need for clarification on certain specific points.

V Particular Procedures

Rule 39: Provisional Measures

(1) At any time after the institution of the proceeding, a party may request that provisional measures for the preservation of its rights be recommended by the Tribunal. The request shall specify the rights to be preserved, the measures the recommendation of which is requested, and the circumstances that require such measures.
(2) The Tribunal shall give priority to the consideration of a request made pursuant to paragraph (1).
(3) The Tribunal may also recommend provisional measures on its own initiative or recommend measures other than those specified in a request. It may at any time modify or revoke its recommendations.
(4) The Tribunal shall only recommend provisional measures, or modify or revoke its recommendations, after giving each party an opportunity of presenting its observations.
(5) If a party makes a request pursuant to paragraph (1) before the constitution of the Tribunal, the Secretary-General shall, on the application of either party, fix time limits for the parties to present observations on the request, so that the request and observations may be considered by the Tribunal promptly upon its constitution.
(6) Nothing in this Rule shall prevent the parties, provided that they have so stipulated in the agreement recording their consent, from requesting any judicial or other authority to order provisional measures, prior to or after the institution of the proceeding, for the preservation of their respective rights and interests.

Rule 40: Ancillary Claims

(1) Except as the parties otherwise agree, a party may present an incidental or additional claim or counter-claim arising directly out of the subject-matter of the dispute, provided that such ancillary claim is within the scope of the consent of the parties and is otherwise within the jurisdiction of the Centre.
(2) An incidental or additional claim shall be presented not later than in the reply and a counter-claim no later than in the countermemorial, unless the Tribunal, upon justification by the party presenting the ancillary claim and upon considering any objection of the other party, authorizes the presentation of the claim at a later stage in the proceeding.
(3) The Tribunal shall fix a time limit within which the party against which an ancillary claim is presented may file its observations thereon.

Rule 41: Preliminary Objections

(1) Any objection that the dispute or any ancillary claim is not within the jurisdiction of the Centre or, for other reasons, is not within the competence of the Tribunal shall be made as early as possible. A party shall file the objection with the Secretary-General no later than the expiration of the time limit fixed for the filing of the countermemorial, or, if the objection relates to an ancillary claim, for the filing of the rejoinder—unless the facts on which the objection is based are unknown to the party at that time.
(2) The Tribunal may on its own initiative consider, at any stage of the proceeding, whether the dispute or any ancillary claim before it is within the jurisdiction of the Centre and within its own competence.
(3) Upon the formal raising of an objection relating to the dispute, the Tribunal may decide to suspend the proceeding on the merits. The President of the Tribunal, after consultation with its other members, shall fix a time limit within which the parties may file observations on the objection.
(4) The Tribunal shall decide whether or not the further procedures relating to the objection made pursuant to paragraph (1) shall be oral. It may deal with the objection as a preliminary question or join it to the merits of the dispute. If the Tribunal overrules the objection or joins it to the merits, it shall once more fix time limits for the further procedures.
(5) Unless the parties have agreed to another expedited procedure for making preliminary objections, a party may, no later than 30 days after the constitution of the Tribunal, and in any event before the first session of the Tribunal, file an objection that a claim is manifestly without legal merit. The party shall specify as precisely as possible the basis for the objection. The Tribunal, after giving the parties the opportunity to present their observations on the objection, shall, at its first session or promptly thereafter, notify the parties of its decision on the objection.
The decision of the Tribunal shall be without prejudice to the right of a party to file an objection pursuant to paragraph (1) or to object, in the course of the proceeding, that a claim lacks legal merit.
(6) If the Tribunal decides that the dispute is not within the jurisdiction of the Centre or not within its own competence, or that all claims are manifestly without legal merit, it shall render an award to that effect.

Rule 42: Default

(1) If a party (in this Rule called the 'defaulting party') fails to appear or to present its case at any stage of the proceeding, the other party may, at any time prior to the discontinuance of the proceeding, request the Tribunal to deal with the questions submitted to it and to render an award.
(2) The Tribunal shall promptly notify the defaulting party of such a request. Unless it is satisfied that that party does not intend to appear or to present its case in the proceeding, it shall, at the same time, grant a period of grace and to this end:

> (a) if that party had failed to file a pleading or any other instrument within the time limit fixed therefor, fix a new time limit for its filing; or
> (b) if that party had failed to appear or present its case at a hearing, fix a new date for the hearing.

The period of grace shall not, without the consent of the other party, exceed 60 days.
(3) After the expiration of the period of grace or when, in accordance with paragraph (2), no such period is granted, the Tribunal shall resume the consideration of the dispute. Failure of the defaulting party to appear or to present its case shall not be deemed an admission of the assertions made by the other party.
(4) The Tribunal shall examine the jurisdiction of the Centre and its own competence in the dispute and, if it is satisfied, decide whether the submissions made are well-founded in fact and in law. To this end, it may, at any stage of the proceeding, call on the party appearing to file observations, produce evidence or submit oral explanations.

Rule 43: Settlement and Discontinuance

(1) If, before the award is rendered, the parties agree on a settlement of the dispute or otherwise to discontinue the proceeding, the Tribunal, or the Secretary-General if the Tribunal has not yet been constituted, shall, at their written request, in an order take note of the discontinuance of the proceeding.
(2) If the parties file with the Secretary-General the full and signed text of their settlement and in writing request the Tribunal to embody such settlement in an award, the Tribunal may record the settlement in the form of its award.

Rule 44: Discontinuance at Request of a Party

If a party requests the discontinuance of the proceeding, the Tribunal, or the Secretary-General if the Tribunal has not yet been constituted, shall in an order fix a time limit within which the other party may state whether it opposes the discontinuance. If no objection is made in writing within the time limit, the other party shall be deemed to have acquiesced in the discontinuance and the Tribunal, or if appropriate the Secretary-General, shall in an order take note of the discontinuance of the proceeding. If objection is made, the proceeding shall continue.

Rule 45: Discontinuance for Failure of Parties to Act

If the parties fail to take any steps in the proceeding during six consecutive months or such period as they may agree with the approval of the Tribunal, or of the Secretary-General if the Tribunal has not yet been constituted, they shall be deemed to have discontinued the proceeding and the Tribunal, or if appropriate the Secretary-General, shall, after notice to the parties, in an order take note of the discontinuance.

VI The Award

Rule 46: Preparation of the Award

The award (including any individual or dissenting opinion) shall be drawn up and signed within 120 days after closure of the proceeding.
The Tribunal may, however, extend this period by a further 60 days if it would otherwise be unable to draw up the award.

Rule 47: The Award

(1) The award shall be in writing and shall contain:

(a) a precise designation of each party;
(b) a statement that the Tribunal was established under the Convention, and a description of the method of its constitution;
(c) the name of each member of the Tribunal, and an identification of the appointing authority of each;
(d) the names of the agents, counsel and advocates of the parties;
(e) the dates and place of the sittings of the Tribunal;
(f) a summary of the proceeding;
(g) a statement of the facts as found by the Tribunal;
(h) the submissions of the parties;
(i) the decision of the Tribunal on every question submitted to it, together with the reasons upon which the decision is based; and
(j) any decision of the Tribunal regarding the cost of the proceeding.

(2) The award shall be signed by the members of the Tribunal who voted for it; the date of each signature shall be indicated.
(3) Any member of the Tribunal may attach his individual opinion to the award, whether he dissents from the majority or not, or a statement of his dissent.

Rule 48: Rendering of the Award

(1) Upon signature by the last arbitrator to sign, the Secretary-General shall promptly:

(a) authenticate the original text of the award and deposit it in the archives of the Centre, together with any individual opinions and statements of dissent; and
(b) dispatch a certified copy of the award (including individual opinions and statements of dissent) to each party, indicating the date of dispatch on the original text and on all copies.

(2) The award shall be deemed to have been rendered on the date on which the certified copies were dispatched.
(3) The Secretary-General shall, upon request, make available to a party additional certified copies of the award.
(4) The Centre shall not publish the award without the consent of the parties. The Centre shall, however, promptly include in its publications excerpts of the legal reasoning of the Tribunal.

Rule 49: Supplementary Decisions and Rectification

(1) Within 45 days after the date on which the award was rendered, either party may request, pursuant to Article 49(2) of the Convention, a supplementary decision on, or the rectification of, the award. Such a request shall be addressed in writing to the Secretary-General. The request shall:

(a) identify the award to which it relates;
(b) indicate the date of the request;
(c) state in detail:

(i) any question which, in the opinion of the requesting party, the Tribunal omitted to decide in the award; and
(ii) any error in the award which the requesting party seeks to have rectified; and

(d) be accompanied by a fee for lodging the request.

(2) Upon receipt of the request and of the lodging fee, the Secretary-General shall forthwith:

(a) register the request;
(b) notify the parties of the registration;
(c) transmit to the other party a copy of the request and of any accompanying documentation; and
(d) transmit to each member of the Tribunal a copy of the notice of registration, together with a copy of the request and of any accompanying documentation.

(3) The President of the Tribunal shall consult the members on whether it is necessary for the Tribunal to meet in order to consider the request. The Tribunal shall fix a time limit for the parties to file their observations on the request and shall determine the procedure for its consideration.
(4) Rules 46–48 shall apply, *mutatis mutandis,* to any decision of the Tribunal pursuant to this Rule.
(5) If a request is received by the Secretary-General more than 45 days after the award was rendered, he shall refuse to register the request and so inform forthwith the requesting party.

VII Interpretation, Revision and Annulment of the Award

Rule 50: The Application

(1) An application for the interpretation, revision or annulment of an award shall be addressed in writing to the Secretary-General and shall:

(a) identify the award to which it relates;
(b) indicate the date of the application;
(c) state in detail:

(i) in an application for interpretation, the precise points in dispute;
(ii) in an application for revision, pursuant to Article 51(1) of the Convention, the change sought in the award, the discovery of some fact of such a nature as decisively to affect the award, and evidence that when the award was rendered that fact was unknown to the Tribunal and to the applicant, and that the applicant's ignorance of that fact was not due to negligence;
(iii) in an application for annulment, pursuant to Article 52(1) of the Convention, the grounds on which it is based. These grounds are limited to the following:

– that the Tribunal was not properly constituted;
– that the Tribunal has manifestly exceeded its powers;
– that there was corruption on the part of a member of the Tribunal;
– that there has been a serious departure from a fundamental rule of procedure;
– that the award has failed to state the reasons on which it is based;

(d) be accompanied by the payment of a fee for lodging the application.

(2) Without prejudice to the provisions of paragraph (3), upon receiving an application and the lodging fee, the Secretary-General shall forthwith:

(a) register the application;
(b) notify the parties of the registration; and
(c) transmit to the other party a copy of the application and of any accompanying documentation.

(3) The Secretary-General shall refuse to register an application for:

(a) revision, if, in accordance with Article 51(2) of the Convention, it is not made within 90 days after the discovery of the new fact and in any event within three years after the date on which the award was rendered (or any subsequent decision or correction);
(b) annulment, if, in accordance with Article 52(2) of the Convention, it is not made:

(i) within 120 days after the date on which the award was rendered (or any subsequent decision or correction) if the application is based on any of the following grounds:

– the Tribunal was not properly constituted;
– the Tribunal has manifestly exceeded its powers;
– there has been a serious departure from a fundamental rule of procedure;
– the award has failed to state the reasons on which it is based;

(ii) in the case of corruption on the part of a member of the Tribunal, within 120 days after discovery thereof, and in any event within three years after the date on which the award was rendered (or any subsequent decision or correction).

(4) If the Secretary-General refuses to register an application for revision, or annulment, he shall forthwith notify the requesting party of his refusal.

Rule 51: Interpretation or Revision: Further Procedures

(1) Upon registration of an application for the interpretation or revision of an award, the Secretary-General shall forthwith:

> (a) transmit to each member of the original Tribunal a copy of the notice of registration, together with a copy of the application and of any accompanying documentation; and
> (b) request each member of the Tribunal to inform him within a specified time limit whether that member is willing to take part in the consideration of the application.

(2) If all members of the Tribunal express their willingness to take part in the consideration of the application, the Secretary-General shall so notify the members of the Tribunal and the parties. Upon dispatch of these notices the Tribunal shall be deemed to be reconstituted.
(3) If the Tribunal cannot be reconstituted in accordance with paragraph (2), the Secretary-General shall so notify the parties and invite them to proceed, as soon as possible, to constitute a new Tribunal, including the same number of arbitrators, and appointed by the same method, as the original one.

Rule 52: Annulment: Further Procedures

(1) Upon registration of an application for the annulment of an award, the Secretary-General shall forthwith request the Chairman of the Administrative Council to appoint an *ad hoc* Committee in accordance with Article 52(3) of the Convention.
(2) The Committee shall be deemed to be constituted on the date the Secretary-General notifies the parties that all members have accepted their appointment. Before or at the first session of the Committee, each member shall sign a declaration conforming to that set forth in Rule 6(2).

Rule 53: Rules of Procedure

The provisions of these Rules shall apply *mutatis mutandis* to any procedure relating to the interpretation, revision or annulment of an award and to the decision of the Tribunal or Committee.

Rule 54: Stay of Enforcement of the Award

(1) The party applying for the interpretation, revision or annulment of an award may in its application, and either party may at any time before the final disposition of the application, request a stay in the enforcement of part or all of the award to which the application relates.
The Tribunal or Committee shall give priority to the consideration of such a request.
(2) If an application for the revision or annulment of an award contains a request for a stay of its enforcement, the Secretary-General shall, together with the notice of registration, inform both parties of the provisional stay of the award. As soon as the Tribunal or Committee is constituted it shall, if either party requests, rule within 30 days on whether such stay should be continued; unless it decides to continue the stay, it shall automatically be terminated.

(3) If a stay of enforcement has been granted pursuant to paragraph (1) or continued pursuant to paragraph (2), the Tribunal or Committee may at any time modify or terminate the stay at the request of either party. All stays shall automatically terminate on the date on which a final decision is rendered on the application, except that a Committee granting the partial annulment of an award may order the temporary stay of enforcement of the unannulled portion in order to give either party an opportunity to request any new Tribunal constituted pursuant to Article 52(6) of the Convention to grant a stay pursuant to Rule 55(3).
(4) A request pursuant to paragraph (1), (2) (second sentence) or (3) shall specify the circumstances that require the stay or its modification or termination. A request shall only be granted after the Tribunal or Committee has given each party an opportunity of presenting its observations.
(5) The Secretary-General shall promptly notify both parties of the stay of enforcement of any award and of the modification or termination of such a stay, which shall become effective on the date on which he dispatches such notification.

Rule 55: Resubmission of Dispute after an Annulment

(1) If a Committee annuls part or all of an award, either party may request the resubmission of the dispute to a new Tribunal. Such a request shall be addressed in writing to the Secretary-General and shall:

(a) identify the award to which it relates;
(b) indicate the date of the request;
(c) explain in detail what aspect of the dispute is to be submitted to the Tribunal; and
(d) be accompanied by a fee for lodging the request.

(2) Upon receipt of the request and of the lodging fee, the Secretary-General shall forthwith:

(a) register it in the Arbitration Register;
(b) notify both parties of the registration;
(c) transmit to the other party a copy of the request and of any accompanying documentation; and
(d) invite the parties to proceed, as soon as possible, to constitute a new Tribunal, including the same number of arbitrators, and appointed by the same method, as the original one.

(3) If the original award had only been annulled in part, the new Tribunal shall not reconsider any portion of the award not so annulled.
It may, however, in accordance with the procedures set forth in Rule 54, stay or continue to stay the enforcement of the unannulled portion of the award until the date its own award is rendered.
(4) Except as otherwise provided in paragraphs (1)–(3), these Rules shall apply to a proceeding on a resubmitted dispute in the same manner as if such dispute had been submitted pursuant to the Institution Rules.

VIII General Provisions

Rule 56: Final Provisions

(1) The texts of these Rules in each official language of the Centre shall be equally authentic.
(2) These Rules may be cited as the 'Arbitration Rules' of the Centre.

Bibliography

Al-Tihyewi (1994), *Arbitration Agreement and its Stipulations in Civil Procedures and Arbitration Act No. 27 of 1994* (Dar El Nahda El Arabia)

Arnaldez, Jean-Jacques, Yves Derains and Dominique Hascher (2002), *Collection of ICC Arbitral Awards, 1996–2000*, vol. 3 (ICC)

Attya, Azmy Abdelfatah (2012), *Kuwaiti Law of Civil Procedures, a Comparative Study with the New French Code, Arbitration Act, Gulf council countries and other Arab countries*, 2nd edn (Kuwait: Dar El Kootob)

de Barros, Cecilia Vidigal Monteiro (2009), 'PPPs in Brazil', *International Construction Law Review*, 26, Part II

Beriry, Mokhtar (1995), *International Commercial Arbitration* (Dar El Nahda El Arabia)

Bernardini, Piero (2007), *Nationality Requirements Under BITs and Related Case Law, Investment Treaty Law, Current Issues II*, edited by Federico Ortino, Lahra Liberti, Audley Sheppard and Hugo Warner (The British Institute of International and Comparative Law)

Bevan, Alexander (1992), *Alternative Dispute Resolution* (Sweet & Maxwell)

Blackaby, Nigel and Constantine Partasides, with Alan Redfern and Martin Hunter (2009), *Redfern and Hunter on International Commercial Arbitration* (New York: Oxford University Press)

Boisséson, M. de (1990), *Le droit Français de l'arbitrage*, 2nd edn (Gide Loyrette Novel)

Bunni, Nael G. (2005), *The FIDIC Forms of Contracts*, 3rd edn (Oxford: Blackwell)

Craig, Laurence, William Park and Jan Paulsson (1985), *International Chamber of Commerce Arbitration* (ICC Publishing)

Dolzer, Rudolf and Margrete Stevens (1995), *Bilateral Investment Treaties, International Centre for Settlement of Investment Disputes* (Martinus Nijhoff Publishers)

Douglas, Zachary (2009), *The International Law of Investment Claims* (Cambridge University Press)

El Ahdab, Abdel Hamid (2009), *Encyclopaedia of Arbitration* (in Arabic) (Beirut: El Halabi Publishing Co.)

El Fakahany and Attyah (1986), *The Administrative Encyclopedia for the Principles of the Supreme Administrative Court and The General Assembly for Legal Opinion 'Fatwa' and Legislation of the Egyptian Conseil d'Etat from 1946–1985* (Cairo: El Dar El Arabia Lel Mosoo'at)

El-Geddawy, Ahmed (1996), 'The Time Limit for Commencing Arbitration under FIDIC Rules Relating to Construction Contracts: Its Nature and Effect in Light of Egyptian law', Paper Presented in the International Commercial Arbitration Conference Organized by CRCICA, Nile Hilton Hotel, Cairo, June 1996.

El Sanhoury, Abdel Razak (1984), *The General Theory of Obligations. Part 3: Expiry of Obligations* (n.p.)

El Sawy, Ahmed (2010), *The Concise in Arbitration*, 3rd edn (Dar El Nahda El Arabia)

El Sharkawy, Abdel Monem (1950), *Civil and Commercial Procedures* (n.p.)

El Sharkawy, Samir (2011), *International Commercial Arbitration, a Comparative Study* (Cairo: Dar El Nahda El Arabia)

El Sharkawy, Soad (2003), *Administrative Contracts* (Dar El Nahda El Arabia)

El Tamawy, Soliman (1991), *General Principles of Administrative Contracts* 5th edn (Dar El Fikr El Araby)

El Wafa, Ahmed Abou (1965), *The Theory of Sentences in the Code of Procedures* (n.p.)

El Wafa, Ahmed Abou (1978), *Contractual and Obligatory Arbitration*, 3rd edn (Alexandria: Monsha'at El Maaref)

Fouchard, Philippe, Emmanuel Gaillard and Berthold Goldman (1996), *Traité de l'arbitrage commercial international* (Paris: Litec)

Fouchard, Philippe, Emmanuel Gaillard and Berthold Goldman (1999), *International Commercial Arbitration* (Kluwer Law International).

Garner, J.F. and B.L. Jones (1985), *Garner's Administrative Law*, 6th edn (Butterworths)

Goldberg, Stephen, Frank Sander and Nancy Rogers (1992), *Dispute Resolution: Negotiation, Mediation and Other Processes*, 2nd edn, Law School Case Book Series (Little, Brown and Company)

Hashem, Mahmoud (1990), *General Theory on Arbitration in Civil and Commercial Provisions, Part I: Arbitration Agreement, A Comparative Study Between Empirical Laws and Islamic Jurisprudence* (Dar El Fikr El Arabi)

Ismail, Mohamed A.M. (2001), 'The Suggested Role of the Egyptian State Council', *El Ahram* 31 July (Cairo)

Ismail, Mohamed A.M. (2003), *International Construction Contracts Arbitration* (Beirut: El Halabi Publishing)

Ismail, Mohamed A.M. (2010), *Public Economic Law and New International Administrative Contracts* (Beirut: El Halabi Publishing, in Arabic)

Ismail, Mohamed A.M. (2010), 'Globalization and New Contractual Regime in International Public Works Agreements in Egypt', *The International Construction Law Review* (UK).

Ismail, Mohamed A.M. (2011), *Globalization and New International Public Works Agreements in Developing Countries* (Farnham: Ashgate Publishing)

Jarrosson, Charles (1987), *La Notion d'arbitrage* (Paris: L.G.D.J.)

Jarvin, Sigvard, Yves Derains and J.J. Arnaldez (1990), *Collection of ICC Arbitral Awards, 1974–1985* (ICC Publishing)

Jones, B.L. (1989), *Garner's Administrative Law*, 7th edn (Butterworths)

Latif, Mohamed Abdel (1996), *Prescription*, 2nd edn (n.p.)

Laubadère, André de, Franck Moderne and Pierre Delvolvé (1983), *Traité des contrats administratifs*, Tomes I & II (Paris: LGDJ)

Leathley, Christian (2007), *International Dispute Resolution in Latin America* (Kluwer Law International)

Leboulanger, Philippe (1985), *Les contrats entre états et entreprises privés étrangères* (Paris: Economica)

Lew, Julian (1978), *Applicable Law in International Commercial Arbitration* (New York: Oceana)

Lew, Julian, Loukas Mistelis and Stefan Kröll (2003), *Comparative International Commercial Arbitration* (London: Kluwer Law International)

Mackie, Karl and David Miles (1995), *Commercial Dispute Resolution: An ADR Practice Guide* (London: Butterworths)

Mahmoud, Dr Mohammed Maged (1993), 'Administrative Contracts and the International Arbitration Clause', *Administrative Sciences Law Journal*, 35

Mahmoud, Dr Mohammed Maged (1997), *Arbitrability in Administrative Contracts* (Kuwait Conference for International Commercial Arbitration)

Meyer-Stamer, Jörg (1997), *Technology, Competitiveness and Radical Policy Change: The Case of Brazil* (London: Frank Cass)

Morduchowicz, Alejandro (2001), *Private Education: Funding and (De)regulation in Argentina*, Occasional Paper No. 36 (Columbia University National Center for the Study of Privatization in Education)

Mounir, Dr Mohammed Kamal (1991), 'Arbitration in Administrative Contracts', *Administrative Sciences Law Journal*, 33:1, 337

Newcombe, Andrew and Lluis Paradell (2009), *Historical Development of Investment Treaty Law, Law and Practice of Investment Treaties: Standards of Treatment* (Kluwer Law International)

Peirano, Claudia and Jaime Vargas (2005), 'Private Schools with Public Financing in Chile' in Laurence Wolff, Juan Carlos Navarro and Pablo Gonzalez (eds), *Private Education and Public Policy in Latin America* (PREAL)

Radwan, Abou Zaid (1981), *General Principles of International Commercial Arbitration* (Dar El Fikr El Arabi)

Rashed, Samia (1984), *Arbitration in Private International Relations* (Dar El Nahda El Arabia)

Redfern, Alan and Martin Hunter (1991), *Law and Practice of International Commercial Arbitration*, 2nd edn (London: Sweet & Maxwell)

Redfern, Alan and Martin Hunter (1999), *Law and Practice of International Commercial Arbitration*, 3rd edn (London: Sweet & Maxwell)

Reed, Lucy, Jan Paulsson and Nigel Blackaby (2010), *Guide to ICSID Arbitration* (Kluwer Law International)

Richer, Laurent (1995), *Droits des Contrats Administratifs* (Paris: LGDJ)

Robert, Jean (1967), *Arbitrage Civil et Commercial*, 4th edn (Paris: Dalloz)

Sarie-Eldin, Hani Salah (1996), *Consortia Agreements in the International Construction Industry* (Kluwer Law International)

Schreuer, Christoph et al. (2009), *The ICSID Convention: A Commentary*, 2nd edn (Cambridge: Cambridge University Press)

Shihata, I. (1986), 'Towards a Greater Depoliticization of Investment Disputes: The Roles of ICSID and MIGA', *ICSID Review*-FILJ 1, 22

Shihata, I. (1991), 'Promotion of Foreign Direct Investments. A General Account, with Particular Reference to the Role of the world Bank Group', *ICSID Review*, FILJ, 6

Snowdon, Brian (2007), *Globalization, Development and Transition* (Cheltenham: Edward Elgar)

Stiglitz, Joseph E. (2004), *Globalization and its Discontents* (New York: W.W. Norton & Company)

Stiglitz, Joseph E. (2007), *Making Globalization Work* (New York: W.W. Norton & Company)

Turpin, Colin C. (1972), *Government Contracts* (Penguin)

Villa, Leonardo and Jesús Duarte, (2005), 'Concessionary Public Schools in BOGOTẤ: An Innovation in School Management in Colombia', in Laurence Wolff, Juan Carlos Navarro and Pablo Gonzalez (eds), *Private Education and Public Policy in Latin America* (PREAL)

Wahab, Mohamed S. (2005), *Cultural Globalization and Public Policy: Exclusion of Foreign Law in the Global Village* (Oxford: Oxford University Press)

Wälde, Thomas W. (2007), *New Aspects of International Investment Law*, ed. Philippe Khan and Thomas W. Wälde (Leiden/Boston: The Hague Academy of International Law, Martinus Nijhoff Publishers)

Wallace, Ian Duncan (1986), *Construction Contracts, Principles and Policies in Tort and Contract* (London: Sweet & Maxwell)

Waly, Fathy (1986), *El Wassit in Civil Law Procedures* (Cairo: Dar El Nahda El Arabia)

Waly, Fathy (1987), *Civil Procedures Law* (Cairo: Dar El Nahda El Arabia)

Waly, Fathy (2007), *Arbitration Law in Theory and Practice*, 1st edn (Monsha'at El Maareef) (in Arabic)

Wolff, Laurence (2005), 'Public Policy and Private Education: Where to Now?' in Laurence Wolff, Juan Carlos Navarro and Pablo Gonzalez (eds), *Private Education and Public Policy in Latin America* (PREAL)

Yardley, D.C.M. (1981), *Principals of Administrative Law* (Butterworths)

Yassin, Hamdy (1987), *The Administrative Acts* (Alexandria: Monsha'at El Maaref)

Yehia, Abdel Wadoud (1987), *Obligations' Stipulations* (Cairo: n.p.)

Websites

BCDR-AAA: www.bcdr-aaa.org/en
CRCICA: www.crcica.org.eg
DIAC: www.diac.ae/idias/
ICC: www.iccwbo.org
ICSID: https://icsid.worldbank.org
Kluwer Arbitration: www.kluwerarbitration.com
LCIA: www.lcia.org
UNCITRAL: www.uncitral.org
UNCTAD: www.unctad.org

Index

References to illustrations are in **bold**

Kolibri 360 GmbH
Ferdinand-Jühlke-Straße 7
99095 Erfurt, Deutschland
produktsicherheit@kolibri360.de